Trafficking and the Global Sex Industry

Program in Migration and Refugee Studies

Program Advisors:
Elzbieta M. Gozdziak and Susan F. Martin,
  Institute for the Study of International Migration

Trafficking and the Global Sex Industry

Edited by Karen Beeks and Delila Amir

LEXINGTON BOOKS
A division of
ROWMAN & LITTLEFIELD PUBLISHERS, INC.
Lanham • Boulder • New York • Toronto • Oxford

LEXINGTON BOOKS

A division of Rowman & Littlefield Publishers, Inc.
A wholly owned subsidiary of The Rowman & Littlefield Publishing Group, Inc.
4501 Forbes Boulevard, Suite 200
Lanham, MD 20706

PO Box 317
Oxford
OX2 9RU, UK

Copyright © 2006 by Lexington Books

British Library Cataloguing in Publication Information Available

Library of Congress Cataloging-in-Publication Data

Trafficking and the global sex industry / edited by Karen Beeks and Delila Amir.
       p. cm. — (Program in migration and refugee studies)
   Includes bibliographical references and index.
   ISBN-13: 978-0-7391-1312-7 (cloth : alk. paper)
   ISBN-10: 0-7391-1312-7 (cloth : alk. paper)
   ISBN-13: 978-0-7391-1313-4 (pbk. : alk. paper)
   ISBN-10: 0-7391-1313-5 (pbk. : alk. paper)
   1. Prostitution.   2. Forced labor.   3. Human smuggling.   4. Slave trade.
   I. Beeks, Karen, 1941–   II. Amir, Delila, 1930–   III. Title.   IV. Series.
HQ281.T64 2006
363.4—dc22   2005027906

Printed in the United States of America

∞™ The paper used in this publication meets the minimum requirements of
American National Standard for Information Sciences—Permanence of Paper
for Printed Library Materials, ANSI/NISO Z39.48-1992.

Contents

Acknowledgments

This book is the outcome of the Trafficking [in persons] & Trade: The Impact of Globalization on Women Conference held in Denver, Colorado, on March 14–15, 2003. The conference was a three-pronged event—a Freedom Network (USA) workshop for law enforcement, advocates, and service providers; paper presentations; and a panel on Burma, with a silent auction to raise money for the women and children in the refugee camps on the Thai–Burma border. Special thanks to all those who participated in this conference to make it the success it was!

Most of the chapters included in this book were presented in a series of panels at this conference. Several authors have been added to fill the gap left by those who moved on to finish school or start new jobs. Thank you to the authors in this volume for their contributions and their patience and ready cooperation in revising and updating their papers for publication, maintaining communication, and meeting deadlines. And a special thank you to our publisher and our editors, Sheila-Katherine Zwiebel, Kathryn Funk, and Serena Leigh Krombach!

It takes thousands of hours of time to plan and coordinate a conference with a follow-up book and I could not have donated the time to this effort had it not been for my family who supported me, financially as well as emotionally, kept me in their prayers, and gave up quality family time for me to sit at my computer; also, friends and colleagues were vital to enable me to stay focused and maintain a sense of humor to facilitate the completion of this book.

And, finally, I want to thank Dr. George DeStefano for his encouragement at the beginning stages of this project, for without it, there would be no book.

Karen Beeks

A Message from Aung San Suu Kyi

$\mathcal{I}$t is an honor to be able to send a message, brief as it is, to this conference.[1] Such a conference reminds us that there is a continuing need to highlight the vulnerable position of women and children even in situations where the protection of basic human rights is the fundamental issue. Unless we address this special need, progress and development in our world could take on an asymmetry that exacerbates the crushing disadvantages with which women and children have to cope the world over.

Trafficking and trade are fuelled by the profit motive. Profit, defined simply, is the gain that is made in the course of a transaction. It is not something that can be seen purely in material terms. People take into consideration such factors as mental effort, loss of leisure, loss of enjoyment, and loss of emotional satisfaction or security when calculating the costs of a particular transaction; they are not likely to undertake it unless they believe their gains will be more than their losses. Too often women are seen merely as goods and chattels at the disposal of a society dominated by male concerns. The more value placed on women by society, the less likely it is that they will be regarded as a cheap commodity to be used and abused with impunity.

As we take practical steps to prevent trafficking in women and to punish those who engage in this most heinous of trades, we also have to work to eradicate deeply rooted customs and prejudices that undermine their position in society. Women have to be so valued that the price of treating them as disposable goods would be so high in emotional, spiritual, and economic terms that any perceived benefits would be greatly offset by a very real loss to family and society.

You who have organized this conference and are participating in it stand as living evidence of the high value of women. I believe your deliberations will result in practical measures that will improve the situation of women in this era of globalization. I would like to extend to you, and to your doughty male colleagues, my warm good wishes and to thank you for what you are doing for the rights of women and, consequently, for the good of the human race.

Aung San Suu Kyi
Rangoon
March 2003

NOTES

Aung San Suu Kyi (pronounced Awng San Su Chee) was born in Rangoon, Burma, in 1945. She is the daughter of Burmese General Aung San, who, after leading his country's military forces to victory in the war against Japan, was assassinated in July 1947. Following the famous 8-8-88 mass uprising of millions of people to protest against the government, which ended with a military crackdown killing thousands of people, she was chosen to lead the National League for Democracy in opposition to the ruling military regime. She was detained in 1989 and held under house arrest until 1995. She was rearrested and detained in May 30, 2003, following a brutal massacre of her supporters and is currently under house arrest. Suu Kyi hopes that international pressure, namely sanctions and tourist boycotts, will be the key to political change in her homeland.

1. Trafficking & Trade: The Impact of Globalization on Women Conference presented by Global Partnerships for Humanity in Denver, Colorado, March 14–15, 2003.

Introduction

Delila Amir and Karen Beeks

$\mathscr{T}$he United Nations estimates that 4 million humans,[1] mostly women and children, become victims of international trafficking each year and are forced to work in construction, farming, mining, fishing, landscaping, domestic and childcare work, or in the carpet, garment and brick industries. They are also used as warriors and camel jockeys and coerced into drug trafficking, begging, and illegal adoptions. Victims of sex trafficking are forced into prostitution, pornography, sex tourism, marriages, and the mail-order bride trade. This book focuses on the women and girls who have become victims of sex trafficking.

The collection of chapters presented in this book is devoted to the description and analysis of the phenomena of the current global sex industry from the operational features at the local community level to its global industrial structures and operations. Most of the specific country papers in this anthology have been researched and written by concerned academians and advocates, not only versed in the issues of the current discourses and debates about the global sex industry, but also knowledgeable and embedded in this particular sociocultural and political milieu.

CONCEPTUAL FRAME WORK

Any document or publication about prostitution at-large and the phenomenon of the sex industry as mostly a gendered phenomenon has to consider the feminist conceptual and political framework, as well as the current debates surrounding this issue. The readers of this book will find them interwoven in the individual country chapters and more pronounced in the discussions of the legal issues or debates regarding prostitution and trafficking. These feminist debates are also in the background of the chapters devoted to the discussion of the policies and activities of international organizations and even more pronounced in the section and chapters devoted to the mobilization to combat criminal activities of smuggling women and the supportive services developed by feminist groups in "importing countries."

While feminist debate focuses mostly on women's and, at times, children's motivational "push" for entering and staying in the trade as embedded in a patriarchal gendered context,[2] our conceptual framework for the book is the global sex industry, in which we have taken the perspective of a contextual-situated gendered analysis within Wallerstein's[3] conceptual framework about the "global industry" and the "world as a Global System." Our reference in this book to the "global" is based on Wallerstein's analysis of the current global system and its local manifestations, as well as the conditions and mechanisms that facilitate the (hegemonic) position of the capitalist economic system to shape and control the global industries. After first reviewing the papers submitted for this book, it became clear to us how the gendered, economic, and political systems in each of the importing countries seem to fit Wallerstein's analysis and how helpful his framework is in sharpening the issues at hand.

In this book, we made a point to include not only papers that describe and analyze the phenomena of the global sex industry, but also papers that explain the global, national, and local counterforces—anti-trafficking organizations, grassroots programs to combat the abusive, exploitative nature of the trade, and programs for alternative options and choices.

SOCIOPOLITICAL BACKGROUND

During the last decade of the twentieth century and simultaneous with the disintegration of the USSR into separate national states, we witnessed the tendency for new regional affiliations and development among nation states. At the same time, political, technological, and economic developments have contributed to strengthen the hold of Western countries on the developing countries. These developments facilitated the spread of the capitalist economic system and the flow of products, capital, and cheap labor. As more people emigrated from poor countries to rich countries in search of employment, women's labor immigration constantly increased and surpassed the rate of male labor immigrants in contrast to previous immigration waves. These developments have all contributed and been instrumental in the growth of the global sex industry and are demonstrated by the country chapters.

This book is about the global sex industry. The authors discuss the socioeconomic, cultural, and gendered background in specific geopolitical locations that make the option of becoming a sex worker—as forced or voluntary employment—an income producing venue for women exploited by the growing local and international activities of organized crime as part of these global trends. The general perspective and the individual papers composing this book view the sex industry as a global phenomenon linked to the general political, economic, and social developments within societies, regionally and internationally.

According to Wallerstein, the organizing capitalist global system exploits the work of one specific social category of people (i.e., women and children) for the benefit and profit of another category or categories of people (i.e., organizers and managers of the sex industry) and caters to the needs or created needs of additional categories of people (i.e., mostly men). Labor immigration and the commerce in humans, as Wallerstein and others argue, is one of its manifestations which methodologically, classical economic classifications taught us, calls for a differentiation between exporting countries and importing countries, or exporting regions and importing regions, communities, and so forth. In this scheme, the exporting countries or regions are peripherally located: mostly poverty ridden, dependent on resources from the center, even for their meager survival. At times, the people's experience of powerlessness and hopelessness is related also to the weakness of the state and its governing apparatuses, which enhance and contribute to the commerce in humans. In addition, a patriarchal gender structure, and at times, the custom of selling children and women, creates the human "material" for sex commerce.

Concomitantly, the economic resource gap between the rich and poor countries and between categories of people in the same society, including the gender gap, and the commodification of sex as organized by the sex industry, creates the global phenomenon, not only of the sex industry, but the commerce of women and children for this sex industry. This growing gap between rich and poor countries such as Mexico, Vietnam, and Nigeria and regions in South East Asia and the former Soviet Union motivates people, including women, to migrate to enhance their chances for a better life or to support their families. On the other hand, the surplus of income in the rich countries supports the consumer's side of the sex industry in their own countries (including Italy, USA, and Israel) and the global phenomenon of sex tourism.

The sex industry found the global capitalist system, which operates on the principal of supply and demand with a maximized profit, the least risky and the most profitable for business. The illegality of prostitution in many importing countries does not create a barrier to the traffickers, who bribe their way into the country and leave the smuggled women with an illegal status and vulnerable to abuse, exploitation, and victimization. This system reinforces the networking and cooperation of international and local criminal groups, as well as the corruption of law enforcement authorities and individuals.

The main goal of this book and the current effort of international and national bodies, as well as civil rights groups and organizations, is to expose the phenomenon of the global sex industry—to break the veil of silence, indifference, and apathy.

The first section of the book focuses on definitions, causes, trafficking routes, policies, and recommendations. In "Ambiguities and Confusions in Migration-Trafficking Nexus: A Development Challenge," Md. Shahidul Haque explains the differences between migration (both voluntary and forced), smuggling, and trafficking within the complex continuum of "population movement." He argues that "over emphasizing trafficking in persons within the general debate on a migratory process and 'mixing' it with legal migration could be counterproductive in addressing trafficking." Efforts to limit trafficking should not limit freedom of movement of people, which makes safe migration difficult for people of developing countries. Restrictive policies of migration in some destination countries pushes flow of migrants underground, making them easy victims of criminal gangs, claims Haque.

Arun Kumar Acharya supports Haque's thesis and says, "tightening of the U.S. borders has not slowed illegal immigration across the Mexican/U.S. borders. To escape the poverty and unemployment, many Mexicans are leaving their homes in search of a better future . . . many illegally." According to Acharya, economic globalization exacerbates the inequalities between nations whereby for many, migration becomes not a choice but an economic necessity. The number of Mexicans crossing the U.S./Mexican border has increased dramatically over the past five years, and one of the main reasons for this increase in numbers is the massive trafficking in women for the sex trade which now frequently involves "sophisticated crime networks." In "International Migration and Trafficking of Mexican Women to the United States," Acharya details some of the causes of trafficking such as the 1994 agrarian conflict between the indigenous people in Chiapas State and the Mexican government and practices such as "harvest time prostitution, weekend prostitution, and vacation time prostitution."

Currently, Vietnam has no precise and coherent understanding of what is meant by trafficking and approaches trafficking as one of the "social evils," a consequence of the open-door policy, change of economic management, process of urbanization, and increasing exchanges with other countries in the region, according to Vu Ngoc Binh in "Trafficking of Women and Children in Vietnam: Current Issues and Problems." During a rapid development process, there has been a negative impact of reforms, which include the disappearance of guaranteed housing, medical services, pensions and other basic services especially among the poorest of the families, says Binh. Because of this, women and girls have become more vulnerable to newly emerging social issues such as neglect, abuse, and exploitation, and trafficking is an outcome.

Similar to Vietnam, Malaysia does not have a word equivalent to the word "trafficking." In the second section of the book, Zarina Othman says the Malaysian government does not consider trafficking as an issue but as a smuggling issue and regards those who have been smuggled as illegal immigrants rather than trafficking victims. Othman and Haque agree that smuggling and trafficking threaten state security. In Othman's chapter, "Human (In)security, Human Trafficking and Security in Malaysia," she discusses how human *insecurity*, such as poverty, hunger and related economic inequities, and inadequate sanitation and healthcare due to an oppressive regime, has led to human trafficking, which constitutes a threat to every state's national security. She hopes to shift the focus from "national security," where the state is a primary entity to be protected, to human security, protecting the humans who live in that state, which in the long term is providing security for the state.

According to Saltanat Sulaimanova in "Trafficking in Women from the Former Soviet Union for the Purposes of Sexual Exploitation," after the collapse of the Soviet Union, political, economic and social changes occurred which resulted in unprecedented levels of poverty and unemployment, creating a new pool of women from which traffickers could recruit. The former Soviet Union Republics, especially Russia, are experiencing an organized crime epidemic—9,000 criminal organizations operate in Russia and control trafficking of humans. Sulaimanova discusses the involvement of government officials and the role of organized crime in Russia, Ukraine, and Kyrgyzstan and the methods used to control women such as violence, threats to family, drugs, withholding passports, and threats of deportation.

Gendered violence is also used in civil conflict in Colombia, which has claimed more than 40,000 (mostly civilian) lives over the past decade and internally displaced thousands more, and fuels the trafficking in women into sex work, according to Abbey Steele, "Insecurity and Opportunity in Colombia: Linking Civil War and Human Trafficking." She says, that while men are the primary targets of lethal violence in Colombia's war, women are the predominant targets of sexual violence. Poverty and unrest heighten the motivation for women to emigrate and be lured into the sex industry.

The third section focuses on laws, legislation, and international involvement. The Philippines experienced a similar problem defining the word "trafficking" as encountered in Malaysia and Vietnam. Carolina S. Ruiz-Austria, "Conflicts and Interests: Trafficking in Filipino Women and the Philippine Government Policies on Migration and Trafficking," critically assesses the laws and policies of a government bureaucracy that views the problem as simply "illegal recruitment" rather than "trafficking" in persons. Many governments are in denial or turn a blind eye to trafficking within their countries as the labor of migrant, sweatshop, sex, and domestic workers contributes significantly to their coffers. Ruiz-Austria says, "Because of a lack of economic opportunities at home and a growing demand for cheap labor in destination countries and with the encouragement of the Philippine government riding on the dollar remittances of overseas Filipino workers to stay afloat, more than 2,300 Filipino women risk traveling abroad daily." A new law recently enacted treats the phenomenon of trafficking as a human rights violation and distinguishes between situations where there is consent and where there is not.

The United States responded to the trafficking of humans through the implementation of the Trafficking Victims Protection Act (2000), which is the first comprehensive federal law to protect the victims of trafficking and prosecute their traffickers. In the chapter authored by Free the Slaves, Washington, DC, and the Human Rights Center at the University of California, Berkeley, and adapted for this book by Austin Choi-Fitzpatrick, "The Challenge of Hidden Slavery: Legal Responses to Forced Labor in the United States," he discusses the value and the shortcomings of the TVPA and says, "The key to the success of the bill is providing immigration benefits and social services to survivors of trafficking and forced labor."

Anne Gallagher takes the discussion one step further in her chapter on "Human Rights and Human Trafficking in Thailand: A Shadow TIP Report," as she discusses the problems with the standards established by the United States in the Trafficking in Persons (TIP) report mandated by the Trafficking Victims Protection Act of 2000. There is disagreement in the global community regarding the merits of these TIP reports, report cards of sorts, which give a "tier grade" to each country stating whether that country is complying with the established standards set by the United States. Using Thailand as an example, she argues that while it is important to have an evaluation and assessment process for each country's performance and progress, it is also important to recognize the limitations in this "unilateralist" approach where one size fits all.

William A. E. Ejalu reviews international conventions and national laws that have been established to eradicate trafficking of human beings such as the Universal Declaration of Human Rights, the Convention on the Rights of the Child, the Protocol to Prevent, Suppress & Punish Trafficking in Persons & Especially Women and Children and others in his chapter, "From Home to Hell: The Telling Story of an African Woman's Journey and Stay in Europe." While governments are able to ratify these conventions, they are not required to have any national laws with specific legislation regarding trafficking of persons. Ejalu says, "trafficking is a transnational crime, which requires the cooperation across borders to eliminate trafficking." Since enforcement agencies do not have jurisdiction beyond their borders, he sees the need for a separate treaty specifically for trafficking to enable law enforcement to punish the perpetrators.

The last section of the book is devoted to the combating of trafficking of women through local and national initiatives. Many diverse actions are being taken in many countries around the globe to tackle trafficking, including awareness campaigns, research, and rescue, rehabilitation, and reintegration programs which include educational and vocational training and employment opportunities for survivors of trafficking. Upala Devi Banerjee, "Migration and Trafficking of Women and Girls: A Brief Review of Some Effective Models in India and Thailand"; Rita Chaikin, "Fighting against Trafficking in Women in the North of Israel"; and Isabel Crowhurst, "The Provision of Protection and Settlement Services for Migrant Women Trafficked for Sexual Puroposes: The Case of Italy," describe the enormous input of the local women's movement and feminist organizations and the struggle to change laws which will enable trafficked women to get a legitimate status, access to services, and protection from abuse while developing support emergency services for sex workers who are interested in getting out of their bondage.

Banerjee says most observers believe there is a direct link between trafficking in persons, particularly women and children, with the ongoing insecurity of food and livelihood crisis, which is discussed in an earlier chapter by Othman. She says the focus should be on linking anti-trafficking programs at the macro level with intensive anti-poverty programs at the local and national levels and reveals several innovative approaches to combat trafficking in India and Thailand.

Isha L'Isha, the Haifa Feminist Center in Israel, initiated a project to provide support to women victims of trafficking and to raise public awareness of the phenomena, according to Rita Chaikin. Although prostitution is on the rise in Israel, their project has had a tremendous impact on the problem by providing the trafficked victims with emotional and practical support, medical insurance, and legal aid and representation. It has established a legislative parliamentary committee and network that works together for stricter legislation to fight trafficking.

Crowhurst provides a critical review of the protection and settlement services to women victims of sex trafficking in Italy from the deliverer's point of view. According to Crowhurst, little has been said regarding the impact these services have on the beneficiaries or to what extent their integration is successful from *their* standpoint. In the first section of the book, Haque stated: "The core of a meaningful counter-trafficking strategy should be based on the principle that women's rights are human rights . . . [it] should be gender sensitive and rights based." Crowhurst chorused these remarks with a concluding statement made by the former UN High Commissioner on Human Rights, Mary Robinson: "[We must] ensure that well-intentioned anti-trafficking initiatives do not compound discrimination against female migrants or further endanger the precariously held rights of individuals working in prostitution."

NOTES

1. Exact numbers of victims of trafficking are difficult to enumerate. The United States Department of State estimates between 600,000 to 800,000 men, women, and children are trafficked internationally each year (2005).

2. Kamala Kempadoo and Jo Doezema, *Global Sex Workers: Rights, Resistance and Redefinition*, London: Routledge (1998): 1–34. In their introduction to the book, Kampadoo and Doezema present the three main feminist perspectives toward the phenomena and issue of prostitution. While in their book they maintain the stance of "sex workers," whether voluntary, forced, trafficked, or immigrated.

3. Immanuel Maurice Wallerstein, *The Modern World System*, New York: Academic Press (1974–1989).

I

MIGRATION AND TRAFFICKING: DEFINITIONS, CONDITIONS, ROUTES, AND POLICIES

• 1 •

Ambiguities and Confusions in Migration-Trafficking Nexus: A Development Challenge

Md. Shahidul Haque

> The problem of trafficking and the web of human rights viola-
> tions it embraces present some of the most difficult and pressing
> issues on the international human rights agenda. Complexities in-
> clude different political contexts and geographical dimensions of
> the problem; ideological and conceptual differences of approach ...
> [the] link between trafficking and migration presents another
> complexity presenting both political and substantive obstacles to
> resolutions of the trafficking problem.
>
> UN Secretary General's Report on "Trafficking in
Women and Girls" presented at the 58th
Commission on Human Rights (2002), Geneva

The dynamics of population movement has undergone fundamental trans-
formations in the twenty-first century adding new multi-faceted dimensions,
complexities, and challenges. The age-old migratory nature of human beings,
which helped conquer the planet, has substantially been reshaped by formation
of nation-states, extreme poverty, economic imbalances, environmental degradation, and security challenges. Today, migration does not only imply "shifting
of population" from one place to another across political or geographical frontiers. Migration is not determined by simple human nature or desire; rather it
is an outcome of a set of interrelated historical, geographical, economic, social,
and political factors. These factors, forces, and processes create a complex migration picture (shown in appendix 1.1). Noticeably, the migration picture developed in mid-1990s did not contain trafficking in persons as a part of migration phenomena. It does not mean that trafficking did not exist then. It was
perhaps, because of lack of understanding and knowledge of intricacies of trafficking and migration that led to the absence of recognition of trafficking as a

case of population movement "gone wrong." These gaps or limitations in understanding pose a critical challenge for states and international communities to manage various types of migration effectively.

Trafficking in persons is the "dark side" of population movement, which places people in a "harm" situation. It is a form of modern-day slavery. It is a coercive and violent form of movement which must be prevented,[1] contrary to safe migration, which should be promoted as a livelihood option and which could be beneficial for all. The trafficking process thrives on individual's vulnerability and it has three core elements, namely, movement, deception or coercion and "harm" outcome or exploitation or slavery-like practice.[2] The interface between migration as the "bright side" and human trafficking as the "dark side" of population movement is far more complex and overlapping than our existing understanding suggests. In addition to the social, economic, and cultural factors, the tensions between the economically rationalized integrative forces, which encourage migration, and the restrictive immigration policies, which discourage such movement, have further compounded the nexus between the two phenomena.

This paper intends to examine the intricate link between migration and trafficking within the complex continuum of population movement. It also attempts to establish the relations between "smuggling in migrants" and "trafficking in persons" to bring in further conceptual clarity. It tries to argue that clear-cut differentiation between migration, smuggling, and trafficking is extremely difficult and attempts to separate them for development of interventions may be counterproductive at the end. The paper concludes that the best possible option is to take a comprehensive and integrated approach for management of migration and addressing the trafficking problem.

CONCEPTUAL AMBIGUITIES, LIMITATIONS, AND CONFUSIONS ABOUT VARIOUS TYPES OF POPULATION MOVEMENT

Involuntary and Voluntary Migration

There are primarily two generic types of population movement. First, there is "involuntary" or "forced" migration in which people are compelled to move out of their home in large numbers in situations of conflicts, both armed and non-armed. People flee or are obliged to leave their home or places of habitual residence out of fear of persecution or events threatening to their lives or safety.[3] There are numerous reasons behind forced migration such as persecution, human rights violations, repression, conflict, military aggression, and natural and man-made disasters. Sometimes people also leave their homes on their own initiative to escape from these life-threatening situations. Often-armed "groups" also force a large number out of their homes to fulfill objectives such as "depopulating" an area or "ethnic cleansing." Those forced to leave their homes either cross international borders in search of refuge or move to another place within the state-borders. The first group is known in general as "refugee," whereas the second group of people is termed as "internally displaced people" (IDP). Refugees move under compulsion, not by choice or for better livelihood. Refugees have a special status in international law under the UN Convention and Protocol Relating to the Status of Refugees administered by UNHCR. By definition, a refugee is a person who, owing to a well-founded fear of being persecuted for reasons of race, religion, nationality, membership of a particular social group or political opinion, is outside the country of his/her nationality and is unable to or owing to such fear is unwilling to avail himself/herself of the protection of that country or return there for fear of persecution.[4]

Second, there is "voluntary" migration in which people move out in search of better livelihood or for other reasons. The voluntary migration is a part of people's strategies to enhance and/or diversify their livelihood. The decision to migrate is often guided by the wider and brighter opportunities abroad. People who migrate are known as "migrants," "labor migrants," or "economic migrants." The migrants are rational persons who are able to judge opportunities abroad. The term "migrant" covers all cases where the decision to migrate is taken freely by the individual concerned, for reasons of "personal convenience" and without intervention of an external compelling factor.[5] But people also migrate because of poverty, lack of employment opportunity, and disaster. The forces of globalization, widening and deepening of trade liberalization, and economic disparities at home combined with ageing and declining of population abroad, influence both internal and international migration. Historically, migration has been an enduring component of human civilization. It has contributed to enriching societies and benefiting economies of both origin and destination countries.

It is estimated that there are about 185 million people living outside their country of birth, amounting to about 2.9 percent of global population.[6] Refugees and IDP constitute a small part of the global migratory population with 17 million refugees and 22+ million IDP.[7] Increasingly, the lines between migrant and asylum seekers are getting confused, as the distinction between migration control and the refugee protection is becoming blurred.[8] But a clearer differentiation between forced and voluntary migrants in the globalized world is needed as asylum seekers and refugees often use the same channel of migration as that of documented or undocumented migrants. The refugees and IDP often join a larger stream of migrants, posing challenges to the refugee regime and migration system. This development challenge is further compounded by the absence of an international regime for managing the broader spectrum of population movement.

Migration versus Trafficking in Persons

Migration and trafficking are two distinct but interrelated phenomena. Migration is a broad general concept and trafficking is only a subset or category of the broader migration concept. Migration is the movement of people from one place to another (in case of international migration one country to another) in order to take up employment or establish residence. It applies to various types of movements guided by diverse causes. International migration (i.e., migration across borders) in particular is a complex and multidimensional phenomenon. The dynamics of international migration is often explained or measured in relation to (either alone or in combination) citizenship, residence, time or duration of stay, purpose of stay, or place of birth. On the other hand, trafficking in persons as a subset of migration is the movement (either internally or internationally) of a person under a situation of deceit, force, threat, debt bondage, etc., involving exploitation and violation of human rights. Trafficking in persons therefore results in abusive exploitation and human rights violations. Studies suggest that a person by placing himself/herself in the hands of traffickers loses control of his/her fate and freedom[9] and ends up in a "harm"[10] situation.

The concept of migration is understood as covering all cases where the decision to migrate is taken freely by the individual concerned, for reasons of "personal convenience" and without intervention of an external compelling factor. It is clear from the definition that migrants are not refugees, exiles, or other persons forced or compelled to leave their home. According to the International Convention on the Protection of the Rights of All Migrant Workers and Members of Their Families, a "migrant worker" is a person who is to be engaged, is engaged or has been engaged, in a remunerated activity, in a State of which he or she is not a national.[11] The definition includes undocumented workers who would also, under this Convention, be entitled to certain rights.[12]

The above elaborations suggest that it is difficult to clearly differentiate between migration and trafficking, as the demarcation between the two phenomena is often not apparent and a question of perception. The efforts attempting to draw a clear line between the two concepts is described as working in a "terminological minefield."[13] In some cases, researchers and practitioners mistakenly use movement, mobility, and migration as interchangeable concepts. The movement or mobility of a trafficked person from one place to another is sometimes misperceived as migration. The movement or mobility may be a common element of the trafficking and migration phenomena, but it is not a criterion to ascertain the difference between the two processes. Rather, the presence or absence of coercion, exploitation, abuse, loss of control on life options, or agency is the determining factors. Absence of some or all of these makes movement of a person migration and the presence of these factor, trafficking. The presence of abuse or non-fulfillment of work contracts or violations of rights are trafficking outcomes irrespective of the nature of mobility with socioeconomic and legal dimensions/consequences. Sometimes attempts, though wrongly, are made to distinguish migration as a labor issue and trafficking as a human rights issue.[14] Any such generalization in identification of the differences between the two concepts can be misleading because both the concepts are overlapping, contextual, and time bound.

Moreover, violations of rights of migrants are addressed by specific sets of legal instruments, which are different for the legal procedure for combating trafficking cases. The national, regional, and global attitude, norms, and practices concerning the migrants and the trafficking survivors also reinforce the assumption that two groups have distinctive causes, purposes, and consequences in their life experiences and expectations.

In simple terms, the difference could be as follows:

- Trafficked persons are deceived or forced (actual or threat) to move, whereas, migrants (even domestic worker) are not usually deceived or forced to leave their place of residence. But sometimes it could be difficult to draw a line between the two concepts, as there are gray areas in between blurring the clear distinction.
- Both trafficking in persons and migration share the same "migratory space"; both involve movement but have very different outcomes, with trafficked persons being exposed to a "harm" situation.
- Trafficking is a development-retarding phenomenon, whereas migration is a development-enhancing process.
- Trafficking is viewed as an antisocial and morally degrading, heinous event. But migration is widely considered as a process that enhances social progress in both the origin and destination countries; if managed properly, it could be an empowering process. Exploitation, profit, and illegality are all central to the idea of trafficking in persons.[15] That is certainly not the case in the migration process.

Trafficking in Persons versus Smuggling in Migrants

In order to better understand the migration-trafficking nexus, we need to look at the concept of "smuggling in migrants" and identify the interfaces between the concepts of trafficking and smuggling. Smuggling in migrants is a phenomenon in which a person acts to facilitate his/her border crossing in an irregular manner, with the help of an entity, by making a financial or other material payment. There are differences between trafficking in persons and smuggling in migrants, both in the process of movement and in the outcome. The critical factor separating trafficking from smuggling is the presence of force or coercion throughout or at some stage in the process—the force or coercion being the purpose of exploitation.[16] In a case where a person was misled about the dangers of the journey and irrespective of the treatment he/she receives at the hands of smugglers, provided there is consent to the original transport and provided an exploitative relationship does not develop or was not envisaged between the two parties, it would be considered as smuggling in migrants.[17] The only situation in which non-coerced movement will be considered as trafficking is when the individual is a child.[18]

However, it may be noted that such distinctions between the two phenomena are not absolute or foolproof. In practice, establishing clear-cut distinction between trafficking and smuggling is a very challenging task. Often it is found that a person leaves the country as a smuggled migrant, but soon becomes victim of an abusive or exploitative situation while even in transit and eventually ends up in a "harm" situation, thereby falling under the definition of trafficking. Although the main purpose of migrant smuggling might be to facilitate the illegal entry of the migrant into another country, there are many cases in which smuggled migrants are exposed to violation and exploitation either during transportation to the destination country or on arrival.[19]

The United Nations draws a distinction between trafficking and smuggling. According to the Protocol to Prevent, Suppress and Punish Trafficking in Persons, Especially Women and Children (popularly known as Palermo Protocol), "trafficking in persons shall mean the recruitment, transportation, transfer, harboring or receipt of persons, either by the threat or use of abduction, force, fraud, deception or coercion, or by the giving or receiving of unlawful payments or benefits to achieve the consent of a person having control over another person, with the aim of submitting them to any form of exploitation [. . .]." On the other hand, according to the Protocol against the Smuggling of Migrants by Land, Air and Sea (other part of Palermo Protocol), "Smuggling of migrants shall mean the procurement of the illegal entry into or illegal residence of a person in (a) (any) State Party of which the person is not a national or a permanent resident in order to obtain, directly or indirectly, a financial or other material benefit."

IOM definitions are close to the above-mentioned UN protocols. According to IOM, trafficking occurs when a migrant is illicitly engaged (recruited, kidnapped, sold, etc.) and/or moved, either within national or across international borders. The intermediaries (traffickers) during any part of this process obtain economic or other profit by means of deception, coercion, and/or other forms of exploitation, under conditions that violate the fundamental human rights of migrants.[20] On the other hand, smuggling occurs when there is only illegal facilitation of border crossing.[21]

It is clear that the primary difference between trafficking and smuggling appears to be in relation to coercion, exploitation, and violation of human rights. Smuggling is clearly the manner in which a person enters a country, and with the involvement of third parties that assist him/her to achieve entry. Therefore, a potential migrant requests and pays a third party for assistance to cross into another State where, she/he has no right of residence and the third party (smugglers) involvement goes no further than the facilitation of the illegal border crossing. Trafficking is a more complex concept as it requires consideration not only of the manner in which a migrant enters a country but also his/her working conditions (outcome). Trafficking involves coercion and exploitation, and the main purpose of trafficking is to place persons in a "harm" situation where their labor can be exploited under conditions that involve human rights abuses. Trafficking has a bigger impact, particularly on women and children and entails trafficking for commercial sex purposes, and also for work in sweatshops, forced labor, begging, domestic or agricultural labor and forced or fictitious marriages. Trafficking is not a single event but a process starting from the recruitment, continuing on with the travel, and ending with the exploitation of the person (outcome). The differences between smuggling and trafficking could be as follows:

- Normally, smuggled migrants are aware of the conditions of the travel and voluntarily engage themselves in the process of irregular migration. Trafficked persons are seldom aware of the entire process. Even if they submit themselves freely to the trafficker, they cannot give consent to the abuses or exploitation or human rights violations they will be subjected to.
- While smuggling of persons indisputably involves international cross-border movements, trafficking could also occur within national borders, although the vast majority happens across international borders.

Experts opined that clear distinction between smuggling and trafficking could be difficult to establish, particularly in analyzing causes, process and outcomes. Smuggling may contain elements of deception and/or coercion as well. Both smuggled and trafficked persons (and even migrants) incur debts with the intermediaries, and the abuse of human rights may occur during the time of smuggling operations also. There is often a gray area in between the two processes. It is not realistic to discuss smuggling without trafficking.[22]

There is, however, a similarity, as both trafficking and smuggling threaten human and State security[23] because of the links with exploitation, organized crime, and violation of national legislation in both the processes. But the threat from trafficking in persons to State security is perhaps much higher as it concerns safety of its citizens. However, States need to provide protection to both smuggled and trafficked persons in terms of return and reintegration, and medical, psychological, counseling, and legal support.

Distinction between Trafficking, Smuggling, and Migration

It is obvious that ascertaining a clear distinction between migration, smuggling and trafficking is an extremely complex undertaking and often impossible. They are intertwined and part of population movement—both conceptually and operationally. It could be rather realistic to conceive all the three phenomena as part of a dynamic "population movement scenario." People on the move could be categorized in nine different categories (see appendix 1.2) depending on their legal and human rights status. Movements back and forth along the two processes are not only possibilities but inevitable, and often that is the case. As shown in appendix 1.2, migrants in an orderly and humane situation could be placed on the left side of the diagram and trafficked/smuggled persons on the right of the diagram.

THEORETICAL FRAMEWORK FOR ANALYZING MIGRATION AND TRAFFICKING

There are several theories to explain reasons for international and internal migration. The migration theories, over the years, have moved from macro-level structural explanations (e.g., spatial differences in the characteristics of capital and labor market) to individual level behavioral explanations (e.g., beliefs, norms and expectations about consequences of migration behavior).[24] Recent theories are looking at migration integrating it with the structural behavioral explanations. The process of migration could be analyzed through macro theory (Push-Push factor), or micro theory, or new economics of migration, or dual labor market theory, or world system theory, or network theory, or institutional theory or migration system theory.[25]

On the other hand, there is not much theoretical work done on trafficking or smuggling phenomena. There is no strong theoretical construction, which could deal with trafficking or smuggling within a broader migration dynamics taking into accounts the process and outcome of trafficking. There are two overlapping approaches to analyze trafficking.[26] First, an economic perspective that considers trafficking as an economic activity approaches trafficking in a broader concept of business in which agents/institutions seek to make profit.[27] Some analysts have suggested that trafficking should be viewed as a consequence of the "commodification" of the process that generates profit out of peoples' mobility. Placing trafficking only in economic and/or legal bounds makes it difficult to identify elements of movements that are associated with quasi-legal or quasi-economic issues. Second, a legal perspective considers trafficking as a criminal activity. It considers trafficking as a violation of legal provisions of the State and/or violation of human rights. It assumes that criminal networks have emerged involving trafficking in persons, which provide labor to the "hidden economy" illegally. The main weakness of the two perspectives is that neither focuses on the outcome of trafficking, e.g., abuses, exploitation, and human rights violations of the person. Therefore, there are discussions on construction of a "humanitarian perspective" or "rights based approach" to deal with the trafficking phenomenon.

The ambiguities in theoretical understanding of the migration-trafficking nexus often lead to unavailability of adequate and reliable statistical data. The researchers face difficulties in choosing appropriate methods of data collection and analysis. The inadequate data in turn impose two types of "limitations" on the researches: first, overdependence on subjective interpretation which could be biased and marred by individuals' perceptions: second, adoption of "ad hoc methods" which sometimes could lead to distorted analysis and outcomes. Since trafficking and irregular migration take place within a broader socioeconomic space, there is a need to be careful in choosing the right terminology in describing the various processes of population movement.

IMPLICATIONS OF MIGRATION-TRAFFICKING AMBIGUITIES ON INTERVENTIONS TO ADDRESS TRAFFICKING IN PERSONS

The situation of migrants with that of trafficked or smuggled persons is often "mixed up," creating difficulties for management of migration. Overemphasizing trafficking in persons within the general debate of population movement and "mixing" it with regular migration could be counterproductive in addressing the trafficking and smuggling-in-persons problem. It may also make regular and safe migration difficult, especially for the people of developing countries. Some of the destination countries sometimes use trafficking and smuggling as excuses to develop more restrictive approaches toward migration. They argue that "trafficking in migrants" is a criminal act and needs strict crime prevention strategies to tackle it. These policies further limit the impacts of interventions attempting to address the trafficking problem.

However, it must be noted that efforts to limit trafficking and smuggling in persons should not limit freedom of movement of people. Migration remains a basic option of livelihood for many families and communities. It also provides opportunities for developing countries to enhance socioeconomic development, among others, through receiving remittances and skill transfers. The UN High Commissioner for Human Rights has recommended[28] that anti-trafficking measures should not adversely affect the common right and dignity of persons, in particular the rights of migrants, internally displaced persons, refugees, and asylum-seekers. It further recommended protection of the rights of all persons to move freely and ensure that anti-trafficking measures do not infringe upon that right.[29]

ALTERNATIVE STRATEGY TO MANAGING POPULATION MOVEMENT

The ambiguities and confusions in identifying different categories of population movement make management of mobile populations a difficult task, especially in an environment where international regime for migration is almost nonexistent. Some countries have developed ad hoc and reactive policies to address the various challenges of population movement. Most of these policies are narrowly based, not mainstreamed and project-centric. They are mostly treated outside the frame of the main development planning of the country. Today, some countries are realizing the limitations of this project approach for migration management, particularly in addressing trafficking and smuggling problem. They are also recognizing the need for an integrated framework to develop larger "program"-based strategies for managing migration. The concepts of "program approach," "sector-wide approach," and "sectoral approach" are often used interchangeably. The "program approach" is a longer-term, coordinated way of developing strategies to manage a particular sector such as health, rural development, or education. It tries to involve all stakeholders, is strategic in perspective, and is flexible in setting goals and implementing mechanisms. It is broader and more comprehensive than the "project approach," which narrowly bases or focuses its efforts on achieving immediate, issues-specific objectives through a relatively rigid implementation process. The programmatic strategy to migration management holds possibilities to manage migration and trafficking in persons in an integrative and comprehensive manner.

In Bangladesh, trafficking in persons has emerged as the priority for the government, and it is considering adopting an operational framework for engaging a wide range of partners and developing comprehensive migration policy responses. A counter-trafficking program strategy has already been developed and was published in June 2004. It focuses on how programming can be planned, implemented, and monitored, who/which agency is responsible for the different program aspects, and the time frame needed to measure concrete progress. Based on that programming, a National Anti Trafficking Strategic Plan of Action is being formulated, linking it to the overall migration management policies of the country.[30]

To effectively manage migration in a comprehensive and integrative manner, a strategy could be conceived through looking at the four-box chart of migration management (see appendix 1.3). The chart has four interlinked thematic boxes, namely, "migration and development," "facilitating migration," "regulating migration," and "forced migration." There are also a number of cross cutting issues. The initiatives also must have policy, legislation, and administrative organizations, both at the national and the regional level. Migration cannot be managed in isolation, and like other aspects of globalization it is more manageable when origin, transit, and destination countries work together.[31] Therefore adoption of a comprehensive systematic approach at the national level is a crucial first step, which needs to be linked at the regional level to ensure effectiveness.

CONCLUSION

The traditional theoretical understanding of population movement can no longer comprehend the complexities of trafficking or smuggling in persons. It cannot analyze and resolve the ambiguities and uncertainties concerning migration and trafficking. It warrants a new theoretical framework for providing a clear picture and analytical understanding on the issue. There is a general recognition that trafficking should be analyzed in its totality ("process" as well as "outcome") and policies addressing trafficking should have provisions for safe migration as well.

The existing migration policy in some origin countries based on bans/restrictions on migration of women abroad for employment purposes (which is otherwise discriminatory and regressive in nature) and the restrictive migration policies of some destination countries cannot effectively and comprehensively manage global population movement, particularly trafficking in persons. Rather, it pushes the flow underground, making innocent people easy prey of criminal gangs.

Another limitation, which often hampers effectiveness of counter-trafficking interventions, is the lack of gender responsiveness of the strategy. Moreover, programs often lack a rights-based sustainable development orientation. This limits efficacy of the interventions and disempowers the survivors. The core of a meaningful counter-trafficking strategy should be based on the principle of human rights. The counter-trafficking interventions should be gender sensitive and rights based. It should also address the difference and specific needs of women and children survivors. To effectively address irregular migration, interventions should also ensure human entitlements and well-being of the vulnerable groups in order to expand their choices and promote and empower them in an equitable and sustainable manner. This could be possible within an integrated and multi-sectoral counter-trafficking program, which would be an integral component of development planning of countries.

In the immigration context, the irregular migration including trafficking could be curbed by progressively "regulating" the flow of migrants. The process requires not only adoption of a migration policy, but also a reorientation of basic strategies and rationale for migration management. A comprehensive, flexible, and balanced mechanism to regulate migration, including irregular flows, can reduce "tension" between States on one hand and between employers and migrant workers on the other. It can also enhance the image of the country and society. The UN Principles and Guidelines on Human Rights and Human Trafficking[32] suggest that States should effectively enforce agreements to help eliminate trafficking and related exploitations.

The new migration-trafficking regime has to be consistent with the development trends and priorities. The international development partners should similarly "rethink" the significance of migration on the socioeconomic development process both in origin and destination countries, especially its potential role in addressing global inequalities. Increasingly, migration is conceived as a "developmental force" as well as an "equalizing force" which could soften the impact of adverse consequences of the globalization process on the developing countries. The development partners should look beyond traditional boundaries of "security," "criminality," "sovereignty," or "immigration" in formulating a creative counter-trafficking policy and strategy.

A program-based migration management structure could be one of the options that the South Asian countries could perhaps examine. A programmatic strategy to deal with both migration and trafficking in an integrated manner could also help countries to strike a right balance between priorities and concerns of State, society, and individual citizens in the area of population movement. It could eventually increase the possibilities of preserving the integrity and development-enhancing role of migration as a natural process of societal advancement.

To meet the demands for a comprehensive balanced and integrated policy approach, we may consider looking at the IOM's migration management strategy. It relates to shaping of clear and comprehensive policies, laws, and administrative arrangements to ensure that the population movements occur in a humane and orderly way to the mutual benefit of migrants, societies, and governments. To this end, migration management must be comprehensive and should take into consideration all forms of population movement, regular and irregular.

Along with the national level comprehensive and coherent approach, it is important to integrate the national efforts into a regional framework. A collaborative endeavor among the States is a precondition for a successful approach to manage population movement in a globalized world. A widely negotiated and mutually agreed arrangement in the form of a "Framework for Cooperation" to manage population movement, both regular and irregular, is a most essential precondition for a sustainable system. The Framework should reflect concerns and interests of all States and parties and should contain principles to guide individual States to formulate and implement their individual migration and counter-trafficking policy. The Framework must have a mechanism to reconcile contradictory priorities and interests of the concerned countries. The success of the "Cooperation Framework" to address broader migration issues and processes will largely depend on balancing the concerns, priorities, and development interests of the trafficked survivors and migrants as well as the origin, transit, and destination countries. In order to develop a consensus on a framework, we need to initiate a regional consultative process, which would be informal in its mechanism. The earlier we recognize needs for such a forum, the better it is for all of us.

APPENDIX 1.1
TYPOLOGIES AND INTERRELATED CAUSES OF MIGRATION

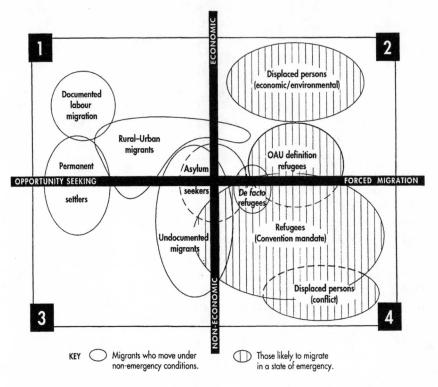

Note: IOM, "Overview of International Migration," Migration Management Training Program, April 1997, Geneva.

APPENDIX 1.2
DYNAMICS OF POPULATION MOVEMENT
IN A PROCESS-OUTCOME SCENARIO

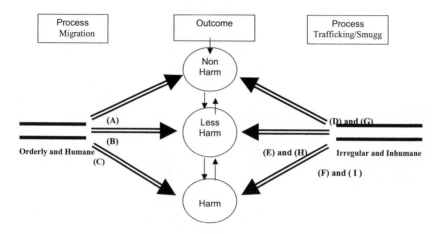

(A) A person who has been migrated to another country with legal documents (orderly process) and is in a "non-harm" working situation (humane outcome).

(B) A person who has been migrated to another country with legal documents (orderly process) but is in a "less-harm" situation (exploitative outcome).

(C) A person who has been migrated to another country with legal documents (orderly process) but is in a "harm" situation (inhumane outcome).

(D) A person who has been smuggled into another country (irregular/in orderly process) but is in a "non-harm" working situation (humane outcome).

(E) A person who has been smuggled into another country (irregular process), and is in a "less-harm" situation ((exploitative outcome).

(F) A person who has been smuggled into another country (irregular process), and is in a "harm " situation (inhumane outcome).

(G) A person who has been trafficked either within his or her own country or another country through a forced, deceptive and abusive process (irregular process) but is in a "non-harm" situation (humane outcome).

(H) A person who has been trafficked either within his or her own country or another country through a forced, deceptive and abusive process (irregular process) and is in a "less-harm" situation (exploitative outcome).

(I) A person who has been trafficked through a forced, deceptive and abusive process (irregular process) and is in a "harm" situation (inhumane outcome).

APPENDIX 1.3
CONCEPTUAL FRAMEWORK FOR
MIGRATION MANAGEMENT STRATEGY

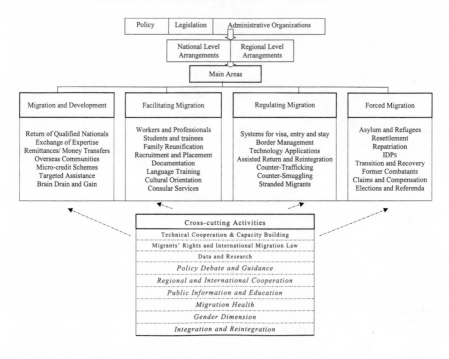

NOTES

An earlier version of this chapter, titled "Ambiguities and Confusions in Migration-Trafficking Nexus: A Challenge for Development Practitioners," was published in December 2002 in *Human Rights and Development*, edited by Dr. Mizanur Rahman. The author is grateful to Umbareen Kuddus of IOM Dhaka for reviewing the paper.

1. Jyoti Sanghera, "Enabling and Empowering Mobile Women and Girls" (paper presented at the Seminar on Promoting Gender Equality to Combat Trafficking in Women and Children, Bangkok, 7–9 October 2002).

2. Jean D'Cunha, "Gender Equality, Human Rights and Trafficking: A Framework of Analysis and Action" (paper presented at the Seminar on Promoting Gender Equality to Combat Trafficking in Women and Children, Bangkok, 7–9 October 2002).

3. Susan F. Martin, "Forced Migration and the Evolving Humanitarian Regime," UNHCR Working Paper No. 20, Geneva, July 2000.

4. 1951 Convention relating to the Status of Refugees.

5. International Organization for Migration (IOM), "Overview of International Migration, Migration Management Training Program," April 1997.

6. IOM, "World Migration 2005: Costs and Benefits of International Migration," Geneva, 2005.

7. UNHCR Discussion Paper presented at Sixth Plenary Meeting of APC, Manila, 5–6 December 2001.

8. UNHCR Discussion Paper, 5–6 December 2001.

9. IOM, "Migrant Trafficking and Human Smuggling in Europe: A Review of the Evidence with Case Studies from Hungary, Poland and Ukraine," Geneva, 2000.

10. "Harm" is the undesirable outcome that places a person in a situation whereby the person finds him/herself in an exploitative and dehumanizing condition, often beaten up, sexually and psychologically abused, made to work long hours without any remuneration. Freedom of mobility and choice are nonexistent. The "harm" results from a situation of forced labor, servitude, and slavery-like practices in which a person is trapped/held in place through force, manipulation, or coercion for a given period of time.

11. Article 2 (3a) of International Convention on the Protection of the Rights of All Migrant Workers and Members of Their Families.

12. For details see Syed Refaat Ahmed, "Forlorn Migrants: An International Legal Regime for Undocumented Migrant Workers," 1999, UPL Dhaka.

13. Ronald Skeldon, "Trafficking: A Perspective from Asia" in *Perspectives on Trafficking of Migrants*, ed. Reginald Appleyard and John Salt (Geneva: IOM, 2000).

14. IOM, "Migrant Trafficking and Human Smuggling in Europe."

15. IOM, "Migrant Trafficking and Human Smuggling in Europe."

16. Advisory Council of Jurists, The Asia Pacific Forum of National Human Rights Institutions, "Consideration of Issues of Trafficking—Background Paper," New Delhi, 11–12 November 2002.

17. Advisory Council, "Consideration of Issues of Trafficking."

18. Advisory Council, "Consideration of Issues of Trafficking."

19. Frank Laczko, "New Directions for Migration Policy in Singapore," *Royal Society Journal,* 2001.

20. IOM, "The Concepts of Trafficking in Human Beings and Smuggling of Migrants," Discussion Paper, Geneva, October 2000.

21. IOM, "Concepts Trafficking and Smuggling."

22. Ronald Skeldon, "Trafficking: A Perspective from Asia," IOM, Geneva, 2000.

23. Security has been used in its broadest possible term including both military and non-military dimensions.

24. IOM, "Moroccan Migration Dynamics: Prospects for the Future," Geneva, August 2002.

25. For an analytical work see S. Douglas Massy et al., "Theories of International Migration: A Review and Appraisal," *Population and Development Review* 19, no. 3, September 1993.

26. IOM, "Migrant Trafficking and Human Smuggling in Europe."

27. John Salt and Jeremy Stein, "Migration as a Business: The Case of Trafficking," *International Migration* 35, issue 4, December 1997.

28. "Recommended Principles & Guideline on Human Rights and Human Trafficking," Report of the United Nations High Commissioner for Human Rights to the Economic and Social Council, New York, July 2002, E/2002/100.

29. UN, "Principles & Guideline."

30. For more details, see "Counter Trafficking Framework Report: The Bangladesh Perspective," 2004.

31. IOM, "Managing Migration Challenges and Responses for People on the Move," World Migration Report 2003, Geneva, 2003.

32. UN, "Principles & Guideline."

• 2 •

International Migration and Trafficking of Mexican Women to the United States

Arun Kumar Acharya

*M*igration is perceived by both men and women as a means to improve their living situation and increase their share in development. Poverty and lack of opportunities represent the major factors leading men and women to move away from their national border. Female emigration is spurred in part by a large wage differential between sending and receiving countries, and the increasing burden placed on women by rising male unemployment at home, as well as by the reduction in demand for male labor in receiving countries due to economic slowdowns, which cause demand to shift to services that usually employ female labor.

Migration is not a new phenomenon. People have always left their home in search of better economic opportunities, both within and outside their own homeland. But economic globalization has put a new spin on global migration, causing global movement and human displacement at an unprecedented scale. Because economic globalization exacerbates the inequalities between nations, migration for many becomes not a choice, but an economic necessity. Today, more than one billion people, or nearly one out of every six people in the world, are crossing national borders as migrants—and 60 percent are women.[1]

This growing female migration flow allows the women to offer better living conditions to their families, whether in the country of origin or destination. This movement seems to have an empowering impact on women in terms of higher self-esteem and increased economic independence both as family members and as economic actors. Also, with women's educational levels improving notably worldwide and with declining fertility rates, women's insertion in the labor market has showed rates of economic participation close to men.

Today, the feminization of international labor migration is a global trend. The percentage of women in the migrant population (both permanent and temporary migrants) has been increasing in the postwar period, and at present they comprise the majority of international migrants. According to Zlotnik,[2] between 1965 and 1990, the number of female migrants around the world increased by 63 percent—from 35 million to 57 million—an increase of 8 percent higher than that of male migrants and in the United States, 53.3 percent of newly admitted immigrants were women in 1998.

Women are no longer just following their fathers or husbands. They migrate on their own capability as workers. However, as the number of migrant women increased, the incidence of abuse and exploitation has also risen. Since most migrant women work at the bottom rung of the occupational hierarchy, they are extremely vulnerable.[3] The vast majority of them work as sex workers, housemaids, entertainers, nurses, and factory workers. Sex workers are especially vulnerable because they work in brothels and bars where there is very little scrutiny by the authorities. Problems include harassment, violence, verbal/physical/sexual abuse, and so on.

Because of these growing problems, many international organizations such as the United Nations Population Conference in Cairo, Egypt (1994), United Nations Fourth World Conference on Women (1995) in Beijing, China, and the United Nations General Assembly and other international conferences and meetings have been addressing the problems that migrant women are facing. The United Nations General Assembly adopted the Resolution on Violence Against Women Workers in 1994. The United Nations Commission on the Status of Women and the Commission on Human Rights also adopted the Resolution and all have taken initiatives to encourage member States to adopt and implement effective measures to protect migrant women.

Despite this growing attention to the issue of female migration, there has not been any systematic research to explain the mechanism and pattern of international female migration in relation to trafficking. Most studies simply compile descriptive cases without systematic comparisons or present theoretical assumptions without providing empirical evidence. This research aims to fill the gap by considering the trafficking of women from Mexico to the United States. Primary information was gathered during fieldwork for my doctoral thesis on trafficking of women in Mexico.

MIGRATION FROM MEXICO TO UNITED STATES

Historically, Mexico and the United States comprise a region of significant population movements. Migration is a factor that often looms large in the region's social and economic life as well as its political discourse. In the postwar period, the region was largely an immigration source with the bulk of outside flows heading to the United States. The situation changed radically during the economic crisis and restructuring of the 1980s, which led to increased geographic and social polarization. Illegal migration appeared to decline during the oil boom, but after that when 4 million new jobs were created in the United States, it increased sharply again.[4]

Meanwhile, the United States and Canada have witnessed attempts at redefining themselves as a "country of immigration," resulting in periodical relaxing and tightening of their immigration policy. Although Mexico remains the single most important source for immigrants to these countries, both the United States and Canada have seen increasing diversity in their immigrant population during the past several decades, with profound implications for illegal migration and migrant trafficking. The undocumented migration to the United States has remained high since the mid-1970s. In 1976, more than a decade after the termination of the Bracero Program in 1964, it was estimated that as many as 12 million persons were residing illegally in the United States; 4 million were from Mexico.[5]

To escape the poverty and unemployment, many Mexicans are leaving their homes in search of a better future. Most of the time the conditions are so grim that they prefer to cross the border at any cost, many illegally. Other contributing factors for the migration from Mexico to the United States include economic changes in Mexico (peso devaluation),[6] rapid population growth, increasing labor market in the United States, changes in the US immigration policy, and fluctuation in US border enforcement.

During 1960–1970, there were approximately 290,000 illegal Mexican migrants, of which 5,200 were women. From 2000 to 2002, the estimated number of illegal Mexican migrants increased to 840,000; 336,000 were women.[7] These numbers reflect the annual increase of illegal Mexican migrants, including women, into the United States. One of the main reasons for this growing number of illegal migrants is the massive trafficking of women for the sex trade in the United States. For the last few decades, the demand for women in the sex trade has increased more than 50 percent. To meet this demand, the traffickers prefer to take the women from Mexico as both countries share the border and there is less risk for a trafficker to traffic a woman from Mexico compared to any other country.

Although migrant smuggling has long existed in the region, it only recently captured wide attention among authorities in the region. Previously, migrant smuggling in the region involved relatively small-scale intra-regional movement abetted by unsophisticated *coyotes* or *polleros*. Since the late 1980s and early 1990s, illegal migration has increased from Mexico to the United

States. Not only is this a route for the growing illegal migration (smuggling) but also trafficking of migrants through the region which now frequently involves sophisticated crime networks taking advantage of the high profit and low risk of their businesses.

Although intra-regional movements continue unabated, the involvement of trafficking syndicates and associated criminality has caused the greatest concern for the law enforcement officials. Migrant trafficking has affected nearly every country in the world as a point of origin, transitional locale, or destination for the victims. Although Mexico is a country that acts as a point of origin, transit, and destination, the United States Department of State has ranked Mexico as a source country in the trafficking of women to the United States. Due to existing poverty, unemployment, and political instability, many Mexican women are migrating to big cities where many become victims of the organized trafficking networks.

TRAFFICKING OF MEXICAN WOMEN TO UNITED STATES

The United Nations Protocols to Prevent, Suppress and Punish Trafficking in Persons, Especially Women and Children, supplementing the Convention on Transnational Organized Crime (2000),[8] defines trafficking as "the recruitment, transportation, transfer, harbouring or receipt of persons, by means of the threat or use of force or other forms of coercion, of abduction, of fraud, of deception, of the abuse of power or of a position of vulnerability or of the giving or receiving of payments or benefits to achieve the consent of a person having control over another person, for the purpose of exploitation. Exploitation shall include, at a minimum, the exploitation of the prostitution of others or other forms of sexual exploitation, forced labor or services, slavery or practices similar to slavery or servitude or the removal of organs."

This definition makes clear that trafficking covers not only the transportation of a person from one place to another, but also their recruitment and receipt so that anyone involved in the movement of another person for their exploitation is part of the trafficking process. It also states that trafficking is not limited to sexual exploitation and also takes place for forced labor and other slavery-like practices. This means that people who migrate for work in agriculture, catering, construction, or domestic work but are deceived or coerced into working in conditions they did not agree to are also defined as trafficked people.

The International Organization for Migration[9] has tentatively defined trafficking in women as:

> any illicit transporting of migrant women and/or trade in them for economic or other personal gain. This includes: (1) facilitating the illegal move-

ment of migrant women to other countries, with or without their consent or knowledge; (2) deceiving migrant women about the purpose of migration, legal or illegal; (3) physically or sexually abusing migrant women for the purpose of trafficking; and, (4) selling women into or trading in women for the purpose of employment, marriage, prostitution or other forms of profit-making abuse.

In relation to international migration, trafficking is considered to exist if an international border is crossed; an intermediary, the trafficker(s), is involved in the movement of the migrant; the recruitment and transporting of migrants or the disposition of such migrants en route or after arrival is accomplished through illicit or abusive means; and the trafficker profits from such activities in terms of economic or other personal gain.

Trafficking has been described as the "trade of human misery." It has increased dramatically during the 1990s, and the United States Department of State estimates that currently 800 to 900 thousand people are trafficked across borders annually.[10] The International Labour Organization (ILO) estimated in 2000, 1.2 million children had been trafficked for sexual or labor exploitation internationally.[11] While estimates of the number of trafficking victims are available, accurate statistics are difficult to obtain because of the clandestine nature of trafficking and the problems involved in detecting and documenting it.

Trafficking cases are hard to uncover as these crimes usually occur behind closed doors and language and cultural barriers usually isolate the victims. The main destination for trafficked women from Mexico is the United States, where approximately 5,000 women aged 17 to 20 years are trafficked annually, primarily for the sex industry (prostitution, stripping, peep and touch shows, and massage parlors), domestic servitude, agricultural labor, maid services at motels and hotels, and to peddle trinkets on subways. The majority of them come from the states of Guerrero, Chiapas, Oaxaca, Michoacán, Zacatecas, Colima, Chihuahua, Sonora, Yucatán, Veracruz, and Quintana Roo.[12]

Though many international organizations, as well as the United Nations and the government of the United States, have focused on the problem of trafficking from Mexico to the United States, evidence shows that the problem is becoming more serious as a violation of human rights due to the commodification of women.

It is a contemporary problem for a poverty-stricken country like Mexico, where women are sold as sex workers and slaves in cities and foreign countries. Along with poverty, other factors such as inadequate employment opportunities, combined with poor living conditions (basically in the indigenous community), including inter-familial violence, family breakdown, and unwanted pregnancies, force young Mexican women to leave their homes. Out of desperation for employment, they become an easy target for traffickers. Similarly, the growing divorce rate in Mexico is also a concern factor in the process of trafficking, where traffickers target divorcees and promise them marriage and/or employment in the United States.

Practices like the voluntary migration for the purpose of prostitution are also a contributing factor behind trafficking of women. For example, *prostitucion en temporada de cosecha* (harvest time prostitution) in the state of Chiapas is the practice of women and young girls from urban centers migrating to the rural areas during the sugarcane harvest where they find a large concentration of agricultural laborers and practice prostitution. During this period the national and international traffickers also arrive at the sites and offer employment to the women and girls. Once they accept the offer, they are trafficked and sent to a brothel.

Also, in the states of Oaxaca, Guerrero, and Morelos, many girls studying in colleges and universities are working as prostitutes on weekends to meet their economic needs. This practice, famous as *prostitution en temporada de vacaciones* (vacation time prostitute) or *prostitutas temporada de fin de semana* (weekend prostitute), has also encouraged the sex trafficking in Mexico.

But research shows these are not the only factors behind this lucrative business. The 1994 agrarian conflict between the indigenous people in the state of Chiapas and the government of Mexico is another contributing factor for trafficking. During this conflict approximately 40,000 indigenous people have been internally displaced and forced to leave their home and lands and living in appalling conditions. Those who remain on their land cannot cultivate their land for lack of sufficient space to farm or for fear of the paramilitaries. This has led to greater poverty in the region and subjected these groups to greater exploitation. To escape from poverty and conflict, some parents have sold their daughters in hope of a better life.[13] Considering all these factors, our research found trafficking of women a *multicausal* phenomenon.

One example is the case of Maria[14] whom we interviewed in Mexico City.[15] Maria is 23 years old and works as a sex worker in La Merced, a brothel in Mexico City. She was trafficked five years prior to our interview to one of the brothels in San Diego, California, from the state of Michoacán. This is Maria's story:

When I was 14 years old, my mother had some serious health problems, for which we admitted her in the hospital. Doctor told us, it was necessary to do operation, other wise she cannot alive. When my father asked about the total cost of the operation, they told it was nearly 60 to 70 thousands pesos (US$6,000–7,000). To get this amount of money, we sold our agricultural land and some part of the house, but it was not sufficient, so we took some money from our village community. In this way, we gather money and did the operation, but after one year of my mother's operation, we cannot save her. She died because we didn't had sufficient money to buy her medicine. One year after her death, the village community ask for their money, but we could not return it. . . .

Luckily or unluckily, one day a person came to our village and he introduced himself in front of the village community as employment agency, and said he gives work to the women in Mexico City and the United States. He mentions that he needs at least ten to fifteen young women. The next day my father went to talk with *mayordomo* (village head) for work for me. Both my father and mayordomo talked with him and after this discussion he assured my father that he will try to find good domestic work for me in the United States. After two days, he came to my house and paid 5,000 pesos (US$500) and told my father this is advance money and this money he will deduct from my salary. One week later, along with other four girls from my village, we started our journey. That was the first time I was going out from my village, though I was feeling fear about the new environment, also feeling happy that now I could help my parents economically. After traveling five hours, in the evening we reached Mexico City, where the agent took us to a hotel. We stayed two days in Mexico City and started our passage towards the United States. After three days of continuous travel, we reached Ciudad Juarez (border city between Mexico and United States) and one week later in the evening, we crossed the border. Once we crossed the border we walked . . . five to six hours until we reached a town (I do not remember the name), where our agent took us to a house and introduced us to another person and told us now his friend will take us to San Diego and arrange the job for us. After that he returned to Mexico.

We were feeling fear because of not having passport and others papers. But two days later that person took us to San Diego and after reaching this city, he took us to a house where we saw a big fat woman who was speaking Spanish. She took us to a room where I found some women with others boys doing the sex. I got afraid about the place . . . and asked that agent about the place, he told me, "I bought you all from my Mexican friend for the sex work, and now you all have to work with this *hermana* (sister) like others girls." After hearing this, I tried to escape from the place, but I could not. Then, they told me, "*ustedes estan en Estados Unidos, estan ilegal aquí, si van a escapar la policía les van a llevar a cárcel*" ("you all are in the United States and all of you are illegal here, if you will try to escape from here, the police will take you to jail"). This gave us lots of fear. Since childhood, I always afraid the police, because they torture very badly. After that they explain about the work, but along with my others friends we refused to work with them. They forced us and even then we didn't accept the work. Then they beat us and locked us in a house for some days, and told us they will not open the door if we will not accept their work.

Two days later, it was morning time and a person came and asked about our decision. When we told no, he beat us and asked his other friends to come inside. Then they locked the door and abused us sexually, also took some photographs and told us if we will not accept the work, they will send these photos to our parents. This gave us terror and we thought about our social prestige and parents. After that we told them that we will agree to work.

Once we accepted their demand, they taught us about the work, how we have to negotiate with clients and they also taught us some English. This training was one week and after that we started working. Every day I was taking more than 10 clients and charging around US$10 to each client for 30 minutes. Some times the madam was asking me to work without condom, for that she was taking US$15 to US$20. Every day the madam was paying me US$10. Many times she was also forcing me to work in midnight and if I told no, she was scolding me. The day when I enter to this profession my life has converted into violence. I am facing violence from madam and sometimes from the clients. When the client did not get satisfied in sex, they beat us. Though I did not have any interest to work, I was working because I do not have any option to go anywhere. I was living at a place, which did not belong to me. I did not know anyone over there. After working little more than five years continuously, one day the agent from Mexico came and asked me to come with him. When I asked for the reason, he told me: "*ya esta vieja, los clients no te quieren más*" ("now you are old, the clients do not wants you any more"). After that he brought me to Mexico and kept me here. He also told me that if I would like return to my village I could, but I refused to return, because, I am feeling impure because of my work, feeling guilty. Also, I do not have courage to face my parents. Since the last one year, I am working here as a sex worker, I do not know how long I will remain here, also, do not know where is my future.

We found a number of girls in Mexico like Maria who had been trapped by different economic and social problems and trafficked to the United States. Based on our study and field experience, we found that 6 out of every 10 trafficked Mexican women are taken to the United States and sold in the different sex markets of this country, while the other four women are sold inside Mexico to meet the national demand.

TRAFFICKING PATTERNS FROM MEXICO TO UNITED STATES

One way to traffic a Mexican woman to the United States is through promises of a good job with high income as we observed in the case of Maria. There are also cases in which women are lured with false marriage offers or vacation invitations and sold by their parents for a cash advance and promises of future earnings. After convincing the woman or girl to accept the offer, the agent makes arrangements for travel and job placement and hires an escort to accompany the woman on her trip. Once the arrangements have been made, the woman has no control over the nature or place of work or the terms or conditions of her employment.

Or, the woman hands over her passport to a trafficker believing that he is a travel agent or recruiter who is handling all of the logistics, including obtaining legitimate work permits. But once in the United States the traffickers do not return the passport or allow the woman to choose her employment.

Mexican *coyotes* commonly used to smuggle illegal migrants across the northern border are also used in leading trafficking victims to the United States. Using the same routes used for smuggling illegal migrants, the victims are transported by foot, van, bus, truck, or boat. Women are bought in Mexico by the Mexican traffickers for US$400–$800 and resold in the United States for US$5,000–$10,000. The price varies according to their age, physical appearance, education, and also virginity.[16] The main destinations for the Mexican women in the United States are: New York, Dallas, Chicago, Los Angeles, San Diego, Las Vegas, Houston, and San Antonio. According to one trafficker, the trip from the southern border of Mexico to the northern border takes more than 11 days. Once they cross the border into the United States, a car or van is used to take the women to brothels in various locations.

But not all the trafficked women are brought across the border illegally. The easiest way to traffic the women from Mexico to the United States is to overstay their visa. In Mexico, it is possible to get a multiple entry visa for ten years; and the PRC 13 student (F1), fiancée (K1), and entertainer visas (P1, P3) are also used to acquire entry. Traffickers illegally purchase 1–20 student forms to facilitate obtaining student visas, then produce fraudulent job letters supporting documentation to obtain the visas to convince a consulate officer that the woman will return.

CONCLUSION

Formerly, international migration was regarded as a relationship between an individual or household moving for their permanent settlement or work and the government acted as the gatekeeper for entry into a country and acquiring citizenship. Today, it is regarded as a diverse international "business," with a vast budget, providing hundreds of thousands of jobs worldwide, and managed by a set of individuals and institutions, each of which has an interest in how the business develops and each of which stands to make a commercial gain.

This global migration business is linked with trafficking in women and prostitution and has developed into a massive, highly organized international trade in the exploitation of women. One of its noticeable features is a great mobility from city to city and country to country. Despite international organizations efforts to combat the trafficking, this mobility makes it difficult to standardize a national response to the problem and to establish joint border cooperation.

Though many things have been done constitutionally to improve the status of Mexican women, they still remain in a subordinate position in this patriarchal society. The Mexican government is aware of the women and girls migrating illegally each year in an organized trafficking network to the United States, Europe, and some Asian countries but to date have not adopted any steps to combat the problem. A comprehensive approach is essential to address the economic, social, and political aspects of trafficking Mexican women. Mexico has also provided information and awareness raising campaigns to alert the public to the seriousness of the problem, but they need to be involved in establishing joint cooperation efforts on a national and international level to deal with the perpetrators, as well as assist the victims of trafficking.

NOTES

1. Dua Enaskhi, "Beyond Diversity: Exploring Ways in Which the Discourse of Race Has Shaped the Institution of the Nuclear Family," in *Scratching the Surface: Canadian Anti-Feminist Thought*, edited by Dua Enaskhi and Angela Robertson (Toronto: Women's Press, 1999).

2. Hania Zlotnik, "International Migration 1965–1996: An Overview," *Population and Development Review* 24, no. 3, 1998.

3. Nana Oishi, "Gender and Migration: An Integrative Approach," The Center for Comparative Immigration Studies, Working Paper no. 49, University of California–San Diego, California, 2002.

4. Luis Herrera Lasso, "The Impact of U.S. Immigration Policy on U.S.–Mexican Relations," *Voice of México*, Universidad Nacional Autónoma de México, México, 2002.

5. Douglas S.Massey and Audrey Singer, "New Estimates of Undocumented Mexican Migration and the Probability of Apprehension," *Demography* 32, 1995.

6. In 1994 the peso devaluation caused the main economic problem and a cash-flow problem that closed 10 percent of businesses, while 250,000 persons lost their jobs. Banks' basic lending rate increased 10 percent points to 50 percent, with some businesses paying 60 to 80 percent interest on loans.

7. Rogelio Hernández, "La Migración, el Tema Incomodo de la Binacional," *Milenio Diario*, México, 2002.

8. Referred to as the "Trafficking Protocol."

9. International Organization for Migration (IOM), "International Response to Trafficking in Migrants and the Safeguarding of Migrant Rights," 11th IOM Seminar on Migration, Geneva, October 26–28, 1994.
10. United States Department of State, 2003 Report on Trafficking of Persons available at www.state.gov/g/tip/rls/tiprpt/2003 (4 September 2004).
11. International Labour Organization (ILO), "Forced Labor, Human Trafficking, Slavery Haunt Us Still," *World of Work* 39, Geneva, 2001.
12. Arun Kumar Acharya, "La Esclavitud Humana; El Tráfico de Mujeres en la India y México," PhD diss., Universidad Nacional Autónoma de México, México, 2005.
13. Arun Kumar Acharya, "Agrarian Conflict, Internal Displacement and Trafficking of Mexican Women: The Case of Chiapas State," (Paper presented at the annual meeting of the Population Association of America, Boston, April 1–3, 2004).
14. Maria is not her real name.
15. Author's interview conducted in 2004.
16. Darío Dávila, "Polleros Crean Una Sofisticada Red Financiera Para Traficar Ilegales," *La Crónica de Hoy*, México, 2003.

BIBLIOGRAPHY

Acharya, Arun Kumar. "Agrarian Conflict, Internal Displacement and Trafficking of Mexican Women: The Case of Chiapas State." Paper presented at the annual meeting of the Population Association of America, Boston, April 1–3, 2004.
———. "La Esclavitud Humana; El Tráfico de Mujeres en la India y México." PhD diss., Universidad Nacional Autónoma de México, México, 2005.
Dávila, Darío. "Polleros Crean Una Sofisticada Red Financiera Para Traficar Ilegales." *La Crónica de Hoy*, México, 2003.
ECPAT International News Letter. "The American Exploitation and Trafficking of Children in Central America." No. 36, September, 2001.
Enaskhi, Dua. "Beyond Diversity: Exploring Ways in Which the Discourse of Race Has Shaped the Institution of the Nuclear Family." *Scratching the Surface: Canadian Anti-Feminist Thought*, edited by Dua Enaskhi and Angela Robertson. Toronto: Women's Press, 1999.
Hernández, Anabel. "Oaxaqueños Fincan Imperio Lenón en EU." *El Grafico*, México, 2003.
Hernández, Rogelio. "La Migración, el Tema Incomodo de la Binacional." *Milenio Diario*, México, 2002.
International Labour Organization (ILO). "Forced Labor, Human Trafficking, Slavery Haunt Us Still." *World of Work* 39, Geneva, 2001.
International Organization for Migration (IOM). "International Response to Trafficking in Migrants and the Safeguarding of Migrant Rights." 11th IOM Seminar on Migration, Geneva, October 26–28, 1994.
Lasso, Luis Herrera. "The Impact of US Immigration Policy on US Mexican Relation." *Voice of México*. México: Universidad Nacional Autónoma de México, 2002.

Massey, Douglas S., and Audrey Singer. "New Estimates of Undocumented Mexican Migration and the Probability of Apprehension." *Demography* 32, 1995.

Oishi, Nana. "Gender and Migration: An Integrative Approach." The Center for Comparative Immigration Studies, Working Paper no. 49, University of California, San Diego, California, 2002.

Rodriguez, Ruth. "AIDS Victims Suffer Abuse." *El Universal*, México, December, 2003.

Shailaja, Abhram. *Going Nowhere: Trafficking of Women and Children in International Sex Trade*, vol. 2, New Delhi, India: Dominant Publishers and Distributors, 2001.

United States Department of State, 2003 Report on Trafficking of Persons available at www.state.gov/g/tip/rls/tiprpt/2003 (4 September 2004).

Zlotnik, Hania. "International Migration 1965–1996: An Overview." *Population and Development Review* 24, no.3, 1998.

———."The Global Dimensions of Female Migration." Migration Information Source; Fresh Thought, Authoritative Data, Global Reach. 2003. www.migration information.org (22 February 2005).

· 3 ·

Trafficking of Women and Children in Vietnam: Current Issues and Problems

Vu Ngoc Binh

$\mathcal{V}$ietnam has experienced dramatic changes in its transition from a centrally planned to a market-oriented economy. Since the launching of *doi moi* (renovation) policy in 1986, the country has made remarkable progress across a broad range of socioeconomic development measures. Vietnam has been able to reduce poverty by more than 30 percent over the past 10 years, one of the sharpest declines of any developing country on record. This achievement has been traced to the high annual economic growth rates of the country in the early 1990s (about 8–9 percent) and, specifically, to Vietnam's strong agricultural performance.

The reform process has also contributed substantially to social development. Life expectancy has increased to nearly 68 years and adult literacy has been maintained at more than 90 percent. In 2002, Vietnam ranked 112 out of 177 countries in terms of the Human Development Index (HDI)—well above what would be expected from its current level of GDP per capita of more than US$400.[1] These impressive achievements lay out a firm foundation upon which Vietnam is expected to gradually become a modern-oriented industrialized country by 2020.

While these reforms have benefited a large number of people through offering new opportunities to Vietnamese families, rapid economic and social changes have also placed new pressures on them. Particularly for the 28.9 percent of the population that continue to live in poverty, these pressures can threaten their economic survival and cohesion, undermining the family's role as the primary social institution. Families have seen their range of choices broadened, but also their responsibilities.

With the weakening of social welfare and traditional safety nets, the burden on families, especially women, has become heavier. The poorest families and children are the first to be hit by the negative impact of reforms. The disappearance of guaranteed housing, medical services, pensions, and other basic services and the reform of the state-owned enterprise system are posing new kinds of economic and psychological stress, especially among disadvantaged families.

Furthermore, in this rapid development process, women and girls have become more vulnerable to newly emerging social issues such as neglect, abuse, and exploitation they had never experienced before.

The trafficking in children and women is one of the social manifestations arising from this growing transformation, and is further exacerbated and compounded by the phenomena of poverty, unemployment, increasing urban/rural disparities, inveterate gender discrimination, urbanization, and migration as commonly experienced in many other countries. The drive toward globalization and the urgent need to achieve international competitiveness is another factor.

DEFINITION AND DATA

At present in Vietnam, there is no precise and coherent understanding of what is meant by the term "trafficking" and to what and whom it should apply. The term means many things to different people and is often not well distinguished from smuggling. The lack of clarity in use of terminology is partly because trafficking covers a wide variety of situations, not all of which involve illegal migration or exploitation. Although trafficking is often linked with women and girls being sold into prostitution, it is now widely recognized that this is only part of a much larger picture which includes trafficking for forced and exploited labor, including begging, sweatshop and domestic labor and other illegal employment, trafficking for forced marriage, and trafficking for adoption.

Currently, efforts are being made to reach a consensus on the following definition used in the 2000 UN Protocol to Prevent, Suppress and Punish Trafficking in Persons, Especially Women and Children, Supplementing the United Nations Convention Against Transnational Organized Crime: ". . . The recruitment, transportation, transfer, harbouring or receipt of persons, by means of the threat or use of force or other forms of coercion, of abduction, of fraud, of deception, of the abuse of power or of a position of vulnerability or of the giving or receiving of payments or benefits to achieve the consent of a person having control over another person, for the purpose of exploitation. Exploitation shall include, at a minimum, the exploitation of the prostitution of others or other forms of sexual exploitation, forced labor or services, slavery or practices similar to slavery, servitude or the removal of organs."

Trafficking in Vietnam remains a hidden problem, as there is considerable lack of information or available data. Although several researches and surveys have been done following increased attention and coverage by the local mass media, there are weaknesses in the data collection by local and national authorities, as well as at the regional and international levels. However, the lack of statistics on trafficking in women and children is not solely explained by poor data collection procedures. It is extremely difficult to estimate the true level of trafficking that occurs in women and children because victims are often reluctant to report what happened to them. Victims do not come forward because they suspect that there is considerable prejudice against prostitutes, illegal migrants, and women and children when they report cases of sexual violence. They may also fear threats of violence from traffickers and humiliation or shame if their families should find out that they have been working as prostitutes.

Few women and children are prepared or able to report to the police of receiving countries what has happened to them. Vietnamese trafficked women and children are often considered ordinary clandestine migrants and, hence, immediately deportable, so victims are discouraged from going forward to authorities. The countries of destination simply deport victims and little is known what happens to these women once they return to their country of origin. Usually it is not possible to identify female victims of trafficking from police deportation figures; thus, their experiences may never be recorded as cases of trafficking.

CAUSES AND TRENDS

While it is difficult to estimate the number of women and children trafficked every year,[2] it is also recognized that trafficking in women and children is a growing problem and there seem to be some clear patterns of movement. Often women and children are brought or abducted from their villages in poor rural areas to the economically more advanced urban areas and sold in big cities, within their home country, across borders or abroad, for prostitution, forced labor, and adoption.

Within the country, poverty is manifesting itself in new ways because of the economic transition. Much of the burden falls on women and children. It is not surprising that many young women have strong economic incentives to seek employment in urban areas or where the young girls were promised marriage. They want to travel to big cities, which for years were inaccessible to them, where living standards are higher than in their home villages.

Recent small studies indicate that sexual exploitation in the country mostly occurs in venues not established for prostitution but rather in nightclubs, bars, beer halls, and other entertainment venues. Poverty and lack of education and employment opportunities are the primary reasons young women are involved in prostitution. Most come from rural areas with low levels of education and do not have the knowledge or self-confidence to protect themselves. In addition to the need for employment, early marriage, divorce, and sexual abuse during childhood are also among the factors that drive girls into prostitution. Thus, apart from being vulnerable to physical abuse, these young women are particularly vulnerable to STDs, HIV/AIDS, and drug abuse. Widespread apprehension about HIV/AIDS has increased the demand for younger girls.

In Vietnam, there is increasing concern about the problem of cross-border trafficking in women and children. If they are fortunate enough to escape or be assisted by the authorities, they often have little prospect of returning to their home because of lack of finances and travel documents and fear of stigmatization.

Trafficking routes and patterns have connected Vietnam as a source and transit country to several other countries in the Mekong region and beyond. The three major known trafficking routes in which Vietnamese are sent across the border or farther abroad are from northern Vietnam to China, southern Vietnam to Cambodia, and farther to other countries.

Within a short period of time, China has become a major receiving country. Official research and statistics are scarce but letters from Vietnamese women in China, police reports made by their families, accounts from women who have managed to return, and articles in local newspapers give some ideas of its scope. It is still impossible to know how many women have been trafficked to China and have not returned.

The victims are usually poor, single women, often with little education and a general lack of knowledge about the situation and living conditions in China. They are recruited as wives or helpers and migrate to work in the northern bordering towns of China. They do not have to travel far and legal entry as a tourist or for business is easy, as visa restrictions no longer apply to them. Eager to escape poverty and social insecurity, they become easy prey and willingly accept the services offered by traffickers for promises of well-paid jobs or marriage to a Chinese man. Once enmeshed within an environment of illegal migration, many become vulnerable to physical and mental abuse and find themselves trapped in a life of slavery, exploitation, or prostitution. Even those who establish a stable family life constantly risk being detected and sent back to Vietnam without any money or support and are often forced to leave their children behind.

It was also reported that many of the prostitutes in Cambodia are from southern Vietnam.[3] Many were very young, only 15 to 18 years of age. Most, though, tend to be older on average and more likely to be married with children. High proportions of all victims were unemployed or never had a job before. Some women and girls were offered legitimate jobs and then tricked into prostitution, while others knew they would work as prostitutes. Regardless of the work expected, however, many ultimately found themselves trapped in prostitution.

While most victims of trafficking are young women who are unaware of the problem and unable to defend themselves, women experienced in the trade and aware of the problem also become victims of unscrupulous traffickers. In many cases, traffickers sexually abuse the young women before departure. Their largest concern is the condition of work and the amount of remuneration.

Forcing women into prostitution can create huge profits for traffickers. Criminal groups operating in the recruiting as well as the destination countries sometimes control the traffic in women business. They are highly organized, extremely violent, and often involved in other criminal activities. Trafficking in humans is much less risky for criminals than other forms of crime, such as drug trafficking. There are few successful convictions, in part, because countries of destination often deport victims immediately, thereby losing valuable witnesses. When traffickers are convicted the sentences against them are generally not severe enough.

In receiving and transit countries, there is a trend to enforce only their immigration laws to punish and deport the women rather than considering them victims of a modern form of slavery. This general practice makes it impossible for trafficked women and children to seek protection and pursue any legal battle against traffickers and accomplices. Being transported with false documentation makes women become stateless people. They are subject to persecution and to the enforcement of immigration laws. They are also subject to arrest and deportation on charges of overstaying their visa. As a result, they are the target of discrimination and prejudice, subject to many forms of physical and psychological violence. The media sometimes focus on the victims rather than the abusers. In countries where prostitution is illegal, such practice reinforces the social stigma toward women and girls.

The recruitment of these women and children is often informal through friends and acquaintances, but, on arrival in the destination country, many of them found themselves indebted to a trafficker or club owner.

Other forms of trafficking include child adoption and marriages with foreigners. Information regarding the extent of this type of trafficking and the means by which people are trafficked remains sketchy, although numerous government and non-government organizations at recent national and international conferences have reported Vietnamese women being coerced and exploited into marriages or sex work. Over the past few years, a number of child trafficking rings providing infants to foreign couples seeking to adopt has also been uncovered. The traffickers regularly purchased babies from desperately poor rural families, provincial hospitals, orphanages, and single mothers.

Intermediaries, besides local agents, are sex tourists who play a vital role in luring women from the sex sector into forced prostitution in other countries or territories, such as Taiwan and Singapore. False marriages and mail-order brides are used as a camouflage to bring women for overseas prostitution. The victims of this pattern of trafficking find it difficult to argue in court that they are victims of trafficking. This is due to the general belief that women and children involved in prostitution cannot be victims of any forms of sexual violence. In other words, the blame rests on them. Intermediaries, who are also sometimes relatives, go into the villages to contact a family who has young daughters to offer them opportunities to work in other parts of the country. Therefore, potential victims do not belong only to the poorest of the poor families.

In sex tourism, clients travel from other countries to Vietnam through several small private travel agencies involved in operating sex tours. At the beginning the women follow the route of other villagers and go to work as domestic helpers in other places. There are young women who are recruited to work outside their community with the promise of high paid jobs either in factories or in restaurants in their places, usually in urban areas. Women as young as 15–16 years are encouraged to migrate by their parents, hopeful that their daughters would earn a high income to help support the family. Many families in poor rural communities get a loan with high interest to pay the fee to local agents for the arrangement of their daughters' trip. In many cases, their parents are tricked into believing that their children will have respectable occupations in urban areas.

The common stereotype of the trafficked victim is a naive young woman who is tricked into prostitution after being offered a legitimate job as "waitress/cook" in the city or marriage to a foreigner. Women and children are recruited quite openly through newspaper advertisements as they regularly contain information about jobs for women as dancers, waitresses, or bar girls in nightclubs. Once they are hired and forced into prostitution they are unable to escape their situation. They are frequently forced into a situation of extreme dependency comparable to that of being a hostage, deprived of their papers, and their movement is controlled or restricted through violence or the threat of violence. They are forced to live on the premises where they work long hours and are not allowed to refuse clients. Many receive no earnings, especially the very young women. Not surprisingly, a high proportion of victims have medical problems. Many, especially the teenagers, contract sexually transmitted diseases, and there is a high incidence of reported mental health problems. The traffickers or club owners withhold all legal papers. They cannot escape.

NATIONAL RESPONSE

Currently, Vietnam approaches trafficking as one of "social evils" which have appeared in recent years as one of the negative consequences of the open-door policy, change of economic management, the process of urbanization, and the increasing exchanges with other countries, particularly those in the region. The Government did not officially recognize trafficking until 1997, when it issued a directive calling for multi-sectoral action toward the trafficking of women and children and for closer cooperation between government agencies, mass organizations as well as international and non-governmental organizations.

Because of the problems the country is facing in trafficking, awareness has been increasing. Vietnam is a state party to several related human rights instruments, such as the Convention on the Elimination of All Forms of Discrimination Against Women (CEDAW), the Convention on the Rights of the Child (CRC) and its Optional Protocol on the Sale of Children, Child Prostitution and Child Pornography, and is currently considering ratification of the Protocol to Prevent, Suppress and Punish Trafficking in Persons, Especially Women and Children, Supplementing the United Nations Convention against Transnational Organised Crime. The Government has also developed relevant long term-strategies for children, the advancement of women, population, nutrition, HIV/AIDS, etc.

Responding to concerns raised at home and abroad, the Government has recently begun encouraging conditions for different organizations and individuals in the country and abroad to help protect and care for women and children. Initiatives to combat trafficking include income generation and vocational training programs, raids on brothels and entertainment areas, surveys on trafficking in selected areas, widespread dissemination of information, educational initiatives, awareness raising campaigns, and community based prevention schemes. The Vietnam Women's Union has worked with other government agencies and NGOs on developing reintegration and reception programs, including shelter, assistance, health care, and training. However, this area remains problematic. Language and cultural differences have made acceptance of assistance for women in Cambodia difficult and some NGOs in Cambodia have expressed concern about possible institutionalization of trafficked victims on return to Vietnam. One reason for that is the lack of experience dealing with this issue. This is especially true for a country like Vietnam, though its Government has started to seriously look at the issue to create an explicit or coherent policy to combat trafficking in women and children. As yet, protection and prevention strategies have not always taken into account the marketability of certain skills or initiatives provided within vocational training and credit programs. Limited job opportunities are an important factor in determining vulnerability. Formal and informal education programs should be relevant to actual employment, vocational opportunities, or the creation of income generating opportunities. Many training programs fail precisely because they are not geared to market realities, and ironically, some may even have the unintended effect of encouraging migration to urban areas as people search for possibilities to match their skills.

Trafficking in humans is considered to be a comparatively profitable crime since existing penalties are relatively lenient, at least compared with trafficking in drugs. As a result many of those trafficked from Vietnam have remained silent, and, at present, trafficking in children and women continues to be a considerably underreported offense. Also, the available laws and measures on combating trafficking emphasize trafficking for commercial sex, and have not accounted for the many other reasons for trafficking such as bonded and illegal labor, domestic work, and begging, which fall under the broader definition of human trafficking. In addition, the current laws tend to be punitive rather than protective for the victim, and response has focused on a few high profile cases (e.g., illegal network of baby adoption), though the 1999 Criminal Code includes provisions regarding the prohibition of sexual exploitation of children and the prevention and punishment of prostitution and trafficking as well as punishment for violators. Weaknesses have been found in the formulation of the laws relevant to trafficking, and the level of awareness among enforcement officials regarding amendments makes systematic enforcement and implementation difficult.

The Government's recent efforts include a national plan of action to make sure that all children are registered. The legal protection of children from trafficking in the area of intercountry adoption has been strengthened in an attempt to halt fraud and child trafficking, as well as child marriage. There is a long way to go and to have a good law is only the beginning.

RECOMMENDATIONS

There is an urgent need in Vietnam to develop strategies to prevent this trade from growing further. As trafficking is a complex problem, a comprehensive approach should be taken to combat the problem through a combination of prevention, increasing the number of prosecutions against traffickers, and provision of greater assistance to the trafficking victims. If the emphasis is on prevention, there is a chance of success at the least cost. It should also be noted that, while measures to combat poverty and the marginalization of women and children are very much needed, poverty alone does not explain why trafficking of women and children is on the increase.

The complexity of the trafficking problem—involving human rights, border control, law and order, gender, children, mental and physical health, labor, organized crime, migration—means that a broad variety of expertise is needed to address the problem comprehensively. Experience has shown that there is no single body to deal with all these aspects. Programs aimed at preventing trafficking will not be singularly successful. They must operate cooperatively with other agencies and programs to address the multifaceted problem of trafficking. Efforts to prevent trafficking should be integrated into the operations of all relevant government agencies including health, education, law enforcement, labor, social welfare, and the judiciary.

At present, the police, border guards and local women's unions are almost solely responsible for prevention as well as identification of trafficking victims. More effort should be made to encourage others, such as local authorities, schoolteachers, lawyers, members of mass organizations, and the victims themselves to report the incidences of trafficking.

In addition to prevention, there is need to work with national and international partners to implement programs to promote the re-integration of trafficked women and children. Assisting trafficked women and children to return home with improved prospects for their futures can reduce the risk that they will be trafficked again. Measures proposed include counseling, temporary shelter, health care, job placement, and training. These programs should be designed in such a way that the women and children concerned are not immediately identifiable as ex-prostitutes. The staff managing these programs should be sensitive to the needs of the women and children concerned. Legal literacy programs should be provided for personnel in order to raise the issue in international human rights fora.

To create an environment of public intolerance toward the trafficking of women and children, established customs and practices, including early marriage and child labor, must be addressed at all levels of society within their possible link to trafficking. Communication interventions may also be required for behavior change. Information campaigns, which warn about the nature of trafficking, should be launched, targeting young women and the general public. The trafficked women and children should also be involved in such programs which are intended to warn other women and children about the danger of trafficking in their areas. In order to be effective in reducing vulnerability, information and awareness raising campaigns need to reach out to target groups in rural areas where there is little access to the mass media and where the risk of trafficking is often especially high. This means developing materials for prevention efforts in national and local languages and presenting them in formats that are easily accessible to the entire population.

Such efforts should ensure that intersectoral linkages, including education, sexual exploitation, health and HIV/AIDS, are interwoven into national and community strategies. Trafficking in women and children is a subject that receives considerable publicity in the media, but needs to be investigated in a scientific manner. More research is needed on prevention strategies and the factors that contribute to the growth of trafficking in women and children.

Tougher penalties are needed to deter traffickers. The crime of trafficking in women and children needs to be more clearly defined in national law to facilitate prosecutions. Social service and labor authorities should improve surveillance of workplaces to ensure compliance with national laws governing working conditions. Migration officers should devote more attention to studying trafficking and identifying viable solutions, and staff working in Vietnamese embassies abroad should be alerted about the potential danger that women and children from their country may face when they migrate.

As cross-border trafficking networks expand and become more organized and sophisticated, there is an increasing need to assess and analyze the complex nature of the situation and develop effective strategies and interventions for prevention, as well as appropriate support to the victims for their recovery, repatriation, and rehabilitation.

Participation at higher regional and international levels to control illegal migration and combat organized crime is necessary in order to reduce trafficking in women and children, including police involvement to dismantle trafficking and the violence associated with it. Though there have been some agreements and discussions regarding the issue of cross-border trafficking between Vietnam and other neighboring countries, the current situation calls for an urgent strengthening of inter-country coordination and cooperation.

NOTES

1. GSO, Result of the Survey on Household Living Standards 2002, Hanoi: Statistical Publishing House, 2004, 25.

2. The number of women trafficked is very unclear; however, it was estimated to be 22,000 during 1991–1999. Oanh, Colonel Cao Ngoc (Mr.), "People-Elected Deputies with Policies and Legislation for Prevention of Violence Against Women," paper presented at the National Seminar organized by Parliament Committee for Social Affairs, Hanoi, February 1–2, 2002.

3. Colonel Truong Huu Quoc (Mr.), "Elimination of All Forms of Trafficking in Women and Children," paper presented at meeting organized by the Vietnam Lawyers Association, December 21–22, 1999.

SELECTED BIBLIOGRAPHY

Vu Ngoc Binh. *Combating the Trafficking and Prostitution of Children*. 3rd ed. Hanoi: National Political Publishing House, 2004.

——. *The Issue of Child Labour*. 5th ed. Hanoi: National Political Publishing House, 2002.

——. "Trafficking of Women—A Growing Problem." Hanoi: *Vietnam News*, no. 1474 (September 1995).

II

NATIONAL SECURITY, ORGANIZED CRIME, AND CIVIL CONFLICT

• 4 •

Human (In)security, Human Trafficking, and Security in Malaysia

Zarina Othman

𝒯he twenty-first century's international political environment has given rise to three major themes in the international security arena. First, nonmilitary security threats have become more prominent on the world's security agendas. Among those nonmilitary threats are poverty, hunger, and related economic inequities; environmental degradation; inadequate sanitation and health care, contagious diseases; lack of education; crime and corruption including trafficking in humans, drugs, and weapons. The second major theme is the awakening of leaders to a better understanding of the roles played by "non-state actors," who may have either economic or political motives in their activities that affect our world's security. The increasing impact of transnational nonmilitary threats—activities that move across borders—do not represent any sovereign state, and yet, have a terrible effect on the human race, as well as on sovereign states of the world. Included among these threats are the activities of terrorist groups and organized crime. Finally, from the above themes emerges the urgent need to investigate the root causes of these threats and to rethink and redesign our security measures accordingly.

One of the issues deemed most important and that has increasingly grown in magnitude is the trafficking in human beings—men, women and children. Human trafficking is not a new phenomenon. It began hundreds of years ago in the form of slavery and forced servitude. While we may like to think that such forms of exploitation have ended, human trafficking has emerged in a new form.[1] This "old wine in a new bottle" is real. Trafficking of women and children, for example, generates the third largest source of profits for organized crime after weapons and illicit drug trafficking.[2] Transnational organized crime (TOC) refers to well-organized and intricately connected networks of "syndicates" that form a sinister web encompassing the globe.

47

The US government estimated that during 2001 approximately 225,000 victims were trafficked from Southeast Asia and another 150,000 came from the countries of South Asia.[3] These numbers are likely to have increased during the past two years. Malaysia is one of the favorite destinations for trafficking victims in Southeast Asia, a region with impressive economic growth in recent times except during the Asian economic crisis in 1997–1998.

Focusing on Southeast Asia, in general, and on Malaysia, specifically, this paper argues that human insecurity has led to human trafficking, which in turn constitutes a threat to every state's national security. It is hoped that the discussion provided in the paper will shed light especially on a shift from focusing on the state as the primary entity to be protected, an approach traditionally known simply as "national security," to focusing even more on protecting the human beings who live in that state. This newer approach is commonly known as "human security." The understanding gained from this new approach is different from the assumptions and perceptions of the traditional security view, in which security most often meant defending territorial boundaries from immediate attack. New insights may contribute to a better design of overall regional security with strategies to address not only human trafficking, but also similar transnational threats—threats that cannot be confronted by one country alone.

SECURITY AND HUMAN (IN)SECURITY

When we examine the exact meaning of the word *security*, the closest meaning to it is "safety." However, in the field of international relations, security has been defined as "protection against threats." As a general rule, states seek security mainly to defend themselves from what they consider to be threats— imagined or real—to their survival. *Survival*, however, may be defined broadly or narrowly. States often broaden their idea of survival to justify aggression that goes well beyond current survival needs. They project into their future and come to believe that long-term survival depends on becoming bigger, or more powerful—or upon eliminating or reducing the strength and power of other states. On the other hand, a state may narrow its definition of survival by not including survival of certain individuals and groups among their citizens.

Given the fact that the world is comprised of nations and states with different cultural and historical backgrounds, as well as geographical settings, the way states seek to preserve their national security will not be the same for all. National security policy varies from one region to another, from one state to another, and from one time to another. It will vary also with circumstances that arise, both planned and unplanned. In other words, national security is not a concept in which "one size fits all." Thereby, what the United States defines as a national security threat may not be an issue at all to Malaysia, and vice versa.

Any discussion of security today would not be complete without including the views of "realism," one of the major schools of thought in the field of international security studies. This school (including its more recent variant group known as neo-realism) attempts to view the world "as it is," and has understood security as "high politics"—the highest priority in any state's agenda. Realists' focus on security is to focus on the security of the state itself. They argue that states are the main actors in world politics and those states rationally pursue their interests by focusing mostly on external threats—threats from outside the political boundaries of the state. In addition, realists recognize that security has been mainly the domain of the military, and they have emphasized the potential, as well as the actual, conflicts between states. Their understanding of national security leads them to conclude that the state has to be stronger than its enemies in a world where war can break out at any time; and peace, defined by them as simply "the absence of war," is always only temporary. Therefore, each state must decide the best means to preserve its national interests, and that always includes being prepared to use force or to go to war in order to survive.

Although the realist theory has a long history,[4] the concept of national security is actually a relatively new idea that U.S. President Harry S. Truman highlighted after the end of World War II in 1949. Today, all states are concerned about their national security, their survival as a state, and about defending themselves from threats—real or perceived, internal or external. Threats can include events, activities, and entities that have the potential to weaken or damage the very core values of the state. In fact, anything that brings change to the basic elements that comprise the state may be considered as a threat.

For the developing countries, categorized by Barry Buzan as "weak states" that are vulnerable to political threats,[5] national security is certainly no less important than to other countries. However, national security for the developing countries differs somewhat from the concept held by the well-developed countries. Developing countries face a different set of problems due to lack of unity within many of a region's states, uneven economic development, and unresolved ideological as well as cultural conflicts. Muthiah Alagappa indicates the need to define the concept of national security differently, because the security issues of developing states "are seldom explored comprehensively and in their own right."[6]

As a developing country, Malaysia has defined its national security mainly in terms of preserving its national boundaries and important core values, and in protecting its most important entities including its parliamentary democracy, constitutional monarch, and national constitution, and its unity as the Malaysian nation.[7] Anything that threatens items on this list will be defined as a threat to Malaysia's national security. The Malaysian government also recognizes that threats do not necessarily originate externally.

Malaysia has long acknowledged "security begins at home," which means we have to be strong on the inside in order to be stronger on the outside.[8] The Malaysian government realized the importance of domestic issues and officially declared illicit drug trafficking (*dadah*) as a threat to its national security as early as 1983, a time when most other countries were still struggling to understand how illicit drugs and related issues could actually affect a nation as a whole, not just the individuals who are directly involved. Nevertheless, even in Malaysia, the focus of national security has largely remained on the state. What we seem to be having trouble understanding is the growing interconnectedness in the world—the growing interdependence between and among states, both rich and poor, developed and developing countries. Issues that are important for one country so often have a spillover impact onto other countries.

In Malaysia, the National Development Policy designed in 1990 replaced the former New Economic Policy that had been established twenty years earlier. Later, in 1991, former Malaysia Prime Minister, Mahathir Mohamad, announced the plan Vision 2020, outlining the goals for changing Malaysia into a "developed" country and presenting the National Vision Policy. All of these policies were designed at least partly to strengthen security at home.

At the international level, the United Nations has acknowledged some of these problems, including the need to change some of our notions regarding the concept of security. In one of its annual reports, *Human Development 1994*, the concept of "human security"[9] was introduced. This term does not focus on traditional "national security"; it highlights instead the importance of protecting the safety, health, and well-being of the human race—not just the security of one's own people, but of all—cutting across distinctions and boundaries of nationality and ethnicity, class, culture, gender, religion, etc. To be more specific, the UN refers to its human security concept as "freedom from fear and freedom from want."

In this paper, I refer to acknowledging and protecting basic human rights and meeting the basic needs of all the people.[10] By human rights, I refer to the freedom to participate in all legal aspects of community life, including government, to express their culture, practice their religion and other manifestations of their identity; and to the granting and protection of other rights necessary to ensure freedom from fear of threats to human survival, health, and well being. By basic needs, I mean adequate food, clean water and sanitation, safe shelter, basic education, and health care. In an interconnected world, both threats and security from threats must take on this focus.

Nevertheless, the idea of human security does not ignore the importance of national/ state entities. Rather, it holds the perspective that in the long run human security is essential to the well-being of the state itself. One entity cannot exist in a sustainable secure state-of-being without the other. When the people of a country suffer from a lack of safety, health, and overall well-being, in other words, when individuals or groups do not experience a state of being secure, the country as a whole, including its sovereignty and ability to protect against outside threats, is at risk. When there is poor health among the populace, not only their physical and mental health, but also poor economic and social health, the health of the nation itself, is also threatened. Providing protection and security to the people is thus seen as an essential means of providing security to the state.

In general, scholars in the field have grouped threats to human security into at least three categories. First, "societal security" includes security for the most vulnerable groups such as the impoverished, the disabled, ethnic minority groups, and women and children. These are threats that originate from within the state itself and can also include the political separatist movements in many countries, such as the Moros in the Philippines, the Kurds in Iraq, the Patanis in Thailand, and so forth.

The second category consists of threats to human security due to development, or what some refer to as globalization. These threats are more complex and include how globalization is driven by a capitalism that affects human security through inequalities in power and resources, often resulting in poverty. This implies that human security cannot be pursued at the expense of others. Likewise, technological developments and rapid expansion of capitalism have contributed to the growth of inequalities between states.

The third category of security threat is comprised of threats to the survival and well-being of individuals. This means that security refers not only to peace and stability, but also and perhaps more importantly, includes the preservation of the quality of life of the people.[11] The very core of this concept is that from our people will come our future leaders, workers, thinkers, and innovators, at all levels of the society. Therefore, the health, safety, and security of our children, and of the families and communities into which they are born and nurtured, will ultimately determine the strength—and probably the fate—of one's country as we travel into the unknowns of the future.

HUMAN TRAFFICKING IN SOUTHEAST ASIA

Southeast Asia has a long coastline with undefended borders, which suggests that law enforcement may be especially difficult in regard to threats that cross those borders. The sea, a factor that further complicates the matter, surrounds all of the countries in the region, except the landlocked Laos. However, before we go further, it is crucial to understand the differences between *trafficking* and *smuggling*. Many people do not fully understand the issues involved with human trafficking, partly because Malaysia and several other countries do not recognize the differences between these two terms. Human trafficking as defined by the United Nations is

> the recruitment, transportation, transfer, harboring or receipt of persons, by means of the threat or use of force or other forms of coercion, of abduction, of fraud, of deception, of the abuse of power or of [another person's] position of vulnerability . . . or of the giving or receiving of payments or benefits to achieve the consent of a person having control over another person, for the purpose of exploitation. Exploitation includes . . . prostitution or other forms of sexual exploitation, forced labor or services, slavery or practices similar to slavery, servitude or the removal of organs.[12]

Trafficking involves the ongoing exploitation of the victims after arriving in a country. They are manipulated and controlled by criminals—organized syndicates or by less widely organized local crime operations to which victims are given or sold by the syndicates who transported them to their destination. Trafficking can also take place within the same state or country, taking victims from one location to another against their will.[13]

Smuggling, on the other hand, refers to an illegal activity in which migrants have agreed to be transported. It ends with the arrival of the migrants at their destinations and it almost always involves the crossing of national borders, or occasionally of other borders within a state. When it comes to people, we are more concerned with trafficking than with smuggling as a threat to security, because human beings are simply being made into another commodity, along with illegal weapons and drugs, from which profit can be made easily.

Generally, causes of human trafficking in Southeast Asia can be divided into push and pull factors.

Push Factors

Poverty.   Food insecurity has been identified as the major cause of human trafficking. Being poor, with insufficient food, makes the victims vulnerable to the traffickers and engagement in criminal activities such as trafficking particularly tempting.

Lack of education.   Traffickers often recruit hill tribe people, especially from the mountainous areas of Myanmar, Thailand, Laos, China, and Vietnam, who have little formal education or exposure to the modern world and to legitimate job opportunities. Without this knowledge and qualifications for legitimate jobs, they fall easy prey to traffickers who deceive them with false promises of jobs in other countries.

Demand.   Economic law of "supply and demand" helps to create conditions ripe for trafficking for profit. In Southeast Asia, transnational organized crime, such as the Chinese Triads, has been identified as being mainly responsible for the trafficking business.[14] Nevertheless, there are also other smaller local syndicates involved, and the region's overall rapid development has led to increasing demands for more labor in the destination countries. This demand provides incentives that help to fuel the illegal supply.

Easy money.   Young girls and women, with no specific training and skills, are easily attracted to this illegal business because it produces 25 times more money than working in the factory.[15]

Insecure environment.   In some countries, such as Myanmar, oppressive regimes have caused frustration among the people in the country. Being trafficked is seen as the easiest way to get out of their country.

History of sexual abuse.   Frustrated with their lives, many victims of sexual abuse are more vulnerable to becoming victims or to involving themselves with the trafficking activities.

High price for a virgin girl.   Some families, especially in Vietnam, willingly allow their young daughters to be trafficked to become prostitutes. This is because the price of a virgin prostitute is high, approximately US$100.00.[16] This amount of money can support a family for several years.

Uneven development.   Southeast Asia is a region with uneven development. Some countries are more developed than others. Likewise, the urban areas are more developed than the rural areas, especially in Myanmar, Laos, Vietnam, and Cambodia. These countries also are in transition from centrally planned to open economies. Many regional and global investors have come in because of this transition process, creating a need for more laborers. In this case, the TOC acted as the supplier.[17] As a result, some countries, usually the poorer ones, became source countries, while others, usually the more well-developed countries in the region, have become the host countries.

Population pressure.   Crowded and poor countries like Indonesia and the Philippines have sometimes forced groups of people to migrate to other countries to search for jobs.

Pull Factors

Globalization.   This phenomenon has exacerbated trafficking activities in the region, and we may continue to witness an increase in human trafficking, especially with the ongoing ASEAN Free Trade Area (AFTA).

Higher wages.   This is one of the factors that attract people to be trafficked. Syndicates usually lure people by promising jobs with high wages; instead they end up as victims in an illegal business in host countries such as in

Malaysia or Thailand. This is also influenced by the fact that the Malaysian *Ringgit* or Thai *Baht* currency is worth more when converted into Indonesian *Rupiah* or Myanmar *Kyat*.

Job opportunities. Because there is a lack of job opportunities in the source countries, many trafficking victims look forward to the destination countries, such as Singapore, Thailand, and Malaysia, where there are many jobs available. Unfortunately, when they arrive they are not allowed to obtain legitimate jobs.

Better quality of life. Destination countries are usually more developed than the source countries and provide not only job opportunities, but also the promise of a better quality of life.

Geography and culture. Factors such as geography and culture also play important roles. Malaysia has been swamped with Indonesian immigrants because the two countries have a similar culture and religion, while Burmese immigrants top the list in Thailand.

Human insecurity factors such as poverty, lack of education, and insecure environment due to an oppressive regime, contribute to human trafficking. These situations have been manipulated by the organized criminal syndicates (TOC) that are based in several countries, "commit their crime in at least one, but usually several, other host countries, usually where market conditions are favorable, and conduct illicit activities which carry a low risk of apprehension."[18] In the academic field of international relations, TOC is categorized as a "non-state actor" because the criminals do not represent any legitimate governments or any sovereign states in the world.

The criminal organizations conducting trafficking activities in the region have indeed exploited the ongoing process of globalization. The expansion of trade, tourism, and various kinds of networks and transportation, all have made it possible for TOC to carry out its illicit activities. The growing integration of the global financial system has also provided more opportunities for TOC to launder illicit money.[19] Money laundering flourishes as a necessary step in most profitable criminal activity. Not only is it needed to reduce the risk of the criminals being caught, but also to enhance their profits. Fighting money laundering helps to fight the criminal organizations that are involved in many of these illegal trafficking activities.[20]

Several research studies have been conducted to try to understand the root causes of the trafficking issue in the region. Although these studies have revealed several different causes or contributing factors, most can be grouped under the category in which threats to individual human beings and groups have contributed to their insecurity, made those people vulnerable, and thus made them more likely to become victims of the trafficking syndicates.

HUMAN TRAFFICKING AND
ITS IMPACT ON MALAYSIA'S SECURITY

As earlier discussed, poverty has been identified as a key factor in source or sending countries, indicating that threats to human economic security contribute to human trafficking, and thus threaten national security. These countries include Myanmar, Cambodia, Laos, Vietnam, Philippines, and Indonesia, as well as the southern part of China, in the state of Yunnan. For example, as reported by the International Migration Organization (IOM), an estimated 15 percent of the children below the age of 15 have been trafficked as prostitutes in the Mekong sub-region area.[21] It has been estimated that 15–33 percent of the children between 9 and 16 years of age have been trafficked annually from Cambodia, a poor country in this region. Nonetheless, about 75 percent of these children are actually Vietnamese immigrants in the country. The Vietnamese culture may more readily allow parents to use their children in an illegal business, such as prostitution, which they justify as a survival need due to chronic poverty. Compared to the Vietnamese, more Cambodian children are trafficked to be beggars in rich neighboring countries, such as in Thailand and Malaysia.

Human trafficking has implications for Malaysia's national security. It empowers the TOC and creates a lot of public disorder within the receiving countries such as Malaysia. Among recent news related to human trafficking appeared "Pat Pong–Style Vice Den Busted"[22] and "China Dolls for Sale."[23] So, why is Malaysia so slow to include human trafficking on its security agenda? Closer investigation reveals the following issues, which complicate the effort to see it as an important national security issue.

First, the Malaysian government does not consider the problem as trafficking, but only as a smuggling issue. Since they define smuggling as meaning the transported persons have agreed to be transported illegally, trafficking victims therefore are considered illegal immigrants rather than trafficking victims.

Second, trafficking is greatly complicated by language. The word "trafficking" has no equivalent in the Malay language. In Indonesia, where the language is most similar to the Malay language, the word "trafficking" has been used interchangeably with "*perdagangan*"(trade),[24] a word that is again more appropriate to smuggling. However, Malaysia does not focus on the concept of "trafficking"; rather, the focus is on the issues surrounding the occurrence. As a result, "trafficking" issues have been looked upon as the same as "smuggling" issues.[25] It may not make much difference whether we use "trafficking," "smuggling," or "trading"—as long as we describe them all as illegal or illicit—when we are talking about transporting weapons or drugs. But it makes a big difference when we are talking about human beings. People should have a choice, and should not be treated as mere unthinking, unfeeling commodities. Therefore, we need to make a concerted effort to distinguish between trafficking and smuggling in every language, even creating new terms when necessary to accurately describe what is happening. Unless this is done, building trust and transparency between the sending and the receiving countries, and working together to tackle the problems of human trafficking among all the countries in the region, cannot proceed successfully.

Third, our research shows that most persons who come from outside the country and are engaged in illegal activities in Malaysia are coming from Indonesia. Unfortunately, available statistics do not distinguish between victims who have been trafficked and those who have been smuggled, and they do not report separately on women and children. Although the United Nations has defined a child as being anyone below the age of 18, official data collection in Malaysia does not allow us to distinguish how many of those persons are victims of trafficking, and from a legal standpoint children are not usually considered able to make a choice about such things as being "smuggled." Therefore, they should be considered either trafficking victims or runaways and returned to their home country. Thus, more work needs to be done to collect and analyze the data differently to rightfully show trafficking as a national security issue. When that happens, human trafficking will be given the attention it deserves and progress can be made to counter it. Nevertheless, it is important to note that not all of the arrests made were of prostitutes who actually had been trafficked, because some enter the country by using a student visa. Thus, not all cases of illegal entry into Malaysia involve organized crime.[26]

Our research also demonstrates that there must be close cooperation between Malaysian and Indonesian governments, and probably other governments as well, to successfully fight the problem. By viewing it as a threat to both national and human security for both the sending (Indonesia) and receiving (Malaysia) countries, cooperation becomes essential. Finally, although Malaysia is among the countries that have ratified the Convention Against Transnational Organized Crime, it has not ratified the protocols.[27] The UN Convention Against TOC promulgated the "Protocol to Prevent, Suppress and Punish Trafficking in Persons, Especially in Women and Children" under its "Trafficking Protocol" and the "Protocol Against Smuggling of Migrants by Land, Sea and Air."[28] This tells us that that there is resistance toward collaboratively making efforts to address the trafficking problem and that resistance becomes itself a new problem to address.

CONCLUSION

For reasons discussed above, the problems surrounding human trafficking make it much more than a law enforcement issue. By looking at the root causes of the problem, we can see that it contributes to widespread human insecurity, which in turn makes it a threat to state, regional, and international security. Thus, it is important to put human trafficking on our security agenda. We know that victims are being trafficked by organized criminal groups and forced into such activities as prostitution and begging, which reap profits for the traffickers and challenge the sovereignty and integrity of civilized nations. The fact that these illegal activities are being carried out by non-state actors certainly suggests that effective ways to counter them will not be found by treating them as a traditional external threat. Similarly, it further supports the idea that the traditional focus of national security needs to shift to include human security.

Therefore, it is crucial to include in planning for security the protection of the individual inhabitants of a country, in addition to the protection of the state itself—recognizing that the people's survival and well-being is essential to the health and survival of the nation. Similarly, if we accept these ideas, and note that regional and international security are also affected by complex transnational threats such as human trafficking, any efforts to address such problems require cooperative efforts on a global scale in order to be effective.

At all levels, human security and quality of life must become a focus in designing security policies. Looking at security problems from the perspective of "human security," which is associated with a "humans first" orientation to policy-making, we will be more likely to gain a broader understanding of all the social, economic, and political factors that impact on the well-being of people and thus on all levels of security.

NOTES

The Faculty of Humanities and Social Sciences, Universiti Kebangsaan Malaysia, has provided the grants for this research.

This paper was also presented at the Fourth Malaysian Studies Conference, 3–5 August 2004, Universiti Kebangsaan Malaysia.

1. Diana Wong, "Border Controls, Illegal Migration and the Sovereignty of the Nation-State," IKMAS, Paper Work Series, No. 10 (UKM: IKMAS, July 2004).

2. Ronald Skeldon, "Trafficking: A Perspective from Asia," *Perspectives on Trafficking of Migrants*, ed. Reginald Appleyard (Geneva: International Organization for Migration and the UN, 2000), 13.

3. CRS Report for Congress, *Trafficking in Women and Children: The US and International Response* (18 March 2002). http://www.ilr.cornel.edulibrary.CRSTrafficwomenchildren.htm (6 June 2003).

4. Included among the classic political philosophers that have discussed the concept of security are Thucydides (471–400 BC) in *The Peloponnessian War*, Niccoló Machiavelli (1469–1527) in *The Prince*, and Thomas Hobbes (1588–1679) in *Leviathan*. See Paul Viotti and Mark Kauppi, *International Relations Theory: Realism, Pluralism, Globalism and Beyond*, 3rd ed. (Boston: Allyn and Bacon, 1999), 57–61.

5. Barry Buzan, *People, States and Fear*, 2nd ed. (Boulder, CO: Lynne Rienner Publishers, 1991), 56.

6. Muthiah Alagappa, *The National Security of Developing States: Lessons From Thailand* (Dover, MA: Auburn House Publishing, 1987), 1.

7. Kamarulnizam Abdullah and Mahmud Embung, "Kepentingan Strategik di Dalam Keselamatan Negara Malaysia." *Sejarah: Jurnal Jabatan Sejarah Universiti, Malaya* 6, (1999): 151–76.

8. Speech given by former Deputy Prime Minister of Malaysia, Musa Hitam, at Harvard Club, Singapore (1986).

9. UNDP, *Human Development Report 1994* (New York: Oxford University Press, 1995).

10. Zarina Othman, Human Security in Southeast Asia: A Case Study of Illicit Drug Trafficking as a Transnational Threat in Myanmar (Burma), Unpublished PhD dissertation (University of Denver, Colorado, USA, 2002).

11. Zarina Othman, *Human Security in Southeast Asia*.

12. UN Convention Against Transnational Organized Crime (2000). http://www.unodc.org.palermo/convmain.html (5 Oct. 2003).

13. United Nations Office on Drugs and Crime, http://www/undoc.org/unodc/trafficking_victim_consents.html (5 Oct. 2003).

14. Sheldon Zhang and Ko-Lin Chin, "Enter the Dragon: Inside Chinese Human Smuggling Organizations," *Criminology* 40, no. 4 (2002); Bertil Lintner, "People Smuggling: The Crime of Flight," *Far Eastern Economic Review* (July 18, 2002): 18–20; Siripon Skrobanek, et al, *The Traffic in Women* (London: Zed Books, 1997); Bertil Lintner, *Blood Brothers: The Criminal Underworld of Asia* (New York: Palgrave Macmillan, 2003).

15. Karen Tumlin, *Trafficking in Children in Asia: A Regional Overview* (February 2000), Bangkok: Institute for Asian Studies, Chulalongkorn University (An ILO-IPEC Paper).

16. Zarina Othman, *Trafficking in Children in Asia: A Regional Overview.*

17. Paul Smith, "Economic Transformation and Labor Migration," In *Fires Across the Water: Transnational Problems in Asia*, ed. James Shinn (New York: A Council of Foreign Relations, 1998).

18. Phil William, "Transnational Criminal Organizations and International Security," *Survival* 36, no. 1 (Spring 1994): 96–113.

19. Robert Schaeffer, *Understanding Globalization: The Social Consequences of Political, Economic, and Environmental Change* (New York: Rowman & Littlefield, 1997).

20. However, not all countries declare or even perceive that money laundering is an illegal activity, which complicates the whole problem of trying to control all kinds of trafficking that are clearly criminal in nature. Laundering money is the processes of converting illegally gained money into forms that make it appear legitimate—moving it into legal businesses such as hotels and real estate.

21. Karen Tumlin, *Trafficking in Children in Asia: A Regional Overview.*

22. "Pat Pong–Style Vice Den Busted," *Malay Mail,* 25 February 2004.

23. "China Dolls for Sale," *Malay Mail,* 25 February 2004.

24. Perhaps the author would like to suggest the Malay word for trafficking to *Dewan Bahasa and Pustaka,* a national institute that officially deals with Malay language.

25. Research conducted on "Trafficking in Women and Children: The Challenge to the National Security of Malaysia" (Code: SK/30/2003).

26. Zarina Othman, "Trafficking of Women and Children in Southeast Asia: Focus on Malaysia," *Journal of Population* (2004), 10, no.1.

27. The protocols deal with Smuggling of Migrants, Trafficking in Persons (Especially Women and Children), and Trafficking in Firearms.

28. UNICEF. http://www.unicef.org/program/cprotection/focus/trafficking/issue .html (5 Oct. 2003).

BIBLIOGRAPHY

Abdullah, Kamarulnizam, and Mahmud Embung. "Kepentingan Strategik di Dalam Keselamatan Negara Malaysia." *Sejarah: Jurnal Jabatan Sejarah Universiti Malaya,* 6: 151–76.

Alagappa, Muthiah. *The National Security of Developing States: Lessons From Thailand.* Dover, MA: Auburn House Publishing, 1987.

Appleyard, Reginald, ed. *Perspectives on Trafficking of Migrants.* Geneva: International Organization for Migration and the UN, 2000.

Buzan, Barry. *People, States and Fear.* 2nd ed. Boulder, CO: Lynne Rienner Publishers, 1991.

"China Dolls for Sale." *Malay Mail,* 25 February 2004.

CRS Report for Congress. *Trafficking in Women and Children: The US and International Response.* 2002. http://www.ilr.cornel.edulibrary.CRSTrafficwomenchildren.htm (6 June 2003).

Hitam, Musa. Speech given at Harvard Club, Singapore, 1986.

Lintner, Bertil. *Blood Brothers: The Criminal Underworld of Asia.* New York: Palgrave MacMillan, 2003.

———. "People Smuggling: The Crime of Flight." *Far Eastern Economic Review,* 18 July 2002: 18–20.

Othman, Zarina. "Trafficking of Women and Children in Southeast Asia: Focus on Malaysia." *Journal of Population.* 10, no. 1 (2004): 31–52.

———. *Human Security in Southeast Asia: A Case Study of Illicit Drug Trafficking as a Transnational Threat in Myanmar (Burma).* Unpublished PhD dissertation, Denver, CO: University of Denver, 2002.

"Pat Pong–Style Vice Den Busted." *Malay Mail,* 25 February 2004.

Schaeffer, Robert. *Understanding Globalization: The Social Consequences of Political, Economic, and Environmental Change.* New York: Rowman & Littlefield, 1997.

Skeldon, Ronald. "Trafficking: A Perspective from Asia." *Perspectives on Trafficking of Migrants.* Geneva: International Organization for Migration and the UN, 2000.

Skrobonek, Siripon, et al. *The Traffic in Women.* London: Zed Books, 1997.

Smith, Paul. "Economic Transformation and Labor Migration." In *Fires Across the Water: Transnational Problems in Asia,* edited by James Smith. New York: A Council of Foreign Relations, 1998.

Tumlin, Karen. *Trafficking in Children in Asia: A Regional Overview.* Bangkok: Institute for Asian Studies, Chulalongkorn University (An ILO-IPEC Paper), 2000. UN Convention Against Transnational Organized Crime (2000). http://www.unodc.org/palermo/convmain.html (5 Oct. 2003).

UNDP. *Human Development Report 1994.* New York: Oxford University Press, 1995.

UNICEF. http://www.unicef.org/program/cprotection/focus/trafficking/issue.html (5 Oct. 2003).

United Nations Office on Drugs and Crime, http://www/undoc.org/unodc/trafficking_victim_consents.html (5 Oct. 2003).

Viotti, Paul, and Mark Kauppi. *International Relations Theory: Realism, Pluralism, Globalism and Beyond.* 3rd ed. Boston: Allyn and Bacon, 1999.

William, Phil. "Transnational Criminal Organizations and International Security." *Survival* 36, no. 1 (Spring 1994): 96–113.

Wong, Diana. "Border Controls, Illegal Migration and the Sovereignty of the Nation-State" (UKM: IKMAS, no. 10, 2004).

Zhang, Sheldon, and Ko-Lin Chin. "Enter the Dragon: Inside Chinese Human Smuggling Organizations." *Criminology* 40, no. 4 (2002): 737–68.

· *5* ·

Trafficking in Women from the Former Soviet Union for the Purposes of Sexual Exploitation

Saltanat Sulaimanova

$\mathcal{T}$rafficking in women is a modern form of slavery that exists in most countries of the world. It is a global transnational problem and is one of the fastest growing criminal enterprises. It is attractive for traffickers because the profits are enormously high and the risks are low. Each year, illicit profits from trafficking in women generate an estimated 7 to 12 billion dollars for organized criminal groups.[1] Thailand and the Philippines have been the main sending countries for many years but Eastern Europe and the former Soviet Union are becoming rapidly growing markets for young women. Political, economic, and social changes, which occurred after the Soviet Union collapsed, resulted in poverty and unemployment, creating a new pool of women from which traffickers can recruit. Thousands of women are lured into prostitution under false pretenses of high paying jobs as waitresses, dancers, models, and au pairs abroad. Impoverished women of the former Soviet Union are an easy target for traffickers, who take advantage of the poverty, high level of unemployment among women, and their lack of a stable future, by enticing the women with lucrative job offers abroad.

Trafficking in human beings is a multifaceted problem and it has various forms—sweatshop labor, domestic servitude, begging, and sexual exploitation. This chapter focuses on trafficking of women from the former Soviet Union for the purposes of sexual exploitation. Trafficking in women is a new phenomenon for this region, which was behind the Iron Curtain for more than seventy years of the Soviet rule. Prior to 1991, there were virtually no reported cases of trafficking in women from the former Soviet republics to the West. Yet, since the breakup of the Soviet Union, this phenomenon has reached epidemic proportions. Consequently, limited research has been done so far in this region, most of the previous research focusing on trafficking from Southeast

Asia. Trafficking in women for the purposes of sexual exploitation is generally a more dangerous form of trafficking in humans compared to sweatshop labor or domestic servitude (although not less inhuman). This is because victims are exposed to serious health risks, including HIV/AIDS, which can be threatening for their lives. Trafficking in children and men also occurs, but the majority of victims are women.

It is hard to find out how many women have been trafficked abroad from the Commonwealth of Independent States (CIS). The trafficking "business" is secretive; the traffickers threaten victims, and there are no official statistics available. The Ukrainian Ministry of Internal Affairs has estimated in 1998 that 400,000 Ukrainian women were trafficked during the previous decade.[2] The estimate of the International Organization for Migration (IOM) is that between 1991 and 1998, 500,000 Ukrainian women had been trafficked to Western countries.[3] As Hughes reports, "there are 6,000 Ukrainian women in prostitution in Turkey, 3,000 in Greece, and 1,000 in Yugoslavia."[4] Ukrainian women are the largest group of foreigners engaged in commercial sex work in Turkey.[5] In the case of Central Asia, approximately 4,000 women from Kyrgyzstan, about 5,000 from Kazakhstan,[6] and 1,000[7] from Tajikistan are trafficked abroad each year.

An estimated 175,000 persons are trafficked from Central and Eastern Europe and the newly independent states of the former Soviet Union annually.[8] Exact statistical data on numbers of trafficked women is not available due to the secretive nature of this criminal activity.

ROOT CAUSES OF TRAFFICKING

In general, women engage in trafficking because of poverty, unemployment, low social status of women in their home countries, lack of opportunities and prospects for the future, and, in many cases, because of an idealistic view of the Western world and the wealthier countries in general.

Poverty in the former Soviet countries has reached unprecedented levels: 53 percent of the Russian population lives on less than US$4 a day as do 82 percent of Moldovans and 88 percent of the Kyrgyz citizens.[9] In Azerbaijan, the monthly minimum per capita consumption budget is US$75, while the average monthly wage is only US$46.[10] Population groups affected by poverty most are women, children, and the elderly. For example, Russian women make up an estimated 80 percent of persons who have lost their jobs due to downsizing and economic shifts.[11] According to the Moscow Center for Gender Studies, 70 percent of the women graduating from higher educational establishments say that they cannot find gainful employment.[12] In Ukraine, women account for more than 60 percent of those who have lost their jobs in recent years.[13]

The National Statistics Committee of Kyrgyzstan reports that 70 percent of women in Kyrgyzstan are suffering from financial difficulties.[14] The unemployment rate in Kyrgyzstan is very high, and even those who are employed make an average of US$28 per month.[15] As the 2000 IOM survey of trafficking victims in Kyrgyzstan reports:

> Seventy-nine percent of the respondents said that unemployment drove them to look for work abroad. The main reasons they were working as commercial sex workers abroad were said to be related to their lack of money and hopes for a better future. The lack of alternative opportunities encourages them to take risks. In focus group discussions, the women said that they want more for themselves and their families than to just earn enough money to feed themselves. They want a better life.[16]

Even when women are employed, they often face job discrimination and sexual harassment at work. In many businesses throughout the CIS region, it is not uncommon for a male boss to demand that his female subordinate engage in sexual relations with him.[17] Newspaper job advertisements targeting women often mention "no hang-ups" (meaning willing to engage in sexual activities) as one of the qualifications required for the job.[18] Not surprisingly, it is not very difficult to entice women with such lucrative "job offers" when women are promised to be paid US$60,000 a year working abroad,[19] an amount they could never dream of at home. The collapse of the Soviet Union resulted not only in poverty and unemployment but also in drastic deterioration of the system of social protection. Many of the social services, which under the Soviet system were a norm, are no longer offered. Before the collapse of the Soviet Union, day care for children, at all levels of education, and medical services were provided free by the government. Now, many day care centers have closed and the remaining ones are not affordable to many parents. Health care and education systems are deteriorating due to lack of funding.[20]

The social status of women in the CIS has been on decline in the last decade. Women are increasingly becoming victims of domestic battering, rape, and sexual harassment.[21] It is estimated that in Russia there are 12,000 to 16,000 domestic homicides per year.[22] More disturbingly, 60 percent of the murdered women are killed by their own husbands.[23]

In Central Asia, since the collapse of the Soviet Union, there has been a revival of "national traditions," which have often come into conflict with Soviet policies that had promoted women's equality. Politicians began advocating a return to "traditional roles" for women, which is also interpreted as an attempt to "drive women out of the labor force and higher education and back into the home."[24] The Parliament in Kyrgyzstan has seriously discussed legalizing polygamy, and rejected this proposal by only a small margin.[25] Unofficially, polygamy is not uncommon in Central Asian republics.[26] The deteriorating economic situation, high unemployment among women, religious and traditional sentiments, as well as the consequences of the civil war (in Tajikistan) are quoted as reasons why polygamy is spreading across Central Asia.[27] One cannot dismiss male chauvinism as another major reason. Such a dramatic decline in women's social status creates a situation favorable for traffickers.

Domestic violence is one of the major reasons why children run away from home. Street children are especially vulnerable to being recruited by traffickers. Young girls from households where domestic violence is a norm grow up "seeing women as inferior beings that men can use and abuse as they please."[28]

In many cases women become victims of trafficking because of their naïveté and unrealistic expectations. According to Aleksandr Strokanov from Interpol-Ukraine, about 75 percent of the women do not realize they will be forced into prostitution when accepting lucrative job offers abroad.[29] In those cases when women know the nature of the job offers, they are not aware of the circumstances and their expectations are usually far from the reality. For example, a Ukrainian woman said she knew she would have to work as a commercial sex worker abroad, but she thought it would be similar to the film *Pretty Woman*, where she would have only one client who would support her.[30] One could argue that this is an extreme level of naïveté, but considering that these countries were totally isolated from the rest of the world for more than seventy years, these kinds of illusions are not surprising. The idea of the lifestyle in Western countries, and especially the United States, is mainly drawn from movies and soap operas that are broadcast on TV on a daily basis. Women watching TV shows such as *Santa Barbara* and *Dallas* expect to have the kind of life they see in the movies once they get to the West. They do not anticipate being manipulated, deceived, or physically abused, and think that nothing bad could happen to them in wealthy countries.

RECRUITMENT OF WOMEN IN THE COUNTRIES OF ORIGIN

Traffickers use the following methods to recruit victims: advertisements in newspapers, marriage agencies or mail-order bride agencies, friends, relatives or acquaintances, the "Second Wave" (trafficked women returning to recruit other women), false marriages (women marrying a false groom who is, in fact, a trafficker[31]), and kidnapping.

Advertisements in newspapers are the most popular recruitment method because traffickers can reach a wide pool of potential trafficking victims. Such advertisements usually offer young women highly paid work abroad as waitresses, dancers, shopkeepers, and so forth.[32] When a woman responds to an advertisement, the traffickers sometimes sign a "contract" with her that promises high earnings but stipulates that the travel expenses as well as room and board will be deducted. Room and board often can eat up half of their daily earnings. Women also must pay back the travel expenses that are "calculated" at a rate often exceeding the real cost of transportation as much as 3 to 5 times. According to the *Global Survival Network*, trafficking networks in Russia and other countries of the CIS charge women anywhere from US$1,500 to US$30,000 for their "services" in facilitating documentation, jobs, and transportation.[33] This puts victims in a huge debt that takes them months and sometimes years to pay off. They are often deprived of all their earnings until the "debt" is paid in full, which makes these women indentured servants.[34]

Mail-order bride and marriage agencies via the Internet have become increasingly popular among women who want to marry a foreigner. Their hope is to improve their economic situation and/or escape their native country, where they see no prospects for the future. Most of these women are somewhat naively searching for happiness, and often become victims of men who "order" them only to sell them to pimps.[35] The paramount problem is that mail-order-bride agencies do not conduct any screening of their male clients, some of whom may have had a history of violence or criminal background. As a result, mail-order brides may become victims of abuse. In a recent case, Anastasia Solovieva-King from Kyrgyzstan, a 20-year-old mail-order bride, was murdered by her American husband, Indle King. He had been married twice before, both times through matchmaking agencies. Within a month of marrying Anastasia, the man was writing to other prospective mail-order brides. Two years later, as his marriage to Anastasia started falling apart, he wrote to more women and began planning to marry another mail-order bride.[36] Following the murder of Anastasia King, the U.S. Congress proposed the International Marriage Broker Regulation Act of 2003, which would allow foreign mail-order brides to check the criminal background (including protective orders issued because of domestic violence allegations) of their potential grooms. If such legislation had been in place, Anastasia Solovieva may have learned that her prospective husband's first wife had obtained a protective order against him in 1995.[37]

There are even so-called marriage camps that have been established by some "entrepreneurs" to set up Norwegian men and Russian women. Russian women are brought in to Norway on tourist visas and they arrive in groups of twenty for three months. Norwegian men then pay a fee to come to the

"marriage camp" to select women, and for an additional fee they can take selected women home for up to three months. If they marry, the women can
obtain Norwegian citizenship after three years of marriage. If they divorce
within those three years, the women will have to return to Russia.[38] Not surprisingly, women in these camps are often treated as exchangeable commodities. It has been reported that Norwegian men view these women almost as
prostitutes "who can be bought, sold, or sent back to Russia if they do not
please the men."[39]

Some victims of trafficking indicated they have been recruited by friends,
relatives, or acquaintances who gain the woman's confidence, then offer highly
paid work abroad often sharing their alleged "experience" and showing off
newly purchased goods and property.[40] "Second wave" recruitment occurs
when trafficked women return home to recruit other women. For some of the
women, this is the only way they could return home—pimps often pose a condition that they should find someone else instead of themselves. Others become recruiters voluntarily to make a profit from other women's victimization.
IOM researchers interviewed a trafficked woman returned to Ukraine who
said: "I will soon visit Germany for the fourth time. One friend of mine will
go with me, a second one has not decided yet. . . . I have honestly informed
them that they will not work as waitresses, that they will serve clients. . . . I'll
assist them in documents' processing and they will pay me later DM500
each."[41] The cycle can be self-perpetuating. There are also cases of women
who have not been recruited being kidnapped off the streets.[42]

TRANSPORTATION TO DESTINATION COUNTRIES AND
INVOLVEMENT OF GOVERNMENT OFFICIALS

In most cases traffickers arrange for a woman's travel documents, visas, and airline or other tickets. Occupations typically listed on a victim's visa applications
include dancer, entertainer, student, or au pair. Tour firms are found to assist in
the trafficking of women and girls abroad, claiming they are "shop-tourists"
who buy goods abroad to resell them in their home countries.[43] Having entered the country with fake passports, women usually overstay their visas,
which makes them even more vulnerable to the local police as they are viewed
as illegal immigrants.

Almost each trafficking network in the CIS has a contact at the passport-
issuing department of the Ministry of Internal Affairs, which makes it possible
for them to obtain genuine state-issued passports.[44] This indicates that some
corrupt local law enforcement officials are an integral part of the trafficking
chain. If a woman does not have a passport or is underage, a false passport is

arranged for a bribe ranging from US$100[45] to US$800.[46] Corrupt law enforcement officials often have a purely monetary motive for facilitating trafficking of women, as salaries at the government agencies are very low. It is likely that government officials in the CIS are reluctant to intervene in human trafficking due to fear of reprisals by organized criminal groups.[47]

It also has been reported that law enforcement officials in some receiving countries are also involved in trafficking. For example, women under the age of 31 are not allowed to enter the United Arab Emirates, which is a major country of destination for women trafficked from Central Asia, unless accompanied by male relatives. When 15- and 16-year-old girls enter the United Arab Emirates with passports that indicate they are over 31, traffickers bribe the immigration officials at the airport for letting the girls pass through the immigration control.[48] Seventy-three percent of the trafficking victims interviewed by IOM in the Kyrgyz Republic reported they were harassed upon return by the customs and law enforcement officers. As one of the women recounts, "When I got to Almaty, the customs officials took US$500 cash off me, they also took my jewelry. They said, 'We know what you are. It's written all over your face.'"[49]

THE ROLE OF THE ORGANIZED CRIMINAL GROUPS IN TRAFFICKING

The former Soviet republics, especially Russia, are experiencing an organized crime epidemic. The Russian Ministry of Internal Affairs said in 1999 that there were over 9,000 criminal organizations in Russia. They employ about 100,000 people.[50] According to a senior official from the Ministry of Internal Affairs, organized criminal groups control 50 percent of Russian private enterprises and about 60 percent of state enterprises. State enterprises are used by the Russian Organized Crime (ROC) to carry out illicit financial transactions.[51] Overall, according to the same ministry, ROC controls 40 percent of the Russian economy. The Center for Strategic and International Studies (CSIS) estimates that some 8,000 criminal gangs operate throughout the CIS.[52] About 200 are now global conglomerates and operate in 59 countries of the world.[53] Twenty-six of them have established a presence in the United States.[54]

Overall, ROC is involved in all types of criminal activities, including but not limited to money-laundering, drug-trafficking, gambling, prostitution, trafficking in women and children, child pornography, contract killings, racketeering, banking and insurance fraud, extortion, and kidnapping for ransom.[55] The trafficking networks, controlled by criminal gangs that provide false documents, security, and logistical support, liaise with brothel owners in many countries.

According to Marco Gramegna of IOM, there are large, medium, and small-scale networks of trafficking in women.[56] Large-scale networks recruit women in a seemingly legal way as language students or au pairs, which leads to the conclusion that these networks have extensive international contacts at a political and economic level. The medium-scale networks usually traffic women from one country, and the small-scale networks traffic a few women at a time when a brothel owner places an "order."[57] In many cases, trafficking is carried out by organized criminal groups with foreign connections.[58]

The fact that organized criminal groups in various states of the former Soviet Union have links with each other allows them to effectively organize trafficking of women. For example, Russian and Ukrainian women are trafficked through Georgia to Turkey and the Mediterranean.[59] Tajik women are trafficked to the United Arab Emirates, Russia, Turkey, and other countries transiting through CIS states.[60] Armenian women are trafficked to Turkey and the United Arab Emirates through Georgia and to Poland and United Arab Emirates through Russia.[61] According to Louise Shelley, Director of the Transnational Crime and Corruption Center at American University, "While the links among the States have declined since the collapse of the Soviet Union, the organized criminals still manage to function effectively together. And in the Russian Far East, you see links with Korean and Japanese organized crime groups that are facilitating the trafficking of women."[62]

METHODS USED BY TRAFFICKERS TO CONTROL WOMEN

The Dutch NGO working against trafficking in women, *Stichting Tegen Vrouwenhandel* (STV), reports that organized criminal groups involved in trafficking are extremely violent and use every kind of threat to intimidate women. The so-called red mafia is said to have made a woman dig her own grave and take the women's family members hostage in order to force them to comply or keep silent.[63] As Shelley points out, "many of the women refuse to cooperate with the authorities because there was little or no protection, and they faced deportation and threats against their families if they cooperate with foreign law enforcement."[64]

Once a woman is in trafficker's hands, the latter uses any and all means to control her: violence, including sexual assault, threats to the victim's and her family's lives, drugs, and threats to turn the woman over to unsympathetic local authorities. Traffickers take away women's passports immediately upon arrival in the receiving country either by force or claiming that they need to extend the visas. Passports are then kept hostage to control victims. According to Human Rights Watch, the most common form of coercion is debt bondage.[65]

Women are told they must work without wages until they repay their purchase price and/or travel expenses. Employers also maintain their power to "resell" indebted women into renewed levels of debt. In some cases, women find that their debts only increase and can never be fully repaid.[66] It seems that pimps/traffickers let some women keep just enough of their earnings to take back home, to attract other potential victims.

Trafficked women who do not obey the rules are treated very severely. The corpses of several hundred trafficked women, strangled, shot, or beaten to a pulp, are detected in Europe every year.[67] Europol believes that many more bodies are never found. The Russian organized criminal groups, which control the trafficking in women from the CIS, are known for their cruelty. As Friedman puts it, "Russian mobsters, in the United States, simply don't play by the unwritten rules of the acceptable uses of gang-land violence."[68] And IOM reports that "The organized gangs of traffickers who lure and smuggle young women into prostitution are ruthless. During the interviews the women discussed cases they had heard of women who had been murdered." As a trafficked victim from Kyrgyzstan testified, "Russian pimps, unlike most European ones, are also hardened criminals. It's no big deal for them to kill someone. They're the greediest, cruelest people in the world. They warned me, 'If you try to go to the police, we'll kill you.' I believed them."[69] As Shelley testified in the U.S. Congress, "the ability to threaten the women under their control and to threaten retaliation against family members at home because of the long reach of the criminal organizations makes the women particularly vulnerable."[70]

The majority of victims are often kept in squalid conditions in a state of virtual house arrest and transported to and from work only. Even when women have relative freedom of movement, their illegal immigration status, inability to speak the local language, lack of documents and fear of being arrested, mistreated, and deported keeps them from seeking help from the local law enforcement authorities. For example, IOM study of trafficking from Azerbaijan reports that, "With one exception, none of the victims have tried to seek assistance from authorities, either in the country to which s/he was trafficked or upon his/her repatriation to Azerbaijan. The primary reason for that is a lack of trust in law enforcement agencies."[71]

THE SIMILARITIES AND DIFFERENCES BETWEEN HUMAN TRAFFICKING AND HUMAN SMUGGLING

Issues of human trafficking and human smuggling are closely intertwined as routes and methods of transportation are sometimes the same; both often involve illegal crossing of borders, and both involve human suffering and exploitation. The major difference, however, is in organization and profit-maximization patterns, especially when it comes to Chinese human smuggling and trafficking in women from the former Soviet republics.[72] Ko-Lin Chin has conducted a comprehensive study of human smuggling from China to the United States, which demonstrates a high level of organization and integration of smuggling networks.[73] For example, the first thing that smuggled Chinese do once they arrive in the United States is to place a telephone call to their families. This is a signal for their families that the migrants arrived to the destination and the smuggling fee should be paid. In contrast, trafficked women from the Newly Independent States of the former Soviet Union are generally not allowed to contact their families at home.

Chinese smugglers maximize their profits running their operations as integrated business operations.[74] Smuggling of Chinese migrants also generates capital that is invested back in China. Human traffickers, specifically former Soviet traffickers, do not return anything to their societies back at home.

Trafficking from the CIS is characterized by the short-term mentality of the organized criminal groups, which also characterizes the attitude toward the post-Soviet economy in general. Post-Soviet organized criminals recruit women and usually sell them at the first point of entry into another country to other criminal groups who subsequently resell women.[75] This leads to greater abuse of the women and to an increase of their debts.

CONCLUSION AND RECOMMENDATIONS

Trafficking in women is a fundamental human rights violation that needs to be combated on both national and international levels. The consequences of trafficking are grave to the women and countries involved. According to Marco Gramegna of the IOM, the results of trafficking include a threat to legal migration and a growth in clandestine immigration.[76] Both of these problems could have solemn implications for political, economic, and diplomatic affairs of sending and receiving countries. Victims of trafficking face intolerable situations, including sexual and physical abuse, and deprivation of their basic human rights and dignity.

The trafficking enterprise is driven by poverty and unemployment of women as well as by the demand in the receiving states. To solve the problem by tackling its root causes would be the optimal solution, which, unfortunately, is an enormously complex and multidimensional task. The international community cannot wait until the economy straightens itself out and all women are employed. It is the responsibility of the international community to confront this issue and take aggressive steps to prevent and stop trafficking in women and girls.

The following steps might be carried out in "sending" countries to help alleviate the problem:

- Foster creation of job opportunities for young women;
- Improve law enforcement efforts to prevent and punish trafficking of women;
- Crack down on official complicity in trafficking of women (including stricter control over issuing passports), and combat corruption which fuels organized crime;
- Carry out information campaigns in media and TV about the nature, realities, and risks of lucrative job offers;
- Provide legal, medical and psychological assistance to victims of trafficking; and
- Guarantee safety of victims who testify against the traffickers through witness protection programs.

"Receiving" countries should consider the following actions:

- Amend laws, including immigration law, to exempt victims of trafficking and/or servitude from being prosecuted for illegal status that has resulted directly from these practices. Deportation may be appropriate, but punitive measures, including detention, should be waived;
- Prosecute traffickers and enable victims to bring lawsuits against traffickers by granting temporary residence permits for the duration of the case;
- Impose tougher penalties for trafficking. The United States has already been taking such measures with the adoption of the Trafficking Victims Protection Act of 2000;
- Protect safety of victims of trafficking through strong witness protection programs;
- Ensure that victims of trafficking have access to essential social services, including shelter and medical care; and
- Distribute information brochures at the receiving countries' embassies abroad with each visa issued to a woman on the realities and risks of being trafficked and what to do if she found herself trafficked and abused abroad (in a local language).

Organized criminal groups in both sending and receiving countries are actively involved in trafficking of human beings. Thus, all countries involved (sending, receiving, and transit countries) should continue their efforts to crack down on organized crime. International cooperation and coordination between law enforcement agencies from sending, receiving, and transit countries is crucial for combating trafficking in women. When possible, information needed to prosecute the traffickers and protect the victims should be made available to all parties.

Trafficking occurs because women are poor and desperate, do not have foreseeable perspectives for improvement in their lives at home, and have illusions and unrealistic expectations about what awaits them abroad. Traffickers take advantage of these circumstances and exploit women. However, trafficking would not be so profitable if there was no demand in the wealthier countries. It is obvious that the government authorities in sending countries are involved in the trafficking process at various levels, but are the authorities in the receiving countries also looking away from the problem? How aggressively governments will combat this problem in the next few years will determine if the international community is going to eliminate this modern form of slavery in the twenty-first century.

NOTES

Earlier versions of this paper have been previously published in *In the Tracks of Tamerlane: Central Asia's Path to the 21st Century*, ed. Daniel L. Burghart and Theresa Sabonis-Helf (Washington DC: National Defense University Press, 2004); and *The Journal of Central Asian Studies* 6, no. 2, 2005.

1. Donna M. Hughes, "The 'Natasha' Trade—The Transnational Shadow Market of Trafficking in Women," *Journal of International Affairs* 53, no. 2 (Spring 2000): 625–651.
2. Hughes, "The Natasha Trade," 628.
3. Hughes, "The Natasha Trade," 628–29.
4. Hughes, "The Natasha Trade," 629.
5. Hughes, "The Natasha Trade," 629.
6. IOM, "Trafficking in Migrants," no. 23 (April 2001), http://www.iom .int//DOCUMENTS/PUBLICATION/EN/tm_23.pdf (12 September 2003).
7. IOM, "Deceived Migrants from Tajikistan: A Study of Trafficking in Women and Children" (2001): 13.
8. Organization for Security and Cooperation in Europe, "*Proposed Action Plan 2000 for Activities to Combat Trafficking in Human Beings*," Warsaw: Office for Democratic Institutions and Human Rights (November 1999).
9. United Nations Development Program, *Human Development Report 2004* (New York: Hoechstetter Printing Co., 2004).
10. IOM, "Away from Azerbaijan, Destination Europe: Study of Migration Motives, Routes and Methods," (2001): 13.
11. Gillian Caldwell, Steven Galster, and Nadia Steinzor, *Crime & Servitude: An Exposé of the Traffic in Women for Prostitution from the Newly Independent States* (Washington, DC: Global Survival Network, 1997):11.

12. Caldwell et al. *Crime & Servitude*, 11.

13. IOM, "Information Campaign Against Trafficking in Women from Ukraine," (1998), http://www.iom.int (5 May 2005).

14. IOM, "Trafficking in Women and Children from the Kyrgyz Republic," 11.

15. Cited in Kyrgyzstan Development Gateway, http://eng.gateway.kg (6 July 2003).

16. IOM, "Trafficking in Women and Children from the Kyrgyz Republic" (2000): 11.

17. IOM, "Trafficking in Women and Children from the Kyrgyz Republic," 12.

18. Donna M. Hughes, "Trafficking for Sexual Exploitation: The Case of the Russian Federation," International Organization for Migration (IOM), 2002.

19. "Slaves of Chicago: International Sex Trafficking Is Becoming Big Business," *In These Times*, January 8, 2001. http://www.inthesetimes.com/issue/25/03/crouse2503.html (1 March 2003).

20. IOM, "Trafficking in Women and Children from the Kyrgyz Republic" (2000): 12.

21. Hughes, "Trafficking for Sexual Exploitation: The Case of the Russian Federation," IOM (2002): 11.

22. Hughes, "Trafficking for Sexual Exploitation," 11.

23. Hughes, "Trafficking for Sexual Exploitation," 11.

24. Human Rights Watch, "Sacrificing Women to Save the Family? Domestic Violence in Uzbekistan" (2001): 3.

25. "The Stolen Brides of Kirgizstan," *The Economist* 341, no. 7993, November 23, 1996.

26. Human Rights Watch, "Sacrificing Women to Save the Family?" Also see "Central Asia: Increase in Polygamy Attributed to Economic Hardship, Return to Tradition," *Radio Free Europe/Radio Liberty*, October 16, 2002, http://www.rferl.org/nca/features/2002/10/16102002163911.asp (6 July 2003).

27. "Central Asia: Increase in Polygamy Attributed to Economic Hardship, Return to Tradition," *Radio Free Europe/Radio Liberty*, October 16 2002, http://www.rferl.org/nca/features/2002/10/16102002163911.asp (6 July 2003).

28. Hughes, "Trafficking for Sexual Exploitation," 12.

29. Hughes, "The 'Natasha' Trade," 636.

30. Hughes, "The 'Natasha' Trade," 636.

31. IOM, "Deceived Migrants from Tajikistan," 15.

32. IOM, "Trafficking in Women and Children from the Kyrgyz Republic," 13.

33. Caldwell, Galster, and Steinzor, *Crime & Servitude: An Exposé of the Traffic in Women for Prostitution from the Newly Independent States* (Washington, DC: Global Survival Network, 1997): 14.

34. Caldwell et al., "Crime & Servitude."

35. Hughes, "The 'Natasha' Trade," 635.

36. Jim Haley, "King Case Coming to End," *Daily Herald*, February 21, 2002, http://www.heraldnet.com (15 March 2002).

37. "Abuse of Mail-Order Foreign Brides Prompts Effort to Oversee Fast-Growing Industry," *Associated Press*, July 5, 2003.

38. Hughes, "Trafficking for Sexual Exploitation," IOM (2002).

39. Hughes, "Trafficking for Sexual Exploitation," 20.

40. IOM, "Deceived Migrants from Tajikistan: A Study of Trafficking in Women and Children" (2001): 15.

41. IOM, "Information Campaign Against Trafficking in Women from Ukraine" (1998): 19.

42. IOM, "Deceived Migrants from Tajikistan," 15; also see IOM, "Trafficking from the Kyrgyz Republic," 14–15.

43. IOM, "Deceived Migrants from Tajikistan," 14.

44. IOM, "Trafficking from the Kyrgyz Republic" (2000).

45. IOM, "Trafficking from the Kyrgyz Republic" (2000).

46. Caldwell, Galster and Steinzor, *Crime & Servitude,* 9.

47. Hughes, "Trafficking for Sexual Exploitation," 5.

48. IOM, "Trafficking from the Kyrgyz Republic" (2000).

49. IOM, "Trafficking from the Kyrgyz Republic" (2000): 45–46.

50. Gary Dempsey and Aaron Lukas, "Is Russia Controlled by Organized Crime?" *USA Today 127*, No. 2648 (May 1999): 32–34.

51. "Organized Crime Said to Control Half of Russian Companies," *Interfax News Agency*, November 10, 1999, found in *BBC Monitoring Former Soviet Union*, London, November 11, 1999.

52. Global Organized Crime Project, *Russian Organized Crime* (Washington, DC: Center for Strategic and International Studies (CSIS), 1997).

53. Global Organized Crime Project, *Russian Organized Crime and Corruption: Putin's Challenge* (Washington, DC: CSIS, 2000).

54. CSIS, *Russian Organized Crime and Corruption.*

55. GSIS, *Russian Organized Crime* (Washington, DC: Center for Strategic and International Studies, 1997).

56. Cited in Andrea Bertone, "International Political Economy and the Politics of Sex," *Gender Issues* 18, no.1 (2000): 4–22.

57. Bertone, "International Political Economy."

58. Testimony of Louise Shelley at the Hearing before the Commission on Security and Cooperation in Europe on "The Sex Trade: Trafficking of Women and Children in Europe and the United States" (June 28,1999).

59. Shelley, "The Sex Trade."

60. IOM, "Deceived Migrants from Tajikistan," 18.

61. IOM, "Trafficking in Women and Children from the Republic of Armenia: A Study" (2001): 25.

62. Shelley, "The Sex Trade," 18.

63. Sietske Altink, *Stolen Lives: Trading Women into Sex and Slavery* (London: Scarlet Press, 1995): 125.

64. Shelley, "The Sex Trade," 17.

65. Human Rights Watch/Asia, *Owed Justice: Thai Women Trafficked into Debt Bondage in Japan* (New York: Human Rights Watch, 2000): 86.

66. Ralph Regan, "International Trafficking of Women and Children," Testimony before the Senate Committee on Foreign Relations, Washington, DC, February 22, 2000), http://secretary.state.gov/www/picw/trafficking/tralph.htm (1 March 2001).

67. "In the Shadows," *Economist* 356, no. 8185 (August 26, 2000): 38–39.

68. Robert I. Friedman, *Red Mafiya: How the Russian Mob Has Invaded America* (Boston: Little, Brown and Co., 2000).

69. IOM, "Trafficking from the Kyrgyz Republic," 27, 47.

70. Shelley, "The Sex Trade," 1999.

71. IOM, "Shattered Dreams: Report on Trafficking in Persons in Azerbaijan" (2002): 25.

72. Louise Shelley, "Post-Communist Transitions and the Illegal Movement of People: Chinese Smuggling and Russian Trafficking in Women," *Annals of Scholarship* 14, no. 2 (2002).

73. Ko-Lin Chin, *Smuggled Chinese: Clandestine Immigration to the United States* (Philadelphia: Temple University Press, 1999).

74. Shelley, "Post-Communist Transitions," 2002.

75. Louise Shelley, "Trafficking in Women and Children: Trafficking and Organized Crime" (presented at the Protection Project Seminar Series, SAIS, Johns Hopkins University, Washington, DC, October 4, 2000), www.protectionproject.org (5 May 2005).

76. Cited in Andrea Bertone, "International Political Economy and the Politics of Sex," *Gender Issues* 18, no.1 (2000): 4–22.

BIBLIOGRAPHY

Caldwell, Gillian, Steven Galster and Nadia Steinzor. *Crime & Servitude: An Exposé of the Traffic in Women for Prostitution from the Newly Independent States.* Washington, DC: Global Survival Network, 1997.

Global Organized Crime Project. *Russian Organized Crime and Corruption: Putin's Challenge.* Washington, DC: Center for Strategic and International Studies, 2000.

Hughes, Donna M. "The 'Natasha' Trade—The Transnational Shadow Market of Trafficking in Women." *Journal of International Affairs* 53, no. 2 (Spring 2000): 625–651.

———. "Trafficking for Sexual Exploitation: The Case of the Russian Federation." International Organization for Migration (IOM), 2002.

International Organization for Migration (IOM). "Trafficking in Women and Children from the Kyrgyz Republic" (2000).

———. "Deceived Migrants from Tajikistan: A Study of Trafficking in Women and Children" (2001).

———. "Trafficking in Women and Children from the Republic of Armenia: A Study" (2001).

———. "Shattered Dreams: Report on Trafficking in Persons in Azerbaijan" (2002).

Shelley, Louise. "Post-Communist Transitions and the Illegal Movement of People: Chinese Smuggling and Russian Trafficking in Women." *Annals of Scholarship* 14, no. 2 (2002).

———. "The Sex Trade: Trafficking of Women and Children in Europe and the United States." Testimony at the Hearing before the Commission on Security and Cooperation in Europe on June 28, 1999.

Sietske, Altink. *Stolen Lives: Trading Women into Sex and Slavery.* London: Scarlet Press, 1995.

· 6 ·

Insecurity and Opportunity in Colombia: Linking Civil War and Human Trafficking

Abbey Steele

$\mathcal{T}$he illegal traffic in arms, drugs, and diamonds fuels civil wars around the world. At the same time, civil wars seem to fuel the traffic in humans.[1] Armed groups force civilians to perform services or labor, ranging from porting equipment, as in Uganda and Burma, to becoming combatants or sex slaves.[2] In post-war Bosnia and Kosovo, women have been trafficked into brothels, some patronized by international peacekeeping forces and contractors.[3] Colombian women are trafficked to Japan and Western Europe for sex work in numbers estimated to be greater than those from any other country in the Western Hemisphere.[4] Yet the links between civil war and human trafficking remain uncertain.

Exploring the connections between civil war and human trafficking is impeded by several well-known challenges. The first set is empirical. Data on trafficking is so murky that it is unclear even what we can infer by comparing the numbers of those trafficked from different countries, let alone regions within countries. The second set of problems, which I refer to as analytic, derives from the first: generalizing about the experiences of victims is problematic and imprudent, if not impossible, since we have no basis on which to infer how representative those experiences might be. To avoid these potential pitfalls, which may lead to erroneous conclusions about trafficking, I will posit underlying bases of the supply-side dynamics of trafficking in analytic terms. I suggest that work in this area might yield substantial advances in our understanding, given the challenges to empirical work that do not seem surmountable in the short term. By suggesting analytical foundations for our assumptions and intuitions about the dynamics of human trafficking, we might be better able to design informed research programs and effective preventative and enforcement policies.[5]

In this chapter, I direct my inquiry to two related but distinct analytical questions: how might civil war exacerbate existing conditions conducive to trafficking, and what kinds of new conditions might civil war create which increase the likelihood and incidence of human trafficking? Emphasizing both the decision-making calculus of individuals and the conditions conducive to the success of criminal networks, I suggest that war alters the connection between trafficking networks and individuals in two ways. First, it amplifies the peacetime conditions favorable to trafficking because civilian populations are more willing to accept risky circumstances to migrate, while at the same time, trafficking networks are more likely to successfully victimize those populations in the context of war. Civil wars have the potential to increase networks' opportunities and decrease individuals' alternative opportunities in such a way that is likely to increase the supply side of trafficking, all else being equal. Second, civil wars also create new conditions favorable to trafficking. The atmosphere of violence generates new demands for trafficking, mostly by armed groups, while it also creates new populations affected by the violence, which seems to change how they consider opportunities.

The remainder of this chapter will proceed as follows. First, I specify the elements of trafficking during peacetime. Next, I provide a general background on the Colombian civil war to contextualize the circumstances that both civilians and criminal networks encounter there. I then outline different ways that the war may be increasing the incidence of human trafficking, both by exacerbating peacetime conditions and by creating unique conditions. Finally, in the conclusion I identify additional questions for future research and suggest implications for policy emerging from the analysis.

PEACETIME TRAFFICKING

For the purposes of this chapter, I will limit my focus to large-scale trafficking operations. It is difficult to assess at this point the proportion of victims trafficked by networks as opposed to individuals, but I think it is reasonable to assume that the former cases are greater in number (potentially substantially so) than the latter.[6] In addition, I will set aside theorizing about the demand side of the trafficking equation and assume that it is relatively constant.[7] As I explore below, however, demand for trafficking might change between peacetime and war *within* the country at war; demand might not only increase, but also change in terms of what victims are demanded for and what groups or individuals are demanding them. I begin with the premise that the basic elements of human trafficking are networks and individuals. In general, criminal networks need to exist in order to traffic humans, and there obviously needs to be a supply of potential human victims. While entirely simplistic, it provides an interesting point of departure that enables careful reasoning about the dynamics of trafficking and civil war. In what follows, I use opportunity as a concept through which to theorize about the necessary conditions for trafficking networks to exist and individuals to decide to migrate.[8] Opportunity operates for networks in two crucial areas: impunity and supply of people. For individuals, the lack of alternative opportunities tips their incentives enough to accept an offer of work abroad or in a different region of the country, and thus, their entrance into the trafficking market.

Women with fewer socioeconomic resources are more likely to accept offers to migrate—even if potentially fraudulent—because the potential relative gains are greater than the costs of leaving compared to women who have opportunities for employment or an extensive social network. At the same time, traffickers are more likely to target women of relatively lower socioeconomic resources because it is less costly to resort to fraud and coercion than force. Networks, I suggest, can resort to tactics ranging from force to coercion to fraud, with the latter end of the spectrum the least costly.

Necessary conditions for a criminal network to operate and survive in a country tend to relate to law enforcement and corruption of state agencies. As law enforcement capacity—in both policing bodies and judicial institutions—decreases, and corruption increases, we would expect to find increased trafficking for two reasons related to the criminal networks. One is that a higher number of networks can be expected to exist in countries with low capacity or will to confront them. The second is that these networks may be able to operate at higher capacity since the risk of being both caught and prosecuted is lower than in countries with stronger law enforcement. In addition, if a network is to set up operations in a country, there should exist a population that it perceives is willing to make choices to migrate in uncertain circumstances.

The dynamic described in the literature on migration is useful in thinking about individuals' decision-making. The underlying insight is that individuals consider factors in both their home community, as well as information about the destination or possible destinations when making decisions. The most straightforward way to conceptualize the process is as individuals weighing the costs and benefits of migrating. The costs can include a range of economic and social factors, such as employment opportunities and family ties. Offers of work abroad—whether by trickery about the nature of the work itself (as is sometimes the case with women who end up in the sex industry), or the conditions of work (although some women may agree to migrate to either continue or begin working in the sex industry, they are not any less victimized by enslavement)—can become increasingly appealing given different economic and social circumstances.

CIVIL WARS AND CONDITIONS FAVORABLE TO TRAFFICKING

I suggest that civil wars increase the likelihood of trafficking because civil wars increase the opportunities for trafficking networks and decrease opportunities for civilians. Increased general impunity is likely, given the state's necessary dedication of resources to fighting insurgents. At the same time, civilians—especially those displaced by violence and those affected by economic downturns usually associated with civil wars—face more constraints in earning an income, finding housing, and securing themselves and loved ones against violence. In these circumstances, even risky offers of work become more attractive. A caveat to this line of reasoning is warranted, however: civil wars might also decrease the likelihood of trafficking if the violence is widespread enough, or if infrastructure damage is extensive enough (especially in terms of roads or airports, for example) because trafficking networks will find it too costly to operate in these circumstances. The context of each civil war in question is an important point of departure for assessing the possible effect on human trafficking. With this in mind, I briefly turn to a general overview of the actors and conditions of the Colombian Civil War before suggesting links between it and trafficking.

Over the past decade, the Colombian civil war has claimed 40,000 lives, the majority civilian.[9] Roughly 1,000 people flee their homes each day.[10] The armed groups competing for territorial control in Colombia are multiple and varied, and some span four decades. The Revolutionary Armed Forces of Colombia (*Fuerzas Armadas Revolucionarias de Colombia-Ejército Popular*, FARC) organized during the final phase of *la Violencia*, a period of violence and civil war from 1946 to 1963. Today the FARC's membership is estimated to range between 15,000 and 20,000 fighters. The other remaining guerrilla group is the National Liberation Army (*Ejército de Liberación Nacional*, ELN), which counts roughly 4,000 combatants. Paramilitary groups formed in opposition to the growing strength of the guerrillas (and as a handful of other guerrilla groups emerged and disbanded over this time period). In April 1997, seven blocs united under the umbrella organization the United Self-Defense Forces of Colombia (*Las Autodefensas Unidas de Colombia*, AUC), which has since splintered.[11] The two largest factions are the AUC and the Peasant Self-Defense Forces of Cordoba and Uraba (*Autodefensas Campesinas de Córdoba y Urabá*, ACCU). Combined, the paramilitary groups are estimated to count between 15,000 and 20,000 members.

Initially, the state's armed forces seem to have worked with or to have been complicit in operations carried out by the paramilitaries against the guerrillas or accused collaborators. Since the peace process between the government and the FARC broke down in February 2002, the military, with the substantial aid of the US government, has redoubled its efforts to engage the illegal armed groups. Because all of the armed groups, with the possible exception of the ELN, finance their operations largely with profits from the trade in cocaine, a central counterinsurgency tactic is the fumigation of coca crops.

As in many civil wars, civilians are often the intended targets of the armed groups vying for territorial control. Direct fighting between the illegal armed groups and the state's armed forces is rare, though it also victimizes civilians caught in the crossfire when it does occur. Both guerrillas and paramilitaries have massacred, assassinated, kidnapped, and displaced civilians. The fumigation of coca has destroyed farms and generated the displacement of thousands of peasants in southern Colombia. Violence and displacement are generally restricted to rural areas, while urban zones receive the internally displaced and suffer from violent crime unrelated to the war. Finally, in its fourth periodic report on Colombia, the Committee on the Elimination of Discrimination Against Women (CEDAW) documented, "Confirmation was found of the existence of national and international networks trafficking in women, of importers and exporters of children and adults, and, of recruiting organizations operating at the interdepartmental level."[12] The US State Department reports "Colombians are trafficked to Central America, Panama, the Caribbean (particularly the Netherlands Antilles), Japan, Singapore, and Europe (particularly Spain and the Netherlands)."[13]

Conditions of impunity and corruption exist in countries experiencing civil wars. While political violence is a pervasive cause of death and displacement in Colombia, the US State Department estimates that common criminals caused 75 percent of the roughly 23,000 murders in 2003.[14] Impunity rates for such crimes reach as high as 95 percent.[15] The US State Department Trafficking in Persons report from 2004 ranked Colombia in the top tier of countries, recognizing the Colombian government's efforts to confront the situation and ebb the estimated 35,000 people trafficked outside the country each year, most of whom are women. Yet despite an apparent will to address trafficking, in 2003 only 14 women were freed, 8 people arrested, 16 prosecuted, and 3 convicted of trafficking.[16] Attributing even some of the state's inability to fight crime and enforce its laws to its involvement in civil war, it seems reasonable to suggest that trafficking networks have an easier time in a Colombia at war than one at peace. In addition, bribing law enforcement officials may be easier because they also face less chance of punishment, given general impunity.

The opportunities for networks may also increase during civil wars in two additional ways. First, law enforcement officials may be more willing to accept bribes and ignore trafficking when the state is unable or unwilling to pay high enough salaries, which, all things being equal, is more likely to be the case during civil war. Second, an increased number of civilians will face tougher choices about migration and employment options. In addition, the atmosphere of violence may also change individuals' risk calculations enough to tip the balance in favor of an uncertain situation. Offering a (false) job opportunity abroad may net more victims in a society experiencing civil war than elsewhere. In the next section, I interrogate the links between economic conditions and cost calculations of individuals; the violence dynamic I explore in the section dealing with how civil wars may create new conditions under which trafficking exists.

Finally, additional networks may be able to operate in such a context. Many different types of networks may overlap in a country, including regional, diffuse ones and international, centralized ones. In Colombia, there has been evidence that both types operate.[17] The Yakuza of Japan is a highly organized, hierarchical network with specialized roles at different levels of the organization. At the same time, individuals may work together loosely to traffic within the region.

The cost-benefit analysis that individuals make in reference to migration possibilities might change for two central, related reasons during civil war. Civil wars alter individuals' and households' usual calculations of migration directly and indirectly. Forced displacement creates a new pool of potential targets for two reasons: job options are scant and undesirable in many destinations, whether in an urban area (which is usually the case in Colombia, or a refugee camp)—this also generates economic dislocations among the residents of receptor locations; also, if an individual or household has migrated once, they are more willing to continue migrating. In other words, given options in both the home region and in the possible destinations, those experiencing the violence of warfare may be more likely to migrate than otherwise. Violence could become a cost for not migrating—and a potentially extremely high cost at that. Certainly, not all areas of a country are affected by warfare in the same way. Yet the effects of war on a country's economy can be devastating. In such circumstances, offers from trafficking networks, even if they appear questionable, may be attractive enough that people are willing to take the risk.[18]

CIVIL WAR GENERATES NEW CONDITIONS FOR TRAFFICKING

Until this point, I have focused on how the supply side of human trafficking may be affected by war. But civil wars also create new demands for trafficked humans and opportunities for new actors to traffic. Two such actors are considered in this section: illegal armed groups and (briefly) peacekeepers and post-war reconstruction contractors. A key difference between trafficking victims in unique wartime circumstances and victims of conditions exacerbated by war is the tendency for the former group to be trafficked within the country, as opposed to abroad. This is mainly due to the source of the difference between unique wartime conditions and all others: the armed groups tend to become a new trafficking network, one that does not exist without the context of civil war. In this section, I will first address new conditions for networks and then turn to the new conditions individuals confront.

In order to sustain a civil war, armed groups need to recruit combatants. In many cases, children are targeted with promises of payment or a better life. In others, children are forced to become combatants. The proportion of child soldiers in any given war who are victims of trafficking might be too difficult to estimate, but some circumstances fall under the UN definition of trafficking. The US State Department and Human Rights Watch International both report that the FARC has trafficked children for the purposes of conscription.[19]

Similarly, some armed groups force women and girls to accompany them. In some cases, forced marriages occur, as is reported about the Lord's Resistance Army in Uganda. In others, these women and children are not "married" to combatants, but are also required to perform services for the armed groups, such as collecting food, preparing meals, and washing uniforms. Some are kept as sex slaves. Again, while it is difficult to estimate how many victims exist in any one armed group or conflict, this is a type of trafficking victim that does not exist in peacetime.

In Colombia, the UN Special Rapporteur on Violence Against Women concluded that "Women are sometimes abducted by armed men and detained for a time in conditions of sexual slavery; they are raped and made to perform domestic chores.[20] Further, the report states, "Guerrilla groups are reported to have abducted young girls as companions for their leaders. Reports have also been received of girls being lured into the FARC and then abused . . . Self-defence groups/paramilitaries are also reported to have kidnapped girls and used them as sexual slaves"[21] A Human Rights Watch (HRW) report on child combatants suggests that the paramilitary group operating in the department of Casanare "has been alleged responsible for abducting young women for sexual purposes."[22] Amnesty International (AI) includes similar allegations:

> Women and girls have also been forced into prostitution. In 2002, in the city of Barrancabermeja, fifteen teenage girls who had been forced to become prostitutes for the paramilitaries reportedly had to leave the area for fear of further abuse. Sex workers also allege that they have been forced to provide sexual services to combatants. In 2002, in Medellín, ten sex workers were reportedly abducted by the FARC and forced to provide sexual services.[23]

The UN Special Rapporteur also "took testimonies from girls who had been recruited and used by the armed groups as sexual slaves, combatants, informers, guides and messengers," but there is no indication of how many of the girls she spoke with might be accurately identified as trafficking victims.[24]

There does not seem to be much evidence to justify claims that imply that abduction and sexual enslavement is common in Colombia, especially in comparison with other civil wars. Amnesty International (AI) offers a handful of testimonies that indicate individual combatants take advantage of their power over civilians to coerce sex or to rape.[25] However, this does not imply that the armed groups routinely abduct women and force them into sexual slavery. This is not meant to discount the occurrence of sexual violence, abuse, and enslavement by the armed groups; rather, the pattern may be one of opportunism more than systematic behavior. Nonetheless, no matter how many are victimized, these are victims unique to war conditions.

Finally, the context of international intervention or post-war reconstruction also creates entirely new situations of overlapping and competing authorities. The experience in the post-war reconstruction of the Baltic states and the related cases of trafficking in women for sex is an example of how these war-related environments create new possibilities for trafficking networks.[26]

Networks trafficking other illegal goods related to civil wars, such as drugs and arms, may enter the human trafficking market because the infrastructure is already in place. Some researchers suggest that the armed groups in Colombia might use the networks that exist to transport illegal arms and drugs to also traffic in women.[27]

The new conditions within which networks operate as a result of civil wars combine with new conditions that individuals face to create new patterns of trafficking. The atmosphere of violence generates people in flight, and research suggests that those victims of displacement by violence are more likely to suffer and less likely to find work than economic migrants.[28] In addition, the violence is gendered. By this I mean that patterns of types of violence are generally determined by the sex of the civilian. As with most civil wars, men are the primary targets of lethal violence in Colombia's war. Women and children, as a result, make up roughly 70 percent of the displaced populations, with women as heads-of-households in more than half of the displaced. In addition, women are the predominant targets of sexual violence. The type of violence used against different groups within a population during a civil war can have important implications for the effects of the war. In terms of trafficking, if trafficking networks were able to target and victimize members of the displaced population, we would expect more women than men to be trafficked. In addition, as with the gendered division of labor that exists in most of the world, we would expect women to be destined for the most lucrative trafficking industry: sex work.

Faced with the threat of an armed group taking over a town, or worse, a massacre, people flee their homes every day in Colombia. By the end of 2003, an estimated 2.73 million Colombians had become internally displaced, while another quarter of a million were seeking refuge abroad; for a country of 44 million, the displaced comprise a substantial proportion of its population.[29] From small towns and villages, the displaced arrive in Bogotá, Medellín, Cali, and Cartagena, as well as smaller regional cities. Without resources or social networks they are ill-equipped to find housing, health care, and employment or to face the continued threats from armed groups. Not wishing to leave any sort of "paper trail," many do not register with the government agencies that might help them. Unknown and unregistered, they pass up the opportunity to receive emergency funding, while unemployment can soar to 60 percent in receptor communities.[30] Compounding the situation, displacement is generally from rural to urban areas, and men and women who supported themselves in agriculture no longer have that option and in most cases must change occupations completely. In these circumstances, this group may be more willing to take risks to obtain an income or to secure themselves and their loved ones, and thus form a substantial pool of potential victims. Indeed, arrival sites in receptor cities might serve as the first possible contact with traffickers. In one neighborhood in Cali that receives up to four displaced families each day, the Hope Foundation found "cases of offers of work abroad in a direct and massive form."[31]

In addition, the ways in which women and men experience displacement differently might also shape the likelihood of both agreeing to migrate and being targeted by traffickers. In terms of occupational change, this shock is in some ways easier for women to confront, having been responsible for the domestic work on farms. Anthropologist Donny Meertens writes, "Finding employment as cooks, laundresses, or domestic servants after their displacement helped [women] insert themselves more easily, if uncertainly, into the urban market of paid (usually domestic) labor." The rate of employment in paid domestic work before and after displacement rose from 4.1 percent to 20 percent.[32] Nonetheless, domestic work is unstable and insecure, considering that job contracts are usually nonexistent in this sphere, and salaries are often below the $130/month minimum wage. One researcher with Colombia's anti-trafficking NGO, the Hope Foundation, observed, "Precisely because it is the women who most often look for [employment] options they can be more vulnerable to an offer [of work] in a different [city, region, or country], with ends of exploitation."[33] Indeed, circumstances of economic crisis combined with increasing numbers of single women newly responsible for the survival of families create a vulnerable and in some cases, desperate, population. For some, sex work could be a viable option for a much-needed income. Indeed, Meertens observes that "The necessity for immediate survival frequently leads to prostitution as the only available resourc."[34] The 1997 UN Committee on the Elimination of Discrimination against Women (CEDAW) report on Colombia claims, "Displaced women are more vulnerable to sexual attacks and may fall more easily into prostitution owing to their lack of social, psychological and economic protection." Interviews with social workers indicate that the number of displaced women working in the sex industry is growing, but no data is available because studies have not been designed, let alone implemented, to estimate the extent of this trend.

Although the empirics are rough, it is interesting to consider the suggested links between displacement, migration, and sex work. A study by the Human Rights Ombudsman's Office in Colombia interestingly found that "Most of the children and young people engage in prostitution in towns away from their homes, and the women traveled to these towns initially to work in domestic service."[35] This finding seems to indicate that entering the sex industry begins with migration, not uncommon in many countries. But given Colombia's massive scale of internal displacement, the migration might have initially been forced. More studies are needed to determine the initial impetus for migration among sex workers from rural areas of the country, where the impact of the conflict is more direct than in the large urban centers. Similar studies are necessary in relation to women who have been trafficked. A study by the Ministry of Justice on international trafficking in women found that 55 percent of the women come from villages, 35 percent from medium-sized towns, and 10 percent from urban centers.[36] This indicates that as many as 9 of every 10 women trafficked out of Colombia were originally from an area of conflict, since much of Colombia's rural areas are plagued by armed groups fighting. Yet, my informal interviews with several advocacy and social service agencies (both governmental and non-governmental) revealed that studies on the relationship between displacement, sex work, and trafficking have not been initiated. One researcher with a prominent organization that focuses on issues surrounding internal displacement stated, "We do not ask [if the displaced] enter prostitution [in their receptor communities] because we do not want to increase the stigmatization of displaced women."[37] The stigma associated with the displaced emerges from a placement of blame on the victim: e.g., they must have been a guerilla to be displaced; they only beg for money and flood the job market. The position of the organization relates to society's negative impressions of both the displaced and prostitutes. But I would argue that a critical role of non-profits, social service providers, and government agencies is to confront harmful stereotypes in order to reach a marginalized and vulnerable population.

Civil war as a source of new trafficking patterns might operate by altering individuals' cost-benefit calculations beyond changing the incentive structures, because of the generalized atmosphere of violence and the special effect it may have on "rational" calculations. Violence may reduce the cost of leaving the region or country, or fundamentally changes how people perceive risks and make decisions. This question is beyond the scope of this paper. Nevertheless, if fundamental decision-making processes change as a result of warfare and violence, then this might be a key explanation for the difference in trafficking rates during peacetime as opposed to wartime.

CONCLUSION

In this chapter, I considered two different ways in which civil wars may increase trafficking: by exacerbating conditions that give rise to human trafficking during peace and by creating entirely new opportunities for trafficking to flourish. In order to address these questions, I began by theorizing about the basic elements of trafficking: individuals and networks. I suggested that approaching these questions from both individual choices and favorable conditions for trafficking networks is an illuminating way to understand the links between trafficking and civil wars, as well as to begin identifying points of intervention and prevention.

The main condition of civil wars that I have highlighted in this paper is displacement. Displacement both increases opportunities for trafficking networks and changes the incentives and opportunities for individuals. The phenomenon during civil wars is also important because of the gendered dynamic of violence that characterizes most civil wars: lethal violence is more likely to be directed towards males, leaving a disproportionate amount of females as the heads of households in search of a means to support their families. The combination of economic need and poor economic conditions may lead to an increase in sex work in some areas. It remains an open question whether and to what extent this leads to trafficking for sex work abroad. In Colombia, a randomized survey of displaced households, as well as prostitutes, would help address these possible relationships. Depending on the outcome, policy implications might involve a range of interventions, from awareness raising among sex workers to alternative employment opportunities for both the displaced and sex workers (admittedly difficult in the context of civil war).

Yet many questions remain. What, for example, might explain variation between civil wars in the likelihood of trafficking? I implicitly suggested one dimension on which this likelihood might vary: network capacity, given the extent of violence in the war and the existence of transport infrastructure. In addition, it seems that armed group preferences and norms matter as well, in terms of explaining why some groups traffic women as "wives" or sex slaves, and children as combatants. Further theorizing about these differences would be useful in order to generate hypotheses about these relationships (whether or not they could be tested with reliable empirical data at this time). At the least a theory based on explicit assumptions of human behavior and criminal networks, as I have tried to outline here, would enable scholars and advocates to communicate effectively and to continue building on our collective insights about these processes. Such deliberations would ideally generate implications about where to direct resources for prevention and intervention.

NOTES

The author would like to thank Stephen M. Engel for helpful comments on this chapter, as well as Jessica Reitz, Jolene Smith, and Kevin Bales for valuable discussions on the topic.

1. Notes on definitions: First, I will refer in this chapter to human trafficking as defined by Annex II: Protocol to Prevent, Suppress and Punish Trafficking in Persons, Especially Women and Children, supplementing the United Nations Convention Against Transnational Organized Crime:

> For the Purposes of this Protocol: (a) "Trafficking in persons" shall mean the recruitment, transportation, transfer, harbouring or receipt of persons, by means of the threat or use of force or other forms of coercion, of abduction, of fraud, of deception, of the abuse of power or of a position of vulnerability or of the giving or receiving of payments or benefits to achieve the consent of a person having control over another person, for the purpose of exploitation. Exploitation shall include, at a minimum, the exploitation of the prostitution of others or other forms of sexual exploitation, forced labour or services, slavery or practices similar to slavery, servitude or the removal of organs; (b) The consent of a victim of trafficking in persons to the intended exploitation set forth in subparagraph (a) of this article shall be irrelevant where any of the means set forth in subparagraph (a) have been used; (c) The recruitment, transportation, transfer, harbouring or receipt of a child for the purpose of exploitation shall be considered "trafficking in persons" even if this does not involve any of the means set forth in subparagraph (a) of this article; (d) "Child" shall mean any person under eighteen years of age.

United Nations, *Convention Against Transnational Organized Crime. Protocol to Prevent, Suppress and Punish Trafficking in Persons, Especially Women and Children*, http://www.odccp.org/_palermo/convmain.html (12 January 2005).

Second, I will refer to and theorize about civil wars, as opposed to war in general, first because civil wars are more common than all other types of wars and, as a result, victimize more civilians. In addition, they feature distinct characteristics, such as the existence of armed groups that recruit (forcibly or otherwise) from the civilian population, which may affect the incidence of human trafficking differently than interstate wars. To be sure, all wars share some characteristics that may influence the incidence of human trafficking similarly, such as negative economic impacts and post-war reconstruction.

2. Human Rights Watch, "You'll Learn Not to Cry: Child Combatants in Colombia," 2003, http://www.hrw.org/reports/2003/colombia0903/colombia0903.pdf (12 February 2005), 13.

3. United Nations Regional Crime and Justice Research Institute, "Trafficking, Slavery, and Peacekeeping: The Need for a Comprehensive Training Program: A Conference Report," 2002.

4. Timothy Pratt, "Sex Slavery Racket a Growing Concern in Latin America," *Christian Science Monitor*, 11 January 2001.

5. The Trafficking Victims and Protection Act of 2001 (TVPA) passed in the United States is a good example of reconciling the legal code and, by extension, law enforcement, with the actual experience of trafficking victims. The law-generated changes in how police forces treat women found in conditions that are indicative of sex trafficking—such women are now entitled to protection under the law as victims, rather than criminals.

6. Examples of individual traffickers include men who marry women through agencies and then enslave them in the home as domestic and sexual slaves. The majority of instances of domestic slavery in the United States seem to have been the result of individuals working independently. In contrast, brothels are maintained not only by one criminal network, but often as a collaboration or division of labor between several, usually across borders.

7. Policy interventions may be more feasible in some industries than others. The most daunting challenge would seem to be curbing the demand for women trafficked into the sex industry. The debate over whether sex work in general should be regulated, prohibited, or criminalized is related to the demand question. At the same time, many proponents of one approach or another fail to coherently address how the legal status of sex work may or may not curb demand for trafficked sex workers. Rather, those opposed to legalization seem to work under the implicit assumption that the effect of either regulation or the lack of criminalization will be tantamount to the legitimization of sex work; such a legitimization will reduce social stigma and punishment and foster an increase in the demand for sex workers. By extension, the demand for trafficked (i.e., cheaper) sex workers will increase. Those opposed to prohibition, in contrast, argue that enabling sex workers to organize and demand rights as laborers will reduce the proportion of trafficked sex workers in any given country because it will be more difficult to restrict the rights of anyone working in the sex industry. Here, the implicit assumption about demand seems to be that it will not be curbed by the legal status of sex workers, and given that, societies should strengthen sex workers' rights to prevent abuse. The competing arguments and underlying assumptions cannot be resolved here. However, it is likely that demand for sex work is a combination of many different factors, not least of which are societal norms surrounding sex, gender, and power. It goes without saying that change in this area is glacial and probably too difficult (and unwise) to engineer by policy alone.

8. The distinction between choice and coercion is an important—if nuanced—one. While many victims of trafficking appear to have been abducted, it is impossible to speculate on the proportion. Based on the basic empirics we do have, it is seemingly

unrealistic to theorize that individuals have no choice at any point in the process. Rather, I think it makes more sense to consider an individual's choice as on a continuum between initial willingness to at least consider the terms of the trafficker, to enthusiasm about the trafficker's offer until the destination is reached and the offer is revealed to be fraudulent. All things equal, I think it is reasonable to assume that trafficking networks would prefer the latter type of victim than the former. Further, it would seemingly be much more costly to operate a network entirely based on abductions, both because the risks of detection by law enforcement would increase, and because the transportation costs involved would increase, assuming the need for constant coercion (such as drugging) of the victim.

9. Uppsala Conflict Data Program, University of Uppsala, 2003, http://www.pcr.uu.se/database/conflictSummary.php?bcID=148 (5 May 2005); *Programa de las Naciones Unidas para el Desarrollo (PNUD). El Conflicto: Callejón con Salida.* (Bogotá, Colombia: Naciones Unidas, 2003), 115.

10. *Consultoría para los Derechos Humanos y el Desplazamiento (CODHES), "Personas Desplazadas: Recepción por Departamento por Trimestre, 1999 a 2005,"* http://www.codhes.org.co/cifra/Dpto_Recp_Pers.pdf (5 May 2005).

11. Charles Berquist, Ricardo Penaranda, and Gonzalo Sánchez G., eds., *Violence in Colombia 1990–2000: Waging War and Negotiating Peace* (Wilmington, DE: Scholarly Resources Inc, 2001), xx.

12. United Nations, "Fourth Periodic Report of the States Parties: Colombia." Convention on the Elimination of All Forms of Discrimination Against Women, (New York: The United Nations, 1997), 57.

13. U.S. Department of State, "Victims of Trafficking and Violence Prevention Act of 2000: Trafficking in Persons Report 2004, Colombia," 2004, http://www.state.gov/g/tip/rls/tiprpt/2004/ (28 April 2005).

14. U.S. Department of State, "Consular Information Sheet, Colombia," 2005, http://travel.state.gov/travel/cis_pa_tw/cis/cis_1090.html, (28 April 2005).

15. Mary Roldán, "Citizenship in a Contested State," PBS *Wide Angle*, 16 September 2004, http://www.pbs.org/wnet/wideangle/shows/colombia/briefing.html (1 May 2005).

16. U.S. Department of State, 2004, "Trafficking in Persons Report: Colombia."

17. Pratt, "Sex Slavery Racket a Growing Concern in Latin America"; Fanny Polanía Molina, "Japan, the Mecca for Trafficking in Columbian Women," www.december18.net/paper30ColumbiaJapan (12 April 2005).

18. Again, implicit in this analysis is the assumption that the bulk of trafficking victims have *decided* to accept an offer of work or travel either abroad or within the country. This obviously does not apply to those victims of trafficking who have been abducted, but at the same time does not negate the possibility of overlapping circumstances of both choice and coercion. Many times, once an individual has decided to migrate she is not permitted to change her mind, and the relationship between the traffickers and targets changes from one of choice to one of force before the victim has arrived at her destination.

19. U.S. Department of State, 2004, "Trafficking in Persons Report: Colombia."

20. United Nations, "Report of the Special Rapporteur on Violence against Women, its Causes and Consequences," E/CN.4/2002/83/Add.3 (New York: The United Nations, 2002), paragraph 38.

21. United Nations, E/CN.4/2002/83/Add.3, 2002, paragraph 51.

22. Human Rights Watch, "You'll Learn Not to Cry," 27.

23. Amnesty International (AI), "Scarred Bodies, Hidden Crimes: Sexual Violence against Women in the Armed Conflict," 2004, http://web.amnesty.org/library/Index/ENGAMR230402004 (12 April 2005).

24. United Nations, E/CN.4/2002/83/Add.3, 2002, paragraph 50.

25. Amnesty International, "Scarred Bodies."

26. United Nations Regional Crime and Justice Research Institute, "Trafficking, Slavery, and Peacekeeping: The Need for a Comprehensive Training Program: A Conference Report," 2002.

27. Sandra Claassen and Fanny Polanía Molina, *Tráfico de Mujeres en Colombia: Diagnóstico, Análisis y Propuestas* (Bogotá, Colombia: *Fundación Esperanza*, 1998).

28. Patricia Neira Vélez, "Desplazamiento Forzoso en Soacha: Se Recuperan los Desplazados del Choque Inicial?" (Bogotá, Colombia: Universidad de los Andes, 2004).

29. U.S. Committee for Refugees and Immigrants (USCR), "World Refugee Survey 2004: Colombia Country Report," 2004, http://www.refugees.org/countryreports.aspx?id=83 (28 April 2005).

30. USCR, "World Refugee Survey."

31. Jaime Díaz Palacios, *"Una Mirada a la Prevención del Tráfico de Personas,"* in *Tráfico de Personas y Prostitución: Memorias* (Medellín, Colombia: Pastoral Social, 2001), 25.

32. Donny Meertens, "Victims and Survivors of War in Colombia: Three Views of Gender Relations," in *Violence in Colombia, 1990–2000: Waging War and Negotiating Peace*, ed. Charles Berquist, Ricardo Penaranda, and Gonzalez Sanchez G. (Wilmington, DE: Scholarly Resources Inc., 2001), 163.

33. Díaz Palacios, *"Una Mirada a la Prevención,"* 25.

34. Meertens, "Victims and Survivors," 163.

35. United Nations, "Fourth Periodic Report of the States Parties: Colombia," 58–59.

36. United Nations, "Fourth Periodic Report of the States Parties: Colombia," 60.

37. Statement made to author, July 2003.

BIBLIOGRAPHY

Amnesty International. "Scarred Bodies, Hidden Crimes: Sexual Violence against Women in the Armed Conflict." 2004. http://web.amnesty.org/library/Index/ENGAMR230402004. 12 April 2005.

Berquist, Charles, Ricardo Penaranda, and Gonzalo Sánchez G., eds. *Violence in Colombia 1990–2000: Waging War and Negotiating Peace.* Wilmington, DE: Scholarly Resources Inc., 2001.

Claassen, Sandra, and Fanny Polanía Molina. *Tráfico de Mujeres en Colombia: Diagnóstico, Análisis y Propuestas*. Bogotá, Colombia: *Fundación Esperanza*, 1998.

Consultoría para los Derechos Humanos y el Desplazamiento (CODHES). 2002. "*Boletín 40: Desplazados en la Encrucijada*." February 2002. http://www.codhes.org.co/boletin_public/boletin_ult.htm. 5 May 2005.

———. 2005. "*Personas Desplazadas: Recepción por Departamento por Trimestre*, 1999 a 2005." http://www.codhes.org.co/cifra/Dpto_Recp_Pers.pdf. 5 May 2005.

Díaz Palacios, Jaime. "*Una Mirada a la Prevención del Tráfico de Personas*." Pp. 23–27 in *Tráfico de Personas y Prostitución: Memorias*. Medellín, Colombia: Pastoral Social, 2001.

Human Rights Watch. "You'll Learn Not to Cry: Child Combatants in Colombia." 2003. http://www.hrw.org/reports/2003/colombia0903/colombia0903.pdf. 12 February 2005.

Meertens, Donny. "Victims and Survivors of War in Colombia: Three Views of Gender Relations." Pp. 151–67 in *Violence in Colombia, 1990–2000: Waging War and Negotiating Peace*, ed. Charles Berquist, Ricardo Penaranda, and Gonzalez Sanchez G. Wilmington, DE: Scholarly Resources Inc., 2001.

Neira Vélez, Patricia. "*Desplazamiento Forzoso en Soacha: Se Recuperan los Desplazados del Choque Inicial?*" Bogotá, Colombia: Universidad de los Andes, 2004.

Phinney, Alison. "Trafficking of Women and Children for Sexual Exploitation in the Americas: An Introduction to Trafficking in the Americas." Inter-American Commission of Women, Organization of American States, 2002.

Polanía Molina, Fanny. "Japan, the Mecca for Trafficking in Columbian Women." www.december18.net/paper30ColumbiaJapan. 12 April 2005.

Pratt, Timothy. "Sex Slavery Racket a Growing Concern in Latin America." *Christian Science Monitor*. 11 January 2001.

Programa de las Naciones Unidas para el Desarrollo (PNUD). El Conflicto: Callejón con Salida. Bogotá, Colombia: Naciones Unidas, 2003.

Richard, Amy O'Neill. "International Trafficking In Women to The United States: A Contemporary Manifestation of Slavery and Organized Crime." 1999. Washington, DC: Center for the Study of Intelligence. http://www.cia.gov/csi/monograph/women/trafficking.pdf. 30 April 2005.

Roldán, Mary. "Citizenship in a Contested State." PBS *Wide Angle*. 16 September 2004. http://www.pbs.org/wnet/wideangle/shows/colombia/briefing.html. 1 May 2005.

U.S. Committee for Refugees and Immigrants (USCR). "World Refugee Survey 2004: Colombia Country Report." 2004. http://www.refugees.org/countryreports.aspx?id=83. 28 April 2005.

U.S. Department of State. "Consular Information Sheet, Colombia." 2005. http://travel.state.gov/travel/cis_pa_tw/cis/cis_1090.html. 28 April 2005.

———. "Victims of Trafficking and Violence Prevention Act of 2000: Trafficking in Persons Report 2004." http://www.state.gov/g/tip/rls/tiprpt/2004/. 28 April 2005.

United Nations. "Fourth Periodic Report of the States Parties: Colombia." Convention on the Elimination of All Forms of Discrimination against Women. New York: United Nations, 1997.

———. "Report of the Special Rapporteur on Violence against Women, its Causes and Consequences," E/CN.4/2002/83/Add.3. New York: United Nations, 2002.

———. *Convention Against Transnational Organized Crime: Protocol to Prevent, Suppress and Punish Trafficking in Persons, Especially Women and Children.* http://www.odccp.org/_palermo/convmain.html.

United Nations Regional Crime and Justice Research Institute. "Trafficking, Slavery, and Peacekeeping: The Need for a Comprehensive Training Program: A Conference Report." May 2002.

Uppsala Conflict Data Program. University of Uppsala. 2003. http://www.pcr.uu.se/database/conflictSummary.php?bcID=148. 5 May 2005.

III

LAWS, LEGISLATION, AND INTERNATIONAL INVOLVEMENT

· 7 ·

Conflicts and Interests: Trafficking in Filipino Women and the Philippine Government Policies on Migration and Trafficking

Carolina S. Ruiz-Austria

Young barrio lass comes to the city to fulfill her dreams and winds up in Japan under an assumed name, with a fake passport, and gets sold off to a nightspot to "work off" her debt as a prostitute.

Public school teacher, wife, and mother to three children goes to Singapore, works as a domestic and is maltreated by her employers. She escapes and is accused of a crime she didn't commit.

Young Muslim woman, barely eighteen, wanting to support her family, leaves for the Middle East as a domestic. She gets raped and beaten. She serves sentence in jail for defending herself and is lashed in public.

Passing herself off as eighteen, a young girl meets her Australian beau through the Internet. She exchanges letters with him and sends photographs. They agree to marry. She is surprised that he doesn't look like his picture but decides she fell in love with the man who wrote the letters. They get married and leave for Australia where she discovers he is already married. She gets sent to work in a brothel along with other Filipino and Thai women.

These stories and many more seem to be stuff of *telenovellas*, life stories on cinema, and hackneyed dime novels, and yet many of them actually still do happen to many Filipino women. At the rate of more than 2,300 Filipino women leaving every day to work abroad as entertainers, domestics, and nurses, these stories or even the recent threat of the SARS epidemic didn't seem to discourage Filipino women from seeking employment or going abroad.[1]

For Filipino women, going abroad spells the difference between getting more or less decent pay for jobs (which don't get paid much in the first place) or starving while doing the same work (care giving, nursing, domestic work) at home. The prospect of getting even double and more than nurses or domestics by becoming "entertainers" (usually in Japan) makes the offer even more irresistible.

Filipino women go abroad in droves precisely because economic opportunities at home are scarce. In a 2003 study on the Economic Mobility of Overseas Filipino workers, research found that "Twenty-seven percent of all men and 68 percent of all women currently employed overseas were unemployed prior to migration."[2]

Meanwhile, a study on the income disparity between male and female migrant Filipino workers reveals that overseas employment is not working out as the great "equalizer" among the genders: "The analysis also reveals that many more women were unemployed prior to migration and that the earnings of women are, on average, lower than those of men, even after controlling for variations in occupational distributions, country of destination, and socio-demographic attributes."[3]

While the export of labor was once viewed as a quick fix and temporary strategy for an ailing economy, now it is clearly the main economic strategy of the Philippine government. [4]

In 1975, Filipino women only constituted around 10 percent of overseas contract workers. By 1987, they made up more than 47 percent of all overseas contract workers. And, by 1995, they made up more than half of the overseas contract worker population.[5]

Riding on the dollar remittances of overseas Filipino workers (OFWs), the Philippine government constantly boasted about staying afloat amid the Asian market crash of 1997. Many economists pointed out this was not the least bit surprising since the Philippine economy never really took off and had nowhere worse to go.

According to *Newsweek* in 2004, government pegs the total annual remittances at $7 billion annually, but that's only official transfers. "A recent Asian Development Bank report put the real figure in the $14 billion to $21 billion range, a sum that dwarfs both foreign direct investment and aid flowing into the country, and amounts to 32 percent of GNP."[6]

While trafficking and migration are different issues, there is a need to look into the close relationship between the two issues. Anti-Slavery International[7] offers the following framework:

> Trafficking, smuggling and migration are separate, but inter-related issues. Migration may take place through regular or irregular channels and may be freely chosen or forced upon the migrant as a means of survival (e.g., dur-

ing a conflict, an economic crisis or an environmental disaster). If the method of migration is irregular, a smuggler who will facilitate illegal entry into a country for a fee may assist the migrant. The smuggler may demand an exorbitant fee and may expose the migrant to serious dangers in the course of their journey, but on arrival at their destination, the migrant is free to make their own way and normally does not see the smuggler again.

Trafficking is fundamentally different as it involves the movement of people for the purposes of exploiting their labor or services. The vast majority of people who are trafficked are migrant workers. They are seeking to escape poverty and discrimination, improve their lives and send money back to their families. They hear about well-paying jobs abroad through family, friends or through "recruitment agencies" and other individuals who offer to find them employment and make the travel arrangements. For most trafficked people, it is only once they arrive in the country of destination that their real problems begin as the work they were promised does not exist and they are forced instead to work in jobs or conditions . . . which they did not agree to.

DEFINING THE POLICY ISSUE

A discussion of the policy and legal environment which impacts on the phenomenon of human trafficking, specifically the trafficking of Filipino women, necessitates a framework for looking at the effects of the globalized economy on women as a whole.

When we discuss the trafficking of Filipino women as an issue, it tends to presuppose that the Philippine Government was always aware of it and considered the problem as one of "trafficking," which is really the sale and profit from human slavery, in this case, the slavery of Filipino women. Yet, this is not wholly accurate. Until the establishment of the Philippine Center on Transnational Crimes (PCTC) in 1999, whose members were some of the delegates to the International Convention on Transnational Crimes, not a single law enforcement agency categorized the problem as such.

The earliest use of the term "trafficking" in written government policy was in fact in 1994 in the Implementing Rules and Regulations of the Anti-Child Abuse Law (RA 7610) and in 1997 when President Ramos issued Executive Order 976 declaring the period January to December 1997 as the "Anti Trafficking of Migrants Year." The Executive Order even uses the term "illegal trafficking," as if there were such a thing as the legally sanctioned "trafficking" of persons:

> Therefore, I, Fidel V. Ramos, President of the Philippines, by virtue of the powers vested in me by law, do hereby declare the period January 1 to December 30, 1997 as the Anti Trafficking of Migrants Year.

> During this period, the Departments of Labor and Employment, Foreign Affairs, Justice, Interior and Local Government, Transportation and Communications and National Defense, are hereby tasked to adopt measures, including allocation of its resources, to the drive against *illegal trafficking*. (Emphasis added)

To date, many in the government bureaucracy still adhere to the view that the problem is simply one of "illegal recruitment."[8] Categorizing "illegal recruitment" presumes that massive labor export as a primary economic strategy is not an issue, but rather that the *illegal nature* of deployment (undocumented and ergo outside the realm of taxation) is the sole and serious concern.[9]

Indeed, that Filipino women lack enough economic opportunities in the local economy is not or has rarely been identified as a major problem by the Philippine government. The gendered (stereotyped) categories of jobs available for Filipino women are well established and documented. In fact, when it comes to overseas work, women who previously held clerical and sales occupations prior to seeking overseas work face a 62.9 percent chance of ending up in low-status occupations or manual and domestic-type jobs.[10] The types of work Filipino women are expected to do are also the types of work for which there is very little or no payment at all if they were to perform it in the context of the local economy. In the same way, these types of jobs (classified as women's work) also offer *cheaper* pay in the context of the host or destination country's economy so that migrant women workers are often in demand.[11]

Yet, the context of this burgeoning demand in host countries (for cheap labor) and employment (livelihood) in the Philippines has been the increasingly restrictive immigration policies of many destination countries. All in all, it is said this contributes to a growing market for irregular migration.[12] This is the context where the trafficking of Filipino women is taking place. Thus, when it comes to overseas work, in many ways, the peril that is trafficking has always been literally considered and somehow *accepted* as a "built-in" risk for Filipino women seeking overseas employment.

PHILIPPINE LAWS AND POLICIES BEFORE THE ANTI-TRAFFICKING ACT

By looking at the laws in place prior to the Anti-Trafficking Law, one can get a holistic view of the directions the "migration" and "trafficking" discourse has taken in Philippine policies.

First and foremost, there was migration for labor. Prior to the passage of Republic Act 9208, there were only three types of laws that bore some relation to the issue of trafficking in the Philippines. A handful of them are penal in nature, imposing fines and imprisonment *after* the fact of trafficking, assuming a victim survives the experience and is in any condition to file or initiate a complaint.

The second type of laws are those administrative in nature, focusing on the regulation and licensing of the labor export industry, as well as coverage of administrative liabilities in "illegal recruitment."

A third set of laws and policies consists of government incentives and schemes of promoting the overseas labor export, which range from medical benefits as well as tax exemptions to OFWs.

Criminal Laws/Provisions

Originally, there were four sets of laws that contained penal provisions in relation to some trafficking activities. These were the Migrant Workers and Overseas Filipinos Act of 1995 or Republic Act 8042, the Labor Code (Presidential Decree 442 as amended), the Anti-Mail Order Bride Law or Republic Act 6955, and the White Slave Trade provision in the Revised Penal Code.

Republic Act 8042 basically takes off from the same premises as those of the Labor Code (it refers to the Labor Code definition and adopts the same) and in fact punishes the same types of *acts* which are, essentially, *illegal recruitment* and a set of *prohibited acts* committed by recruiters (i.e., contract substitution, collection of usurious fees and rates, etc.) Both laws defined illegal recruitment essentially as deployment activities[13] undertaken by non-holders of license or authority.

The crime is essentially the act of deployment *without authority*, the main damage of which is tax evasion. In effect, existing penal laws focused on "illegal recruitment" hardly focus on the problem as it is actually experienced by the survivor/victim of trafficking. The essence of the "harm" or "loss" defined is the State's loss of income: that is, legal taxes due.

The narrow definition often interpreted by investigating prosecutors actually posed a problem when it came to prosecuting acts of illegal recruitment perpetrated by officially licensed agencies and individuals connected with such agencies. This type of illegal recruitment in fact is so commonplace that OFWs with long-standing records of overseas work and experience are very familiar and on guard about the practice of licensed agencies which change their business names and offices quite often to evade liability.[14]

Because the provision is penal in nature, courts are wont to strictly construe provisions in the interpretation of the law. And unless the licensed recruiter is also proven guilty of the other prohibited acts, it is not likely to be convicted of "illegal recruitment" even if the act was essentially illegal recruitment, that is, deploying the worker through the back-door channels or under assumed and fake names and documents.

In one section, the law purports that the country will only deploy workers to countries that have signed bilateral agreements as well as ratified international conventions for the protection of migrant workers.[15] At the rate of more than 7 million Filipinos (documented) working abroad,[16] it is not surprising that the provisions of this law are scarcely being observed at all.

By the Secretary of Labor's own admission, there are hardly any bilateral agreements for the protection of OFWs in many of the countries where the Philippines deploys workers.[17] Likewise, many of these states have yet to ratify existing international agreements on the protection of migrant workers.[18]

The maximum penalty is life imprisonment under RA 8042 and a fine of not less than 500,00 pesos (but not more than 1,000,000.00 Php[19]) under two circumstances: if the act constitutes *economic sabotage*, and if the victim of illegal recruitment by the non-licensee is less than 18 years old.[20] The same law defines economic sabotage as follows:

> Section 10. Crime Involving Economic Sabotage.—Illegal recruitment when committed by a syndicate or in large scale shall be considered an offense involving economic sabotage. Illegal recruitment is deemed committed by a syndicate if carried out by a group of three (3) or more persons conspiring or confederating with one another. It is deemed committed in large scale if committed against three (3) or more persons individually or as a group. (RA 8042)

The other law that penalizes some acts of trafficking is the Anti-Mail Order Bride Law or Republic Act 6955. The following acts are prohibited under the law:

> Section 2. Pursuant thereto, it is hereby declared unlawful:
> (a) For a person, natural or juridical, association, club or any other entity to commit, directly or indirectly, any of the following acts:
> (1) To establish or carry on a business which has for its purpose the matching of Filipino women for marriage to foreign nationals either on a mail-order basis or through personal introduction;
> (2) To advertise, publish, print or distribute or cause the advertisement, publication, printing or distribution of any brochure, flyer, or any propaganda material calculated to promote the prohibited acts in the preceding subparagraph;
> (3) To solicit, enlist or in any manner attract or induce any Filipino woman to become a member in any club or association whose objective is

to match women for marriage to foreign nationals either on a mail-order basis or through personal introduction for a fee;

(4) To use the postal service to promote the prohibited acts in subparagraph 1 hereof;

(5) For the manager or officer-in-charge or advertising manager of any newspaper, magazine, television or radio station, or other media, or of an advertising agency, printing company or other similar entities, to knowingly allow, or consent to, the acts prohibited in the preceding paragraph.

Apart from the fact that this law does not have a set of implementing rules and regulations, there has never been a single case successfully prosecuted using this law.

One high-profile case initiated by the Department of Justice involved the trafficking of Filipino women who were "married" to Korean nationals (many of them in absentia—*a prohibited practice in Philippine laws on marriage*) at a mass wedding conducted by the Moonies (United Church of Rev. Sun Myung Sam) here in Metro Manila in 1997. The Department of Justice (DOJ) conducted an on-site investigation in Seoul, Korea, that even included a highly publicized rescue of one of the Filipino brides. A year later, the DOJ Secretary reversed his own findings when the Moonies, represented by Attorney Rene Saguisag,[21] used the defense of "free expression" and "religious freedom" for conducting the so-called inter-cultural marriages. The woman, who was promptly dropped from the DOJ's witness protection program, was later taken in by women's NGOs since she was not even told about the reason for her discharge, let alone the news about the case's dismissal.

While the same law mentions "other media," the law has yet to be amended to likewise specifically cover trafficking activities perpetrated through the Internet. The E-commerce Law of 2000 does not have a provision regarding sex trafficking even though the Internet is actually the leading means of facilitating sex trafficking activities today.

Another law that penalizes some acts of trafficking is the White Slave Trade provision in the Revised Penal Code:

Article 341. White slave trade.—The penalty of prison mayor in its medium and maximum periods shall be imposed upon any person who, in any manner, or under any pretext, shall engage in the business or shall profit by prostitution or shall enlist the services of any other person for the purpose of prostitution. (As amended by Batas Pambansa Blg. 186, March 16, 1982.)

Notably, this is the only law that focuses on the act of profiting and enlisting the services of any person for prostitution. However, there has never been any recorded case filed using this law against pimps or procurers in prostitution. Between 1901 and 2002, only three cases involving white slavery reached the Supreme Court. The most recent was not even a prosecution for white slavery but an administrative case brought against a judge accused of facilitating the same acts.

Administrative Laws Regulating the Industry of Recruitment/Placement

The Labor Code as well as the revised implementing rules of the Labor Code regarding the POEA is still the controlling law on overseas placement, licensing, and regulation. However, Republic Act 8042 (The Migrant Workers and Overseas Filipinos Act of 1995) officially ushered in the demands of globalization to eventually "de-regulate" the export of labor. RA 8042 conspicuously provides for the phase-out of regulation now being done by the POEA.[22] The law actually provides that deregulation should have begun in 2001.

On March 20, 2002, Regional Trial Court Judge Lucas Bersamin of Quezon City handed down a decision ordering the POEA and the DOLE to desist from continuing its activities regulating overseas placement and recruitment.[23] Earlier, Judge Jose G. Paneda of the QC RTC Branch 220 issued a similar order on March 12, 2002, in response to a civil case filed by the Asian Recruitment Council Philippine Chapter, Inc. (ARCOPHIL). The same rulings came in the wake of a case filed by talent managers, their associations and trainers in the recruitment and placement industry questioning the DOLE Secretary's orders, as well as demanding the courts to compel the DOLE and POEA to adopt a deregulation plan. These cases are still pending in the Supreme Court.

Meanwhile, on May 23 of the same year, the Supreme Court issued a temporary restraining order (TRO) against the injunctions issued by Branch 96 and 220 of the Quezon City Regional Trial Courts against the DOLE and POEA orders. Once this happened, the DOLE and the POEA resumed the implementation of its revised regulations.

To date, it is unclear to what degree the phase-out of POEA's functions has been accomplished or whether the deregulation and phase-out provided for in the law has begun. In fact, in the context of RA 8042's provisions on workers' welfare, gender sensitivity, references to international conventions and the establishment of a fund for repatriation, the "phase-out" and "deregulation" policies stand apart from the rest of the "welfare" provisions.

Yet, the agenda is clear. The push toward deregulation can be understood in the context of the demands of the globalized economy wherein capital economies will profit from the inevitable crash of labor costs in a deregulated labor market.

In fact, very early into her term, President Gloria Macapagal Arroyo had already agreed to cuts in wages for Filipinos in Hong Kong and Taiwan just as the government also sanctioned the "trainee" scheme for OFWs in Taiwan where by they are not entitled to minimum wages as "trainees."[24] In midst of growing protests, Hong Kong officials backtracked and announced that the cuts would not take effect until March of 2003.

With the prospect of a fully deregulated labor export industry, labor standards (minimum wage requirements, employment conditions) can be expected to worsen. In such a context, Filipino women already in vulnerable occupations will become even more prone to being trafficked. Ironically, even the Department of Labor and Employment itself recognized this danger in its own petition to the Supreme Court.[25]

Workers' Benefits and Welfare

The third body of laws is the policies that extend benefits to Overseas Filipino Workers. These consist of the tax exemption,[26] the overseas workers investment fund,[27] a Medicaid program for OFWs and their dependents,[28] and loan amnesty,[29] as well as key provisions of RA 8042 regarding free legal assistance and the emergency repatriation fund. Many of these policies do not cover undocumented migrants or workers although, again, RA 8042 does not make the distinction between documented and undocumented workers in the provisions on repatriation. Yet, it is not uncommon to hear about deported trafficking survivors who have had to raise their own funds to come back because the Philippine embassy in the host country cited the lack of funds for their travel.

In September 2003, the Philippine Overseas Workers' Welfare Administration (OWWA), the lead agency that implements welfare and benefit programs for Filipino overseas workers, issued Omnibus Policies on welfare assistance premised on a narrow definition of membership. This prompted a coalition of NGOs to take the secretary of the DOLE (which administers the OWWA as its attached agency) to court on charges of grave abuse of discretion.

The civil case is premised on illegality of the DOLE and OWWA's action in issuing the Omnibus Policies, which limit the coverage for overseas workers assistance, a limitation not reflected in the laws from which OWWA derives its mandate.

Citing cases of overseas workers who contributed to the fund while they were abroad but since were disqualified under the new Omnibus Rules after their return, as well as undocumented migrant workers in need who approach the OWWA in the host country, the petitioners also called for transparency in the management of the burgeoning workers' fund, which was already estimated at 8 billion as of June 2004.[30] Early in 2004, the election spending controversy surrounding the policy changes in management of the OWWA fund also figured in the local media.[31]

THE ANTI-TRAFFICKING LAW
OF 2003: PROSPECTS AND CHALLENGES

On May 6, 2003, the Anti-Trafficking Bill, Republic Act 9208, was finally passed by the joint houses of the Philippine Congress and Senate in a bicameral conference. It took effect on May 17, 2003, following its publication. The passage of the bill took a total of nine years. Initially filed by *Abanse Pinay*[32] Partylist Representative Patricia Sarenas before the 10th Congress (1997), the bill was not really an unpopular measure per se nor did the usual forces of the conservative church, which usually oppose women's rights legislation, controversially oppose it. Lawmakers within the Philippine Congress did not oppose it the way the amendments to the rape law were opposed from 1991 to 1997. Lacking in priority and unable to muster political will, the trafficking bill was stalled in both the 10th and 11th Congress due to government inaction.

Meanwhile, issues were also arising among advocates regarding the bill's focus on women and children. At various points in time, until the final draft bill reached the Senate for final deliberations, child rights advocates raised the possibility of filing a separate measure for the trafficking of children.[33] These issues plus other provisions which were constantly questioned by lawmakers (particularly in the Senate) bring to the fore the position of the same law on yet another controversial issue related to trafficking, which is prostitution.

Salient Features of the Anti-Trafficking in Persons Act of 2003

Republic Act 9208, the Anti-Trafficking in Persons Act, embodies a human rights framework. It treats the phenomenon of trafficking as a human rights violation. It also takes off from the Protocol to the UN Convention against Transnational Organized Crime's definition of *trafficking*, which does not distinguish between situations where there is consent or none. This same feature was one of the more hotly debated provisions of the bill when it was in the Senate.

Consent to "trafficking" has often been used, and in fact is constantly raised even during illegal recruitment cases, as a defense by traffickers. When this bill was being debated, one of the major messages the advocates sought to drive home was the fact that the issue of "consent" hardly alters the character of the act of trafficking (i.e., exploitation for forced labor, slavery, servitude, sexual exploitation, the exploitation or prostitution of others, or the removal or sale of organs) as a human rights violation. For this reason alone, trafficking is penalized because its purpose is to profit from human slavery.

Yet, admittedly, the ticklish issue in the definition even within the global women's rights movement is the issue of prostitution. For those who support the active lobby to legalize prostitution, whether or not all forms of prostitution are equivalent to exploitation and in effect human rights violations, is at the core of the debate. Indeed, the long-standing critique from many Western feminists against conservative and even fundamentalist cultures, which suppress (and denigrate) women's sexuality, challenges the prohibition of prostitution.

On the other hand, local feminists who advocated for the new law were also responsible for the introduction of legislation *decriminalizing* prostitution.[34] Insisting on and claiming a position rooted in the context of Filipino women's realities, that is, as third world women, these advocates maintain that *prostitution is still in many ways commonly experienced as exploitation by Filipino women, locally and abroad*. In turn, this difference in socioeconomic and cultural contexts makes up for many obvious differences in defining concepts such as "choice," "consent," and "prostitution."

The new law on trafficking changes Philippine law on prostitution in part by defining what prostitution is under the law. The penal code only defines who prostitutes are.[35] By placing prostitution as one of the ends or purposes of trafficking, it introduces two new concepts: (a) A definition of prostitution which treats the prostituted as a "victim" (the Revised Penal Code only defines prostitutes as women as criminals); and, (b) The punishable act of trafficking for the purpose of prostitution (to supplement the Penal Code provision on white slavery in establishing the criminal liability of pimps and procurers).

While the law does not directly amend the Revised Penal Code's provisions, it introduces new concepts. The old law was, after all, based on the original Spanish provision lifted from the Kodigo Penal (1897) and traces its roots to the *Siete Partidas* of King Alfonso. In this context of religious morality, women who fell outside the category of chaste women were prostitutes and thus *criminals*. In the new law, the category has literally been changed from "criminal" to "victim." And yet, echoing feminist critiques against "victimization": Are women really any better off as *victims* (?), that is, under the law?[36]

The law also introduces standards for the protection of trafficking survivors such as confidentiality and closed-door trial, witness protection, exemption for filing fees (in civil cases for damages) for victims, the confiscation of the proceeds of trafficking, and the creation of a trust fund for reintegration and rehabilitation, and creates the interagency council against trafficking and overall raises the penalties and fines.

Other features of the law that introduce changes to existing laws on trafficking include the specification of the Internet as one of the means to promote trafficking in persons (amending the mail-order bride law) and categorizing certain acts as "qualified" acts of trafficking, to include the use of the Adoption Act as the means for trafficking, as well as the involvement of military or law enforcement in trafficking, among other things.

Since its enactment, a host of issues have emerged around the effective implementation of the law. Upon its enactment into law, the new programs and services provided for in law remained unfunded because the 2004 Philippine Budget was a reenacted budget. By accessing grants, some agencies, including the Department of Justice (DOJ), which leads the Inter-Agency Task Force, began some projects focusing on capability building (training) activities, law enforcement, and the prosecution of cases.

For the most, the continuing challenge remains in making use of the new law to advocate for change in how trafficking is viewed and in turn approached by government-run programs.

Emerging Issues: Conflicts and Interests

On the surface, the enactment of a Philippine anti-trafficking law demonstrates a somewhat shifting policy framework in addressing the issue. No longer is trafficking merely a "built-in" risk in labor migration. As defined in the law and in accordance with the language of the UN Protocol, it is a human rights issue precisely because exploitation and slavery and slave-like conditions are human rights issues. Yet, it is hardly this simple.

Migration policies prior to (as well as after) the Anti-Trafficking Law demonstrate the barely shifting stance of the government on overseas deployment. If anything at all, the entire gamut of incentives and benefits beginning in the mid-1980s up to the mandate of "deregulation" in the 1995 Overseas Workers' law, highlights the government's role in pushing the labor migration trend. Coupled with the recent enactment of a dual-citizenship law[37] and the Overseas Absentee Voting Act, which goes as far as granting overseas workers the right to vote in local elections, the government's unrelenting push for encouraging this trend has reached full circle.

In 2004, *Newsweek* noted:

> In the past, the Philippines was shamed by its inability to create enough good jobs to keep its people at home. But hard economic reality, a 14 percent unemployment rate and one of the highest poverty indexes in the world (nearly half the population subsists on less than $2 a day) has shifted the sentiment. Today, in a move that countries like Indonesia and Bangladesh are likely to emulate, the government takes the position that, like it or not, overseas workers constitute the nation's biggest comparative advantage in an increasingly borderless world.

Not All Trafficking in Women is Sex Trafficking

With its unequivocal interest in deploying as many Filipino workers, specifically Filipino women (with the global demand for women workers in the service and health industries), how likely is it that trafficking is no longer considered a mere built-in risk for women seeking overseas employment? How likely is it that it isn't considered an *acceptable* risk for a government hell-bent on propping up an ailing economy with foreign exchange remittances?

Indeed, the vulnerability of women to trafficking as a result of low-status, low-income positions has long been the subject of research but there seems to have been very little impact on the policy directions in addressing trafficking for exploitative labor.[38] For instance, a Canadian study[39]—focusing on the phenomenon of mail-order brides and the Canadian Local Caregivers Program (LCP)—highlighted the precarious status of women entering Canada under the two situations. At present, 76.92 percent of immigrant live-in caregivers arriving in Canada under the LCP come from the Philippines. And while "legal" entry into the LCP program will not necessarily fall under "trafficking" under Philippine law, the study categorizes the highly exploitative situation of migrant workers as falling within the ambit of exploitative labor:

> By "trafficking in women," we mean a situation of exploitation relating, in particular, to a woman's paid or unpaid labor or services. Exploitation is engendered by the imbalance between the benefits to each of the parties occasioned by a relationship of inequality, which takes a variety of forms: gender inequality, ethnic inequality, economic inequality, age inequality, and so on. Because there is a fundamental inequality between the parties, one of them is enriched at the expense of the other. Exploitation is manifested by threats, violence, the abuse of vulnerability and dependence, and other violations of the victim's fundamental rights. Exploitation can arise in the case of mail-order brides and immigrant live-in caregivers.[40]

State Regulation of Sex: Programmed Responses

On the other hand, trafficking for the purpose of sexual exploitation, while by no means less serious, has often been approached with less ambiguity (though not surprisingly) on the part of Philippine government. Given the current context of sexual puritanism (as reflected on government policies on sexual rights),[41] various forms of newly defined acts of "sex trafficking" have led to the usual programmed responses of heightened state scrutiny and surveillance, leading to a host of violations against women's autonomy.

Recently, the Anti-Trafficking Law's provisions that put forth a definition of pornography came into focus. While there are always several pending bills in Congress on pornography (at present there are four drafts in Congress), the new law incorporates a definition which is a departure from the "context"-specific "test" adopted by the Philippine Supreme Court in the past.[42] Instead, the new law includes an all-inclusive definition of pornography, which states:

> *Pornography*—refers to any representation, through publication, exhibition, cinematography, indecent shows, information technology, or by whatever

means, of a person engaged in real or simulated explicit sexual activities or any representation of the sexual parts of a person for primarily sexual purposes.

This general categorization of all representations of sex and sexual acts as pornography has been the basis for ongoing raids on so-called cybersex dens. And while the link between the pornography industry and sex trafficking is relatively well established, the all-inclusive definition of pornography, coupled with the irrelevance of "consent" in trafficking, has given rise to a host of issues in relation to women's sexual rights.

In one recent state-sponsored raid,[43] owners of a local cybersex shop were arrested for violation of the Anti-Trafficking Law for their act of operating an Internet café where women were allegedly employed to perform sexual acts in front of a web cam, to paying clients who accessed their websites. According to new reports, the women were earning as high as a thousand dollars in less than a month's time. While the anti-trafficking law clearly did not categorize the women as "criminals," they were nonetheless promptly "rescued" and held at the Department of Social Welfare and Development (DSWD), according to the women, against their will. And while none of the women were reportedly minors, the women had to have legal counsel file a habeas corpus case against the DSWD to gain their release from custody.

The irony of this situation is that the new definition of prostitution (as exploitation) in the law came from women's human rights advocates who wanted to introduce the concept of "decriminalization" of women in prostitution, precisely to promote the rights of women in prostitution. However, to feminists who have engaged state policy and the state itself to promote women's rights, this should not come as a surprise.

In the context of a conservative state, it is not surprising at all that a puritan administration will end up violating the rights of the marginalized. This is after all the same context where curfews (for women and minors) imposed through local ordinances are the staple and "programmed" responses to incidences of violence against women, or even reports of prostitution.

In the end, even as the policy discourse on trafficking in women has managed to reflect a shift from being treated as "built-in risk" in what is considered "necessary" labor out-migration, to arguably what is now viewed as an issue of women's human rights (as far as written law is concerned), it still does not follow that the government (or any state for that matter) is automatically committed to the policy. Neither does it mean that the state will abandon its former strategies.

This is where initiatives and strategies that tend to highlight unchecked state authority will lead us right back where we started: more violations of women's rights and an all too powerful state. Neglecting to scrutinize and counter the "programmed" reactions and responses of the state (that is, overzealous protective and police-led measures coupled with restraints on civil liberties—especially of the marginalized) will lead us nowhere near empowering women in the exercise of their rights.

In coming to terms with policies and strategies against trafficking in women, feminist advocates also come to terms with the fact that the creation of enabling conditions for the exercise of rights is not (and apparently never has been) the Philippine state's strong card (not in a long while at least). Check again. A welfare state is something the Philippine state (as a lot of others like it worldwide) has not even been aspiring to become in the last few decades.

NOTES

1. Patricia Sto. Tomas, Secretary of Labor, Statement at Lyceum University, March 2002.

2. Moshe Semyonov and Anastasia Gorodzeisky, "Occupational Destinations and Economic Mobility of Filipino Overseas Workers," *International Migration Review,* Spring 2004.

3. Moshe Semyonov and Anastasia Gorodzeisky, "Labor Migration, Remittances and Household Income: A Comparison Between Filipinos and Filipina Overseas Workers," *International Migration Review,* Spring 2005.

4.

The case of the Philippines illustrates the way this has occurred. The Philippines once had the second highest standard of living in Asia, behind Japan. It is now one of Asia's poorest nations. The country became impoverished after then-President Ferdinand Marcos bankrupted the country in the late 1960s and early 1970s. The solutions the government adopted then to address the country's problems included: (1) establishing export production zones, (2) developing the tourism industry, and (3) contracting out surplus labor. They received loans from the IMF and WB to develop tourism and export production zones. The external debt ballooned from $.5B to $26 billion in two decades.

Jean L. Pyle, Ph.D., Keynote Address at the Third International Congress on Women, Work & Health, Stockholm, Sweden, June 2, 2002.

5. "Occupational Destinations and Economic Mobility of Filipino Overseas Workers," *International Migration Review,* Spring 2004, quoting S. P. Go, 1998; "Toward the 21st Century: Whither Philippine Labor Migration," pp. 9–44 in *Filipino Workers on the Move: Trends, Dilemmas, and Policy Options,* edited by B. V. Carino; and J. A. Tyner, "The Social Construction of Gendered Migration from the Philippines" *Asian and Pacific Migration Journal* 3, no. 4: 589–617.

6. George Wehrfritz and Marites Vitug, "Workers for the World," *Newsweek International,* 4 October 2004.

7. Mike Kaye, "The Migration-Trafficking Nexus: Combating Trafficking Through the Protection of Migrants' Human Rights," United Kingdom, *Anti-Slavery International*, 2003, 3.

8. The Philippine National Police, The National Bureau of Investigation (Law Enforcement Agencies) as well as the Philippine Overseas Employment Administration (POEA) used to only have "Illegal Recruitment" Divisions, which focused on the illegal nature of "deployment," more than anything else.

9. Statement of Labor Secretary Patricia Sto. Tomas at Lyceum University, March 2002:

> We are not oblivious, of course, to the attendant costs of overseas employment. Family displacement and its consequences is the price paid by Filipino workers who get separated from their families for a substantial length of time. We also need to strengthen efforts to curb illegal recruitment and at the same time address the plight of unrecorded or undocumented workers. Id. at 1.

10. Moshe Semyonov and Anastasia Gorodzeisky, "Occupational Destinations and Economic Mobility of Filipino Overseas Workers," *International Migration Review*, Spring 2004.

11. The data reveal that the vast majority of Filipino contract workers are recruited to fill low-status—manual and service—occupations in the host society. Most of those who were unemployed in the Philippines (64.4 percent among men and 85.7 percent among women) ended up in the low-status unskilled and domestic help category. Among the professional and semi-professional (high status), 35 percent of the men and 41 percent of the women experienced downward occupational mobility. Similarly, 45 percent of the men and over 60 percent of the women who held jobs in the intermediate occupational status categoiy had been recruited to the low-status job category. Almost all those who had low-status occupations in the country of origin (88 percent) retain their low-status occupations in the host society. Apparently, labor migration from the Philippines, while providing opportunities for employment, is strongly associated with employment in the low-status—manual and service—occupations. "Occupational Destinations and Economic Mobility."

12. Annette Lansink, "Trafficking: Law, The Female Body and Commodification" (paper presented at the Workshop: Law and Society, University of the Witwatersrand, September 25–26, 2003), wwwserver.law.wits.ac.za/workshop/workshop03/WWL-SLansinka.doc (19 April 2005).

13. Republic Act 8042 "Sec 6. Definition.—For purposes of this Act, illegal recruitment shall mean any act of canvassing, enlisting, contracting, transporting, utilizing, hiring, or procuring workers and includes referring, contract services, promising or advertising for employment abroad, whether for profit or not, when undertaken by a non-licensee or non-holder of authority contemplated under Article 13(f) of Presidential Decree No. 442, as amended, otherwise known as the Labor Code of the Philippines: Provided, That any such non-licensee or non-holder who, in any manner, offers or promises for a fee employment abroad to two or more persons shall be deemed so engaged. It shall likewise include the following acts, whether committed by any person, whether a non-licensee, non-holder, licensee or holder of authority."

14. A long-time OFW who returned to the Philippines to get married and raise a family in 2001 disclosed that among OFWs who have had several years of experience getting contracts abroad, a "blacklist" of sorts is common knowledge when it comes to "notorious" agencies with reputations for constantly changing their names and/or offices. (Interview with the author)

15.

Section 4. Deployment of Migrant Workers.—The State shall deploy overseas Filipino workers only in countries where the rights of Filipino migrant workers are protected. The government recognizes any of the following as a guarantee on the part of the receiving country for the protection of the rights of overseas Filipino workers: (a) It has existing labor and social laws protecting the rights of migrant workers; (b) It is a signatory to multilateral conventions, declarations or resolutions relating to the protection of migrant workers; (c) It has concluded a bilateral agreement or arrangement with the government protecting the rights of overseas Filipino workers; and, (d) It is taking positive, concrete measures to protect the rights of migrant workers. (Republic Act 8042)

16. Philippine Overseas Employment Administration 2003 Stock Estimates. Office Website. http://www.poea.gov.ph/docs/ofwStock2003.doc (6 May 2005).

17. The only agreements already concluded were with Austria way back in 1982, United Kingdom and Spain in 1989, France in 1994, and Canada in 1996. Other treaties are at present in their various stages of negotiations. Ratified in November 1997 is the RP-Quebec Understanding on Social Security covering around 5,000 Filipino migrant workers. On the other hand, for signing are bilateral agreements with Belgium and Italy which are expected to cover more than 100,000 OFWs. Arrangements for possible ties with the USA, Greece, Cyprus, and Saudi Arabia have been initiated by SSS. The SSS has also coordinated with the DFA to explore possibilities of bilateral agreements with other countries. (Social Security System Website)

18. As of 20 June 2002, the International Convention on the Protection of the Rights of All Migrant Workers and Members of Their Families had been ratified or acceded to by nineteen States, namely, Azerbaijan, Belize, Bolivia, Bosnia and Herzegovina, Cape Verde, Colombia, Ecuador, Egypt, Ghana, Guinea, Mexico, Morocco, the Philippines, Senegal, Seychelles, Sri Lanka, Tajikistan, Uganda, and Uruguay.

In addition, eleven States, namely, Bangladesh, Burkina Faso, Chile, Comoros, Guatemala, Guinea-Bissau, Paraguay, Sao Tome and Principe, Sierra Leone, Togo, and Turkey, signed the Convention. The Convention will enter into force when at least twenty States have ratified or acceded to it. Therefore, only one more ratification or accession is needed for the Convention to enter into force. Distr. General A/57/2919 August 2002.

19. Currently, approximately 20,000 USD.

20. The penalty of life imprisonment and a fine of not less than five hundred thousand pesos (P500, 000.00) nor more than one million pesos (P1, 000,000.00) shall be imposed if illegal recruitment constitutes economic sabotage as defined herein. Provided, however, that the maximum penalty shall be imposed if the person illegally recruited is less than eighteen (18) years of age or committed by a non-licensee or non-holder of authority. Republic Act 8042.

21. Also legal counsel to the former President Joseph Estrada.

22. "VII. Deregulation and Phase-Out: Section 29. Comprehensive Deregulation Plan on Recruitment Activities.—Pursuant to a progressive policy of deregulation whereby the migration of workers becomes strictly a matter between the worker and his foreign employer, the DOLE, within one (1) year from the effectivity of this Act, is hereby mandated to formulate a five-year comprehensive deregulation plan on recruitment activities taking into account labor market trends, economic conditions of the country and emerging circumstances which may affect the welfare of migrant workers.

Section 30. Gradual Phase-out of Regulatory Functions.—Within a period of five (5) years from the effectivity of this Act, the DOLE shall phase-out the regulatory functions of the POEA pursuant to the objectives of deregulation. Republic Act 8042.

23. WHEREFORE, judgment is hereby rendered: 1. Dismissing the petitions for *certiorari* and prohibition; 2. Granting the writ of *mandamus,* and ordering respondents DOLE Secretary Patricia Sto. Tomas; POEA Administrator Rosalinda D Baldoz; and Director-General Lucita Lazo of the Technical Education and Skills Development Authority: a) To forthwith comply with Sec.29 and Sec.30, Republic Act No.8042, otherwise known as the Migrant Workers & Overseas Filipinos Act of 1995; and, b) To rescind DOLE Department Order No. 10 and POEA Memorandum Circular No. 15, Series of 2001, and all orders, circulars, and issuances not tending to implement the deregulation plan to be adopted by DOLE hereafter; 3. Enjoining permanently respondents DOLE Secretary Particia Sto. Tomas; POEA Administrator Rosalinda D. Baldoz; and Director-General Lucita Lazo of the Technical Education and Skills Development Authority, from regulating the migration of workers.

24. Migrante (an organization of overseas Filipino workers) has come down particularly hard on President Gloria Macapagal-Arroyo and her spokesman Rigoberto Tiglao, claiming they have sold out Filipino workers in Hong Kong and Taiwan by secretly agreeing to across-the-board wage cuts that came into effect last November. In Hong Kong, current wages were cut by 15–30 percent, while in Taiwan all newly hired OFWs face salary cuts of 20 percent from previous levels. According to Migrante, GMA agreed to these significant wage cuts on the condition that Hong Kong, Taiwan, and South Korea would not cut back on the total number of Filipinos they hire every year. The group also charges that the Philippine government is supporting the new trainee schemes in South Korea and Japan, in an effort to keep OFW deployment figures up at any cost. *Philippine Daily Inquirer.* http://www.inq7.net/vwp/2001/dec/22/text/vwp_1-1-p.htm (21 December 2001).

25. Sections 29 and 30 of RA 8042 must be understood and interpreted in the light of the constitutional mandate and duty of the government to afford full protection to Filipino workers locally or overseas. Contrary to the lower court's ruling, deregulation does mean the total phase-out of the POEA's regulatory power over the recruitment of overseas Filipino workers (OFWs) that would put migration beyond the pale of State or government regulation or legal scrutiny, the DOLE petition said. It stressed that to rule otherwise would run afoul of the basic tenet that a statute should be interpreted in harmony with the Constitution, particularly the duty of the government to afford full protection to labor.

The immediate, total phase-out of the POEA, the DOLE stressed, would cause chaos, confusion, and disorder to the disadvantage of OFWs and the nation. This would defeat the very objective of RA 8042 to establish a higher standard of protection and promotion of the welfare of migrant workers and their families. The five-year deregulation plan mandated under RA 8042 was not absolute as it was subject to the condition that the country first attains the status of a newly industrialized country (NIC) by the year 2000. Department of Labor and Employment (DOLE) Website http://www.dole.gov.ph/news/pressreleases2002/April/133.htm (6 May 2005); See also http://www.poea.gov.ph/html/news_certiorari.html (6 May 2005).

26. Executive Order 25 (1986).

27. Republic Act 7111 (1991).

28. Executive Order 195 (1994).

29. Executive Order 329 (2000).

30. 2004 Figures. Department of Labor and Employment (DOLE) Website http://www.dole.gov.ph/news/pressreleases2004/october04/322.htm (20 April 2005).

31. *Philippine Daily Inquirer*, http://www.inq7.net/opi/2004/mar/06/opi_ralsamh-1 .htm(6 May 2005); See also: http://www.newsflash.org/2004/02/hl/hl100714.htm (last viewed 6 May 2005).

32. Translation: Filipino Women Advance (or Move Forward).

33. At the time the bill had already passed the lower house and was in the Senate for final deliberations, a child's rights group submitted a new bill on the trafficking of children to a Senator for sponsorship.

34. The Coalition Against Trafficking in Women–Asia Pacific led the proponents of the bill.

35. Revised Penal Code of the Philippines.

Article 202. Vagrants and Prostitutes -Penalty.—The following are vagrants: (1) Any person having no apparent means of subsistence, who has the physical ability to work and who neglects to apply himself or herself to some lawful calling; (2) Any person found loitering about public or semi-public buildings or places or tramping or wandering about the country or the streets without visible means of support; (3) Any idle or dissolute person who lodges in houses of ill fame; ruffians or pimps and those who habitually associate with prostitutes; (4) Any person who, not being included in the provisions of other articles of this Code, shall be found loitering in any inhabited or uninhabited place belonging to another without any lawful or justifiable purpose; and, Prostitutes; (5) for the purposes of this article, women who, for money or profit, habitually indulge in sexual intercourse or lascivious conduct are deemed to be prostitutes. Any person found guilty of any of the offenses covered by this article shall be punished by *arresto menor* or a fine not exceeding 200 pesos, and in case of recidivism, by *arresto mayor* in its medium period to *prision correccional* in its minimum period or a fine ranging from 200 to 2,000 pesos, or both, in the discretion of the court.

36. Feminist critiques on victimization point out that the tendency to essentialism. See: Ratna Kapur, "The Tragedy of Victimization Rhetoric: Resurrecting the 'Native' Subject in International/Post-Colonial Feminist Legal Politics," *Harvard Human Rights Journal* 15 (Spring 2002), http://www.law.harvard.edu/students/orgs/hrj/iss15/kapur .shtml (9 May 2005).

37. Republic Act 9225 (2003). With the adoption of the "The Citizenship Reten-tion and Reacquisition Act of 2003," the Philippines joins the ranks of over 20 nations (as of 2004) which have extended the right to dual citizenship to their citizens. An ac-companying law, Republic Act 9189 (2003), meanwhile extends the right to suffrage to Filipinos overseas despite the Constitutional requirement of six months' residency prior to the election. The Supreme Court upheld the law's constitutionality holding that "residency" under the context of the law is merely "domicile," or place of perma-nent residence, and therefore not actual presence.

38. Saskia Sassen, "Countergeographies of Globalization: The Feminisation of Sur-vival" (paper presented at the conference on "Gender Budgets, Financial Markets, Financing for Development," Heinrich-Boell Foundation, Berlin, February 19–20, 2002). http://e-education.uni-muenster.de/boell/Sassen.doc (9 May 2005).

39. Louise Langevin and Marie-Claire Belleau, "Trafficking in Women in Canada: A Critical Analysis of the Legal Framework Governing Immigrant Live-in Caregivers and Mail-Order Brides," Université Laval: Québec City, Quebec, CIDA Website, http://www.swc-cfc.gc.ca/pubs/066231252X/index_e.html (6 May 2005).

40. Marie-Claire Belleau and Louise Langeuin, Trafficking in Women in Canada: A Critical Analysis of the Legal Framework Governing Immigrant Live-In Caregivers and Mail-Order Brides, Faculty of Law, Université Laval, Quebec, October 2002 http://www.swc-cfc.gc.ca/pubs/pubspr/066231252X/200010_066231252X_22_e .html (9 May 2005).

41. Recent government policy restricting access to various Family Planning meth-ods considered unacceptable by the Roman Catholic hierarchy as well as state empha-sis on Natural Family Planning (NFP) is one of the hallmarks of the current Arroyo administration. See: Newsbreak http://www.inq7.net/nwsbrk/2003/jul/21/ nbk_7–1.htm (6 May 2005); http://www.filnurse.com/greymatter/archives/ 00000045.shtml(6 May 2005); Catholics for Choice Website, http://www.catholics forchoice.org/new/incathcircles/iccbottompg2vol6no1.htm (6 May 2005).

42. In the Philippines, the law on pornography is replete with contradictions. A Movie and Television Review Board is all but authorized to censor as it has done so for many years. But the issue of whether the power of censorship, regarding movies or film, is "judicial" has often been an issue before the Supreme Court. In its most recent ruling on pornography, the court adopted the Miller Test, 413 U.S. 15, 24–25 (1973) from the US in *Pita vs. Court of Appeals* G.R. No. 80806 October 5, 1989:

Whether the average person, applying contemporary adult community standards, would find that the work, taken as a whole, appeals to the prurient interest (i.e., an erotic, lascivi-ous, abnormal, unhealthy, degrading, shameful, or morbid interest in nudity, sex, or excre-tion); and whether the average person, applying contemporary adult community standards, would find that the work depicts or describes, in a patently offensive way, sexual conduct (i.e., ultimate sexual acts, normal or perverted, actual or simulated; masturbation; excretory functions; lewd exhibition of the genitals; or sado-masochistic sexual abuse); and whether a reasonable person would find that the work, taken as a whole, lacks serious literary, artis-tic, political, or scientific value.

43. Chris Navarro, "Cops Arrest 20 in 'Cybersex' Den Raid," *Sunstar Network Online.* htttp://www.sunstar.com.ph/static/net/2004/11/10/cops.arrest.20.in.cybersex .den.raid.html (6 May 2005).

BIBLIOGRAPHY

Belleau, Marie-Claire, and Louise Langevin. *Trafficking in Women in Canada: A Critical Analysis of the Legal Framework Governing Immigrant Live-in Caregivers and Mail-Order Brides.* Université Laval: Québec City, Quebec, October 2002. http://www.swc-cfc .gc.ca/pubs/pubspr/066231252X/200010_066231252X_22_e.html (9 May 2005).

Kapur, Ratna. "The Tragedy of Victimization Rhetoric: Resurrecting the "Native" Subject in International/Post-Colonial Feminist Legal Politics." *Harvard Human Rights Journal* 15 (Spring 2002). http://www.law.harvard.edu/students/orgs/hrj/ iss15/kapur.shtml (9 May 2005).

Sassen, Saskia. "Countergeographies of Globalization: The Feminisation of Survival." Paper presented at the conference on "Gender Budgets, Financial Markets, Financing for Development," Heinrich-Boell Foundation, Berlin, February 19–20, 2002. http://e-education.uni-muenster.de/boell/Sassen.doc (9 May 2005).

Semyonov, Moshe, and Anastasia Gorodzeisky. "Labor Migration, Remittances and Household Income: A Comparison Between Filipinos and Filipina Overseas Workers." *International Migration Review,* Spring 2005.

Wehrfritz, George, and Marites Vitug. "Workers for the World." *Newsweek International,* 4 October 2004.

• 8 •

The Challenge of Hidden Slavery: Legal Responses to Forced Labor in the United States

Free the Slaves, Washington, DC, and
The Human Rights Center, University of California, Berkeley

> Forced Labor: All work or service, which is exacted from any per-
> son under the menace of any penalty and for which the said per-
> son has not offered himself voluntarily.
>
> —International Labor Organization (ILO) Convention
> Concerning Forced Labor No. 29

*T*he United States is at a critical juncture in its struggle to end forced labor.
In 2000, the U.S. government enacted new laws to hold perpetrators of forced
labor accountable and to assist survivors freed from captivity. Since then, both
prosecutions of suspected wrongdoers and the number of social and legal service providers assisting survivors have increased exponentially. As efforts to
stamp out forced labor gather speed, there is a need to evaluate the record to
date and to propose new measures that will further strengthen eradication of
this egregious practice.

To this end, Free the Slaves and the Human Rights Center at the University of California, Berkeley, with the assistance of the Center for the Advancement of Human Rights at Florida State University, conducted a study of
the nature and scope of forced labor in the United States to assess efforts of
government and nongovernmental organizations to address the problem and to
recommend measures to improve the United States' response to forced labor.
This chapter is an edited and condensed version of that report, Hidden Slaves:
Forced Labor in the United States, and focuses on both the United States' legal response to forced labor and the implementation of these laws.

FORCED LABOR IN THE UNITED STATES

For most Americans, the occasional newspaper headline is the only indication that forced labor exists in the United States. And yet, at any given time, ten thousand or more people work as forced laborers in scores of cities and towns across the country. It is likely that the actual number is much higher, possibly reaching into the tens of thousands. Each year forced labor generates millions of dollars for criminals who prey on the most vulnerable—the poor, the uneducated, and the impoverished immigrant seeking a better life. Held as captives, victims of forced labor are enslaved for months and even years with little or no contact with the outside world. Those who survive enslavement face enormous challenges as they struggle to regain control over their shattered lives. Because forced labor is hidden, inhumane, widespread, and criminal, sustained and coordinated efforts by U.S. law enforcement, social service providers, and the general public are needed to expose and eradicate this illicit trade.

Forced Labor Is Hidden

Each year thousands of men, women, and children are trafficked from 35 or more countries into the United States and forced to work without pay in deplorable conditions. Most of them are rarely seen in public places. Hidden from view, they toil in sweatshops, brothels, farms, and private homes. To prevent them from escaping, their captors confiscate their identification documents, forbid them from leaving their workplaces or contacting their families, threaten them with arrest and deportation, and restrict their access to the surrounding community.

Forced Labor Is Inhumane

Victims of forced labor have been tortured, raped, assaulted, and murdered. They have been held in absolute control by their captors and stripped of their dignity. Some have been subjected to forced abortion, dangerous working conditions, poor nutrition, and humiliation. Some have died during their enslavement. Others have been physically or psychologically scarred for life. Once freed, many will suffer from a host of health-related problems, including repetitive stress injury, chronic back pain, visual and respiratory illnesses, sexually transmitted diseases, and depression.

Forced Labor is Widespread

Forced labor exists in at least ninety cities across the United States. It is prevalent in five sectors of the U.S. economy: prostitution and sex services (46%), domestic service (27%), agriculture (10%), sweatshop/factory (5%), and restaurant and hotel work (4%). Forced labor persists in these sectors because of low wages, lack of regulation and monitoring of working conditions, and a high demand for cheap labor. These conditions enable unscrupulous employers and criminal networks to gain virtually complete control over workers' lives.

In the last five years alone the press has reported 131 cases of forced labor in the United States involving 19,254 men, women, and children from a wide range of ethnic and racial groups.[1] Chinese comprised the largest number of victims, followed by Mexicans and Vietnamese. While reported in at least ninety U.S. cities, forced labor operations tend to thrive in states with large populations and sizable immigrant communities, such as California, Florida, New York, and Texas—all of which are transit routes for international travelers. These states are not the only place where forced labor takes place. Some victims are born and raised in the United States and find themselves pressed into servitude by fraud or deception.

Forced Labor Is Criminal

Forced labor is universally condemned and outlawed. Its practice in the United States violates a host of laws including indentured servitude, money laundering, and tax evasion. Yet criminals find it a highly profitable and lucrative enterprise. Their workers are forced to be docile, and when problems arise, "employers" know they can rein workers in with threats and physical violence. Criminals have also learned that the odds are good that they will never be held accountable in a court of law.

Forced labor exists in the United States because factors in the U.S. economy, the legal system, and immigration policy support it. Forced labor is a problem that is driven by a growing "informal economy" in the United States. The International Labor Organization (ILO) defines an informal economy as "all remunerative work—both self employed and wage employment—that is not recognized, regulated, or protected by existing legal or regulatory frameworks and non-remunerative work undertaken in an income-producing enterprise."[2] Forced labor exists in both legal and illegal industries that are poorly regulated and fail to comply with U.S. labor laws. "Employers" in such industries are often criminal entrepreneurs for whom forced labor may be one of a number of illegal activities. Over time, such employers have found that forced labor can be a lucrative business made possible through the ready availability of free labor, better and more varied transport, new methods of secure communications, and the increased permeability of borders.

Nongovernmental organizations (NGOs) in the U.S. deserve the lion's share of credit for exposing the existence of forced labor in the United States.

The first major bust of a forced labor operation in recent years took place in 1995 when labor rights groups uncovered a sweatshop operated by a Chinese-Thai family in El Monte, California, a small community near Los Angeles. Outrage over the case fueled efforts of a relatively small group of advocates and government officials to end such practices. The U.S. Congress responded by adopting the Victims of Trafficking and Violence Protection Act of 2000 (Trafficking Act). One effect of this process is that policymakers and advocates have taken the lead in the struggle to end forced labor. The challenge now is to raise the public's awareness of the problem and to educate and equip state and local law enforcement to recognize and destroy forced labor operations.

Public awareness of forced labor is practically nonexistent in the United States. Occasionally the police or a group of rights advocates will expose a forced labor operation, and invariably the media will depict it as a single and shocking event. But rarely do such exposés educate the public about its place and function within the U.S. economy.

Like the public, U.S. law enforcement is largely unaware of, or poorly informed about the nature of, forced labor and the plight of its victims. Because most victims of forced labor are undocumented workers or illegal aliens, law enforcement often regards them as criminals rather than victims ensnared in an illicit trade. This is largely because trafficking into forced labor is considered a federal crime. As a result, state and local law enforcement personnel lack basic training on identifying the crime, protecting victims, and bringing perpetrators to justice. Ironically, treating forced labor victims as criminals only makes it easier for an "employer" to get away with the crime because prosecutions rarely succeed without cooperative eyewitnesses.

THE U.S. LEGAL RESPONSE TO FORCED LABOR

Throughout U.S. history perpetrators of forced labor have been one step ahead of the law. In 1865 the Thirteenth Amendment of the U.S. Constitution outlawed chattel slavery and involuntary servitude.[3] Yet in the years following the American Civil War, Southern white landowners lured thousands of newly freed slaves and immigrants into peonage as sharecroppers on their plantations and farms. In response, the U.S. Supreme Court issued a series of opinions stating that the Constitution's prohibition against slavery was intended to go beyond situations of ownership to stamp out "any other kind of slavery, now or hereafter."[4] In 1874, in response to a new form of human trafficking, Congress adopted the "Padrone Statute"[5] to combat the practice of kidnapping boys in Italy to be used as shoeblacks, street musicians, and beggars on the streets of American cities.[6] In 1910, in an effort to curb prostitution, Congress passed the

Mann Act, which imposed stiff penalties on traffickers of women within U.S. borders.[7]

Still, unscrupulous employers continued to find new ways of compelling workers—many of whom were newly arrived immigrants—to work under slave-like conditions. In the early 1940s the Supreme Court ruled that employers could not force workers to remain in their jobs. Nor could they penalize them for leaving their employment.[8] Congress went on to enact a federal law in 1948 specifically criminalizing "peonage,"[9] or the practice of holding someone to work off a debt, and involuntary servitude,[10] whereby an individual was *forced* to work against his or her will. Despite this landmark legislation, U.S. courts generally interpreted the law to mean that criminal sanctions could only be imposed against perpetrators who used physical force or threats and *not* psychological coercion or trickery to hold victims in bondage.[11] This limitation in the application of the law was eliminated with passage of the Trafficking Act of 2000.

Domestic Legislation: The Trafficking Act

The 2000 Trafficking Act is a bold departure from prior approaches to trafficking and forced labor in the United States. Recognizing that these crimes are global problems, the law established the Office to Monitor and Combat Trafficking in Persons in the U.S. State Department to oversee a wide range of efforts to end human trafficking abroad. The Trafficking Act criminalizes procuring and subjecting another human being to peonage, involuntary sex trafficking, slavery, involuntary servitude, or forced labor; provides social services and legal benefits to survivors of these crimes, including authorization to remain in the country; provides funding to support protection programs for survivors in the United States as well as abroad; and includes provisions to monitor and eliminate trafficking in countries outside the United States.

Most important, the law distinguishes smuggling—a victimless crime by which migrants cross borders without authorization—from trafficking—a practice by which individuals are induced by force, fraud, trickery, or coercion to enter the United States and then forced to work against their will. The law clearly specifies that those caught up in trafficking and forced labor should be recognized as *victims* of a crime rather than treated as unauthorized migrants who must be returned to their countries of origin.

Labor and human rights activists welcomed the passage of the Trafficking Act in 2000 for many reasons. First, the new law sharpened the legal teeth of existing sanctions for involuntary servitude, peonage, and slavery by adding new crimes of human trafficking, sex trafficking, forced labor, and document servitude (withholding or destroying documents as part of the trafficking scheme).[12] Trafficking is defined as the activity of an individual who provides or obtains labor or services for peonage, slavery, involuntary servitude, or forced labor. The law contains a provision that prohibits trafficking adults into the sex industry through force, fraud, or coercion (in the case of victims under eighteen years old, there is no requirement of force, fraud, or coercion).

Second, the act not only strengthened laws so that traffickers could be held accountable for their crimes, but it provided specific measures to address the unique needs of trafficking victims. To begin with, it offered temporary immigration status to victims of a "severe form of trafficking" (minors who are trafficked for commercial sex and trafficking of adults through deception to work against their will). Through the T visa nonresidents who are willing to cooperate with law enforcement to prosecute their traffickers would be eligible to remain in the United States and to receive the same social service assistance offered to refugees, even where victims have entered the United States without proper immigration documents.

Finally, the act enlarged the repertoire of law enforcement tools to combat trafficking. It broadened the definition of "coercion" for the new crimes of forced labor and sex trafficking to include *psychological manipulation*. This meant alleged perpetrators could be held accountable if they caused a victim to believe that his or her failure to comply with their orders would result in serious harm to the victim or to others. As noted above, psychological coercion was previously insufficient to prove involuntary servitude. The law also criminalized the confiscation or destruction of identity or travel documents, a practice traffickers often use to control their victims, and enabled prosecutors to pursue not just the ringleaders but all those involved in a trafficking operation, including recruiters, drivers, and other intermediaries.

Such progress notwithstanding, the Trafficking Act does have some notable shortcomings. Advocates and service providers criticize the essential framework of the Trafficking Act, which conditions benefits on the cooperation of survivors with federal law enforcement. Qualified trafficking survivors are eligible for two types of immigration relief—"continued presence" and a T visa—both of which grant authorization to work and entitle survivors to receive social service benefits but which require assistance from law enforcement personnel to obtain. Only federal law enforcement may request continued presence. Survivors may apply for a T visa on their own. Applicants for a T visa over fifteen years old must document that they are cooperating with law enforcement. Although not strictly required, an endorsement from federal law enforcement is the preferred evidence of cooperation. State and local law enforcement agencies that encounter trafficking victims are encouraged to refer these cases to the federal government.[13]

RELATION OF THE UNITED STATES
TO INTERNATIONAL TRENDS

In many ways the United States has been at the forefront of the fight against modern slavery and forced labor. Unlike international law, U.S. domestic legislation recognizes that slavery is defined primarily by the power of an individual to control another for economic gain.[14] Historically, the federal government has expanded this principle by adopting laws specifically to respond to the evolving nature of forced labor and enslavement. Moreover, while the definitions and philosophy of trafficking in the U.N. Trafficking Protocol and the United States Trafficking Act are similar, the U.S. has adopted a more aggressive, proactive approach to the problem than the one outlined in the international agreement. For example, unlike the Trafficking Protocol, the Trafficking Act contains international monitoring and sanctions provisions. Similarly, while the protocol does not allow victims to seek relief from perpetrators, the Trafficking Act establishes mandatory restitution from convicted traffickers. A recent amendment to the Trafficking Act allows survivors to sue their former captors for civil damages for violations of the statute.

Despite their strengths, both international and U.S. anti-trafficking laws suffer similar weaknesses when it comes to protections for victims. Although the U.N. Protocol and the U.S. Trafficking Act are explicit in recognizing that trafficked individuals are *victims of a crime* rather than illegal migrants, they are by no means consistent in this victim-centered approach. The Trafficking Protocol makes state provision of immigration relief, social services, and compensation to victims discretionary as opposed to mandatory. While the United States law goes further and establishes regulations to provide immigration status and social services to victims, it provides these benefits only to victims of a "severe form of trafficking" that are involved with the prosecution of their traffickers. Furthermore, conditioning immigration relief and social services on cooperation with prosecution creates the perception that victims are primarily instruments of law enforcement rather than individuals who are, in and of themselves, deserving of protection and restoration of their human rights.

The Trafficking Act also contains "definitional inconsistencies" that may weaken intended protections for trafficking survivors. For example, survivors must show they are a "victim of a severe form of trafficking"—a victim of sex or human trafficking—to be eligible for immigration relief and benefits. According to some advocates, the federal authorities have failed to issue certifications to some trafficking survivors because they felt the allegations of abuse were not "severe enough."[15]

IMPLEMENTATION AND ENFORCEMENT OF U.S. LAWS

Several years after passage of the Trafficking Act, U.S. law enforcement personnel, policymakers, and labor rights advocates are still wrestling with the legal mandates established under the new law. Our research suggests that effective implementation and enforcement of the Trafficking Act will depend on several factors, including training law enforcement officers, particularly at the local level, to identify victims and forced labor operations; improving cooperation and information sharing between federal and state agencies charged with combating forced labor; revising procedures for the handling of survivors; and finding more effective measures for providing survivors with protection, benefits, and compensation.

Identifying Victims

One of the greatest challenges U.S. law enforcement faces is developing the skills to identify victims of trafficking and forced labor. Finding victims, a federal prosecutor in the U.S. Department of Labor said, is "devilishly difficult to do."[16] There are many reasons why victim identification is complicated. Victims are usually reluctant to approach local police because they fear retribution from their traffickers or "employers." This fear often stems from their experiences with corrupt law enforcement personnel in their countries of origin. Invariably, exploiters play on this fear by warning their captives that U.S. law enforcement is no different. In some cases, "employers" have given their workers false identities as a means of passing through U.S. immigration.

Law Enforcement

Law enforcement, particularly at the local level, must develop the capacity to identify not only victims of trafficking and forced labor but also the very operations themselves. "Police don't know trafficking when they see it," said a former representative of Human Rights Watch.[17] Indeed, the problem is so pervasive the U.S. Department of Justice (DOJ) has launched a federal training program to help investigators working for the Federal Bureau of Investigation (FBI), the Department of Homeland Security's Immigration and Customs Enforcement (formerly the Immigration and Naturalization Service, or INS),[18] and the Department of Labor detect forced labor operations.

To date, the Department of Justice has taken a targeted approach aimed at training state and local law enforcement officers located in areas of the country where forced labor is pervasive. Yet, given the sheer number of police departments in the United States—over seventeen thousand—many state and local law enforcement agencies lack knowledge and training for human trafficking. The daunting task of training all of the local law enforcement agencies in the United States is amplified by the frequent turnover of officers, which on average is every few years.[19]

Fragmentation of Law Enforcement

The approach now taken by federal and state agencies to combat forced labor in the United States is fragmentary and inconsistent. This is largely because trafficking is considered a federal crime that must be handled by federal agents. Indeed, until passage of the recent amendments to the Trafficking Act, federal agents had primary authority to certify that a survivor met the definitional threshold to be eligible to receive benefits and protections under the act. This process can be cumbersome and time-consuming and, ultimately, frustrating for the survivor. Likewise, the process of seeking federal certification can involve a great risk to the survivor.

If agents are unwilling to issue such a certification, then the survivor is left exposed. Her trafficker may be aware that she has approached the authorities and seek retribution against her. Without certification, she cannot stay in the United States legally and she faces a grim choice. She must either live in the United States as a permanent undocumented individual, flee to a third country, or risk returning to her home country where the trafficker continues to wield great influence and power.

Not only is the certification process coordinated through the Department of Justice, the department is also responsible for keeping track of statistics under the act. Federal statistics regarding trafficking cases will not include federal cases that are not appropriately charged, for example, by a federal agency other than DOJ, nor do they include trafficking or forced labor incidents that come to the attention of the state prosecutors. Thus, there is concern among service providers that a lack of coordination between the federal government agencies makes it difficult to establish accurate numbers of prosecutions and may prevent survivors from accessing benefits and protection. A related problem is that local police and state officials unable to identify a forced labor operation necessarily fail to refer such cases to federal agents.

Today there are greater protections for survivors of forced labor, largely because of the T visa program and an agreement reached between the Department of Labor and the Department of Homeland Security, which protects undocumented workers from action by immigration officials in connection with labor department investigations. In 1999 the Department of Justice and Department of Labor created the Worker Exploitation Task Force to improve coordination and to increase the prosecution of forced labor cases. In 2001, as required by the Trafficking Act, President George W. Bush created the Inter-Agency Task Force to Monitor and Combat Trafficking. The mandate of this task force is to coordinate and implement executive policy in order to combat trafficking. In March 2003 the task force created a Senior Policy Advisory Group to advise the task force on important policy issues.[20]

There is the hope that this interagency approach will make the process of investigating and adjudicating trafficking and forced labor cases more efficient and less burdensome for survivors. One encouraging sign is the creation of regional task forces under the umbrella of the Worker Exploitation Task Force throughout the United States. These task forces serve as forums for agencies to share information and coordinate approaches to specific trafficking and forced labor cases.

Despite this progress, government officials familiar with the work of such task forces believe coordination among members of the task force could be improved. They point to interagency rivalries, different approaches to cases based on agency priorities, and the challenges of coordinating a large number of agencies and participants. Despite these criticisms, most agree that such task forces serve an important function and emphasize that there has been more interagency cooperation around trafficking than most other issues. As one member of the Worker Exploitation Task Force noted: "I frankly think that [the task force] works reasonably well at this point. It could always work better . . . what I've given you is the model. The closer we come to that, the better off we are."[21]

Nongovernmental organization advocates support the idea of greater federal interagency cooperation and information exchange in addressing trafficking and forced labor cases. Advocates believe that greater cooperation will lead to the development of alternative ways of providing victim relief for those cases that are not taken up by federal prosecutors. One NGO representative has noted that only three or four of the agency's twenty or thirty trafficking cases have been chosen for federal prosecution. In an interagency scheme, she would like to see the Department of Labor, as a federal enforcement agency, take a greater role in addressing trafficking cases by being able to request benefits and issue certificates of endorsement. "Trafficking," she says, "is as much a labor issue as it is a criminal one." She would like to see other federal agencies such as the Department of Labor "have the ability to confer victim status, especially when a case is rejected for criminal prosecution by the Department of Justice."[22]

Ironically, as awareness about trafficking and forced labor has increased at the level of local law enforcement, new tensions have arisen between state and federal agencies. Victims who cooperate with local authorities are technically eligible for a T visa but run into problems because the Trafficking Act favors documentation of cooperation from federal law enforcement over an endorsement from state officials. The new amendments to the Trafficking Act make state and local endorsements equivalent to federal ones but the new law has not yet been fully implemented.[23] Advocates are watching the certification process carefully. Without access to federal immigration and welfare benefits, victims in state prosecutions are unable to regularize their status and must fall back on state benefits—if available—or private support. The NGO advocate recounted that victims "are surviving on the good will of local citizens to take care of them, and they have no legal status."[24]

NGO advocates also report that federal officials often refuse to issue endorsements of T visa applications. One service provider attributed this reluctance to the mistaken belief among law enforcement that the benefits are too generous and that "they are giving away a green card" by providing certification.[25] Moreover, agents may wait until the Department of Homeland Security has determined that a victim is a legitimate victim of severe trafficking, or until a prosecution has begun, to issue an endorsement, causing victims to wait months before receiving much-needed benefits. Advocates report that for some victims the dependency on federal authorities for immigration relief, compounded by the pain and discomfort of testifying about their experience, does not serve their needs and dissuades them from cooperating with law enforcement.

NGO advocates also note that middle management in federal investigatory agencies often hinders the enforcement of the Trafficking Act by downplaying the severity of crimes involving forced labor. On several occasions such officials have reassigned experienced and knowledgeable investigators to other higher priority crimes. Advocates note that investigative resources are beginning to be provided but are not yet sufficient.

New Approaches to Law Enforcement

Bringing the needs of victims of trafficking and forced labor into sharp focus and prosecuting their abusers requires a reorientation of all levels of law enforcement as well as an unprecedented degree of coordination between state and federal justice departments. By any standard it is an enormous undertaking but fortunately one that has enjoyed significant support from both the Clinton and Bush administrations.

The Trafficking Act has also helped law enforcement personnel recognize that those ensnared in trafficking and forced labor are *victims* and not criminals. This approach has paid dividends in a rapid increase in the number of forced labor cases prosecuted in the past five years.[26] Key to this increase has been the change in the relationship between law enforcement and victims. Prosecutors understand that to win forced labor cases and appropriately punish offenders requires the trust and cooperation of victims and witnesses. "Obviously, without the cooperation of the victims we can't win cases," says an official from the DOJ section that prosecutes forced labor cases.[27]

Treatment of Survivors

Much of the criticism of the United States' approach to forced labor stems from the link between prosecution of perpetrators and serving victims. According to one top-level federal prosecutor, attitudes among prosecutors toward forced labor victims vary from "humanitarian"—where the focus is to alleviate the suffering of the victim—to "instrumental"—where victims are seen as necessary to win criminal cases. Under the Trafficking Act prosecutors are pivotal to meeting the needs of victims for social services and fulfilling the criminal enforcement aims of the statute. Yet these aims can at times clash, leaving victims unacknowledged or underserved, perpetrators non-indicted, and service providers and law enforcement agents feeling frustrated.

What makes for a good prosecution does not always serve the immediate safety needs of victims. On average, the investigation and prosecution of trafficking and forced labor cases take between eight months and three years to complete, during which time victims may remain in situations of forced labor or in fear of their captors and associates.

When victims are liberated from situations of forced labor, their treatment by law enforcement varies greatly. For example, in a forced prostitution case occurring before the passage of the Trafficking Act, victims found themselves imprisoned in detention centers while their perpetrators ran free. An FBI agent involved in one case explained: "We couldn't let the witnesses loose because they want to go home—we'd lose them all. It just happened that way."[28] This detention was bad for both the victims and law enforcement. The prosecution team needed to earn the trust of the women freed from forced labor so they would testify against their captors. Yet, their detention confirmed to them what the perpetrators had always told the women: if they were caught by the authorities, they would be "in prison for the rest of [their] lives."[29]

Benefits, Protection, and Compensation

Because of the passage of the Trafficking Act, law enforcement can now offer immigration protection to victims and thus assuage their fear of deportation. These alternatives to the detention of victims (such as the "stay of removal" or "continued presence" provisions) are vital to achieving the humanitarian and law enforcement goals of the Trafficking Act.

Yet for every victim who is willing to come forward and testify for prosecutors, there are many who are unable or unwilling to do so. As a result, the victims will not receive immigration relief or other benefits under the Trafficking Act. One service provider estimates that only 50 percent of their clients wish to cooperate in the prosecution of their perpetrators. "Even though somebody has been beaten and abused," she says, "it may not be a priority for them to see . . . [the perpetrator] go to jail."[30] Some survivors simply desire to return home and never see their traffickers again. Many advocates believe that immigration relief and permission to work should be granted to survivors automatically and not linked to cooperation with a prosecution.

Survivors of forced labor often fear pressing charges against their former captors because it could result in harm to themselves and their families. Associates of the accused have gone to great lengths, in one case attempting to gain access to victims while disguised as armed police officers, to threaten and intimidate potential witnesses. Even after conviction, survivors and their families may remain in danger, whether they return to their home countries or remain in the United States. In some cases escaped perpetrators have returned to their hometowns where they live alongside former captives and their families. Vulnerability of family members abroad causes much anxiety and grief to forced labor victims in the United States. For victims, pursuing justice raises the stakes, and the threats of perpetrators—often powerful and well-connected members of the communities in which they live and recruit—are quite credible.

Despite these real dangers and the Trafficking Act's mandate to protect trafficking survivors, federal authorities have been unable to protect family members of survivors from retribution in their countries of origin. U.S. law enforcement has no authority to intervene directly when acts of retribution take place beyond its borders. While family members have the option of relocating to the United States through the T visa process, that process can take years and is not suited to addressing crisis situations. The inability to meet a global problem with a global response may leave victims of forced labor reluctant to step forward and thus jeopardize future arrests and prosecutions of perpetrators.

A consequence of forced labor is that when freed, survivors are usually left with little or no resources to rebuild their lives. While no comprehensive figures are available, some survivors have sued their former captors to collect the money they are owed. The record so far has been mixed.

LESSONS LEARNED AND FUTURE CHALLENGES

The United States government has recognized the problems of forced labor and human traffickings, and its actions to combat these abuses, both in the U.S.

and overseas, constitute a significant platform on which to build. Already there have been important successes in enforcing laws that bring perpetrators of human trafficking and forced labor to justice. There has also been a marked change in approach and practice. Those caught in forced labor are now more likely to be recognized as victims of crime, with rights and needs that are specific to the nature of the abuse and exploitation they have endured. Nongovernmental organizations (NGOs), service agencies, legal advocacy groups, worker organizations, and other community-based groups are now accumulating invaluable experience in supporting victims of forced labor and trafficking and in participating in multisectoral efforts to combat these crimes. Yet these actions will not be fully effective until the United States raises public awareness about human trafficking and creates transnational law enforcement networks to tackle the problem head on. While much remains to be done, there are lessons to be learned, which can strengthen U.S. efforts to eradicate forced labor.

Domestic Laws Can Create Strong Legal Platforms

Passage of the Trafficking Act in 2000 was a watershed event, providing a comprehensive legal framework to tackle human trafficking in the United States. This legislation established a comprehensive set of regulations to ensure that criminal traffickers are prosecuted and that their victims are treated as such. The record to date shows that the new law enforcement tools have paid off: the number of investigations and prosecutions of traffickers has increased dramatically (four- and two-fold, respectively).[31] Key to this success is providing immigration benefits and social services to survivors of trafficking and forced labor. Greater cooperation would occur if the government issued regulations for the U visa established by the TVPA to allow survivors who provide limited assistance to law enforcement personnel to receive temporary legal status and benefits. There remains a need to refine U.S. laws to close gaps in enforcement and care for survivors of forced labor. For example, increased opportunities for regularized migration would help decrease vulnerability of workers to forced labor, and gender-sensitive migration policies would protect women in potentially exploitative situations.

Training Is Critical

Law enforcement, NGOs, worker organizations, government monitoring agencies, and service providers are learning more and more about the signs of trafficking and forced labor. This study finds that identification of victims increases as those likely to encounter survivors gain expertise in the various signals of forced labor conditions.

The number of professionals with trafficking and forced labor expertise is still relatively small, but growing. Their experiences serve as a vital resource for the creation of training materials as well as their dissemination. With time, training should be extended both in breadth and depth to more agencies and professionals in order to identify, liberate, and support survivors. In particular, worker and employer organizations are important audiences to target for training on the signs of forced labor. Because victims are often isolated, these sectors may have access to victims and could function as monitors.

Witness and Survivor Protection

The safety of survivors is critical to creating conditions under which they will be able to rebuild their lives and, if they choose, to cooperate fully with law enforcement. This study links the effective response of U.S. law enforcement and service providers to the promotion of witness cooperation. Service providers indicated that housing forced labor survivors in homeless shelters or with victims of domestic violence was inappropriate.[32] Creation of temporary housing specifically for survivors of trafficking and forced labor has just begun and promises to address many of the special needs of survivors just emerging from servitude.

While law enforcement has been able to protect survivors in the United States, it has proved difficult to provide effective protection to family members of survivors abroad. Nongovernmental organizations and worker organizations, working transnationally, may prove to be an effective tool for protecting forced labor survivors and their families. NGOs and worker organizations in origin countries could form part of an early warning system by monitoring the status of families of witnesses as well as survivors who return home. These groups could alert government authorities at home and in the United States about reported threats or abuse. Calling attention to problems early would send an important message to both traffickers and survivors.

Social Services Provision to Survivors

A wide range of social services is needed to assist trafficking survivors. This study found that most experienced and successful service providers cover a host of needs, often working with clients for a long period. In particular, seasoned service providers have learned to screen survivors of forced labor and trafficking for specific needs resulting from their forced labor situation. Another proven practice of service providers is to identify a lead agency and point of contact that will remain responsible for coordinating between service providers and, when a survivor is cooperating with law enforcement, between prosecutors and investigators.

Research

Knowledge of the criminal aspects of forced labor and human trafficking in the United States is still very limited. This study shows that law enforcement, social service providers, and legal advocates have gained most of their understanding about trafficking and forced labor on a case-by-case basis. Organized research will inform and strengthen the response by sectors already involved in combating forced labor as well as promote inclusion of other groups, such as medical professionals and worker and employer organizations.

RECOMMENDATIONS

Forced labor remains a widespread problem in the United States because there is public ignorance of the crime, a lack of sensitivity to victims, insufficient legal action, and a public demand for cheap goods and services. Yet for all its severity and breadth, forced labor can be stopped. The record of accomplishments is striking, particularly considering that the Trafficking Act has been in effect for less than five years. It is clear, however, that much remains to be done. In particular, the U.S. government should

- Start a broad-based awareness-raising campaign, with special attention to reaching immigrant communities in the United States;
- Improve institutional capacity to respond to forced labor and trafficking;
- Ensure better protection for workers in sectors vulnerable to forced labor and trafficking;
- Correct aspects of immigration policy that encourage the practice of forced labor; and
- Strengthen protection and rehabilitation programs for survivors.

At the time of this chapters' writing, several states have passed anti-trafficking laws. Scores of federally funded state and local human trafficking task forces have been formed. An increasing number of citizens are becoming aware of the surreptitious enslavement of people in forced labor in the United States. The U.S. government's record of accomplishments to combat forced labor and human trafficking is a firm foundation for implementing the above recommendations.

NOTES

Originally published as "Hidden Slaves: Forced Labor in the United States," Free the Slaves, Washington, D.C. and Human Rights Center, Berkeley: University of California, September 2004; also under the same title in the Berkeley *Journal of International Law* 23, no. 1 (2005), 47–111. The original report is available online at www.freetheslaves .net.

This chapter was edited and adapted by Austin Choi-Fitzpatrick, Free the Slaves, 2005.

    1. Of these 131 cases, 105 listed the number or the estimated number of persons who had been found in a situation of forced labor.

    2. International Labour Organization, Employment Sector, *Women and Men in the Informal Economy: A Statistical Picture* (Geneva, 2002), 12.

    3. U.S. Constitution, Thirteenth Amendment. The amendment states: "Neither slavery nor involuntary servitude, except as a punishment for crime whereof the party shall have been duly convicted, shall exist within the United States, or any place subject to their jurisdiction."

    4. *Slaughter-House Cases*, 83 U.S. 36, 72 (1872).

    5. *U.S. Statutes at Large* 18 (1874): 251.

    6. *United States v. Kozminski*, 487 U.S. 931, 947 (1988).

    7. See, generally, *U.S. Code* 18 (2003), §§ 2421–2424.

    8. *Pollock v. Williams,* 322 U.S. 4 (1944).

    9. *U.S. Code* 18 (2003), § 1581.

    10. *U.S. Code* 18 (2003), § 1584 (outlaws sale into involuntary servitude) and *U.S. Code* 18 (2003), § 1583 (outlaws enticement into involuntary servitude).

    11. See, for example, *United States v. Shackney*, 333 F.2d 475 (2d Cir. 1964); *United States v. Kozminski*, 487 U.S. 931 (1988).

    12. *U.S. Code* 18 (2003), §§ 1589–1592. The Trafficking Act definition of forced labor is narrower than ILO Convention No. 29 as it sanctions compelled labor secured through specific types of threats, rather than labor secured through the more general "menace of penalty." ILO Convention No. 29 stipulates that the work of convicted prisoners should be carried out under the supervision of a public authority and that the prisoner is not to be hired to or placed at the service of private individuals, companies, or associations. Like the ILO Convention No. 29, the Thirteenth Amendment to the United States Constitution also recognizes punishment for a crime as an exception to slavery and involuntary servitude. The United States permits prison labor in a variety of contexts, and this practice has been the subject of prior ILO studies. See International Labour Office, *Stopping Forced Labour: A Report of the Director General*, International Labour Conference, 89th session, Report I (B), 2001, 60.

    13. On December 19, 2003, President George W. Bush signed a new law that makes it easier for survivors cooperating with state and local law enforcement to qualify for immigration relief and benefits. Even with the new law, however, advocates question the wisdom of making access to benefits subject to cooperation with law enforcement because of the additional burdens it puts on survivors who are extremely vulnerable. Trafficking Victims Protection Reauthorization Act of 2003, HR 2640, 108th Cong., 1st session, Public Law No. 108–193.

    14. Nevertheless, there is a growing tendency in international law to expand the definition of slavery. For example, the U.N. Working Group on Contemporary Forms

of Slavery provided, in 1997, that "slavery" covers a range of contemporary human rights violations, including exploitation of child labor, debt bondage, and traffic in persons. See Office of the United Nations High Commissioner for Human Rights, *Fact Sheet No. 14, Contemporary Forms of Slavery*, June 1991, www.unhchr.ch/html/menu6/2/fs14.htm.

15. Anonymous trafficking expert at a nongovernmental organization, interviewed by Laurel Fletcher, Human Rights Center, Univ. of California, Berkeley, June 4, 2003.

16. Anonymous official at the United States Department of Labor, interviewed by Laurel Fletcher, Human Rights Center, University of California, Berkeley, and Jolene Smith, Free the Slaves, July 1, 2003.

17. Martina Vandenberg, attorney, Jenner and Block, formerly researcher, Women's Rights Division, Human Rights Watch, interviewed by Laurel Fletcher, July 5, 2003.

18. The U.S. government recently restructured its immigration agency. Beginning March 1, 2003, the functions of the Immigration and Naturalization Service were transferred to the new Department of Homeland Security (within the Directorate of Border and Transportation Security and U.S. Citizenship and Immigration Services). *Report to Congress from Attorney General John Ashcroft on U.S. Government Efforts to Combat Trafficking in Persons in Fiscal Year 2003*, May 1, 2004, 15.

19. U.S. Department of Justice, *Report to Congress from Attorney General John Ashcroft on U.S. Government Efforts to Combat Trafficking in Persons in Fiscal Year 2003*, May 1, 2004, 41–42.

20. For an account of the activities of the Senior Policy Advisory Group, see U.S. Department of Justice, *Assessment of U.S. Activities to Combat Trafficking in Persons*, 41–42.

21. Anonymous official at the U.S. Department of Labor, interviewed by Laurel Fletcher, Human Rights Center, University of California, Berkeley, and Jolene Smith, Free the Slaves, July 1, 2003.

22. Jennifer Stanger, Media/Advocacy Director, Coalition to Abolish Slavery and Trafficking, interviewed by Rachel Shigekane, Human Rights Center, University of California, Berkeley, July 7, 2003.

23. The Trafficking Victims Protection Reauthorization Act of 2003 directs immigration officials to consider statements from state and local law enforcement officials when certifying a survivor's compliance with a request for assistance in the investigation or prosecution of crimes attributed to the trafficker. However, immigration officials await further guidance to implement this directive. William R. Yates, Associate Director of Operations, Memorandum to Paul Novak, Director, Vermont Service Center, 15 April 2004. *Re: Trafficking Victims Protection Reauthorization Act of 2003*, Washington, D.C.

24. Jennifer Stanger, Media/Advocacy Director, Coalition to Abolish Slavery and Trafficking, interviewed by Rachel Shigekane, Human Rights Center, University of California, Berkeley, July 7, 2003.

25. Stanger, Interview, July 7, 2003.

In fact, the benefits to which victims are actually entitled are fairly modest. In California, for example, victims receive refugee assistance for a period of eight months. This aid consists of $300 per month in refugee cash assistance and $120 per month in food stamps, as well as access to medical care during this period. By way of comparison, this totals just over half of the official poverty threshold for an individual, $748 per month. U.S. Department of Health and Human Services, *2003 Heath and Human Services Poverty Guidelines*, http://aspe.hhs.gov/poverty/03poverty.htm.

26. U.S. Department of Justice, *Report to Congress from Attorney General John Ashcroft on U.S. Government Efforts to Combat Trafficking in Persons in Fiscal Year 2003*, May 1, 2004, 18.

27. Anonymous official, U.S. Department of Justice, interviewed by Laurel Fletcher, Human Rights Center, University of California, Berkeley, June 3, 2003.

28. Anonymous FBI special agent, interviewed by Steven Lize, Free the Slaves, May 2, 2003.

29. Maria, pseudonymous trafficking survivor, statement, U.S. Senate Foreign Relations Committee, Near Eastern and South Asian Affairs Sub-Committee, Hearings on the International Trafficking of Women and Children, April 4, 2000, http://usinfo.state .gov/topical/global/traffic/00040502htm.

30. Jennifer Stanger, Media/Advocacy Director, Coalition to Abolish Slavery and Trafficking (CAST), interviewed by Rachel Shigekane, Human Rights Center, University of California, Berkeley, July 7, 2003.

31. U.S. Department of State, *Trafficking in Persons Report*, 2005. http://www.state .gov/g/tips/rls/tiprpt/2005/46618.htm.

32. Kathleen Kim, Skadden Fello, Lawyers' Committee for Civil Rights of the San Francisco Bay Area, and Mie Lewis, AED, New Voices Fellow, Asian Pacific Islander Legal Outreach (Co-chairs of the Bay Area Anti-Trafficking Task Force), interviewed by Natalie Hill, Amnesty International, and Rachel Shigekane, Human Rights Center, University of California Berkeley, June 16, 2003.

SELECTED BIBLIOGRAPHY

Bales, Kevin. *Disposable People: New Slavery in the Global Economy*. Berkeley: University of California Press, 1999.

——. *Understanding Global Slavery: A Reader*. Berkeley: University of California Press, 2005.

"Florida Responds to Human Trafficking." Center for the Advancement of Human Rights, Florida State University, 2003. http://www.cahr.fsu.edu/hreporte.html.

"Global Alliance Against Forced Labour," ILO, 2005. www.ilo.org/dyn/declaris/ DECLARATIONWEB.DOWNLOAD_BLOB?Var_DocumentID=5059.

"Hidden Slaves: Forced Labour in the United States." Free The Slaves and Human Rights Center, University of California Berkeley, September 2004. http://www .freetheslaves.net/resources/whitepapers/.

Kim, Kathleen, and David Warner. "Civil Litigation on Behalf of Victims of Human Trafficking." Legal Aid Foundation of Los Angeles, 2005. http://www.lafla .org/clientservices/specialprojects/VictimsTrfficking0405.pdf.

"Like Machines in the Field: Workers Without Rights in American Agriculture." Oxfam America, 2004. www.oxfamamerica.org/pdfs/labor_report_04.pdf.

· 9 ·

Human Rights and Human Trafficking in Thailand: A Shadow TIP Report

Anne Gallagher

Since 2001, the United States Government has issued annual reports on the situation of trafficking in every country (except its own) deemed to have a significant problem in this area. These reports have been hugely influential in terms of constructing and directing the global trafficking discourse as well as prompting individual governments to do something about trafficking and related exploitation.

The focus of this study is on the standards against which a State's counter-trafficking performance should be measured. For the purpose of its reports, the United States has established a certain standard and then identified criteria for determining whether or not an individual country is meeting that standard. There are two problems with this approach. The first relates to the inherent limitations in capturing a national trafficking response through application of highly detailed criteria in less than a page. Priorities that must remain unacknowledged become a necessity, and the integrity of the assessment system is inevitably compromised. The second problem concerns the legitimacy of the standard and the criteria by which it is established. In the present case, neither is claimed as deriving from international agreement but is an extrapolation of U.S. law and U.S. perceptions regarding both the nature of the problem and preferred solutions. This calls into question their applicability and their legitimacy. It also inevitably includes acceptance of any conclusions on which they are based.

International law provides detailed and substantive guidance on the obligations of States when it comes to trafficking. Unlike the U.S. criteria, these obligations are contained in international agreements developed and accepted by the majority of States and the international organizations they have established to represent their collective interests. This essay seeks to go beyond what is attempted in the United States Trafficking in Persons (TIP) report: to isolate the key international obligations related to trafficking; to identify their origin and scope; and to apply them to a concrete situation. Thailand has been chosen as a case study because of the complexity of the trafficking situation in that country as well as its relatively long and interesting history in dealing with trafficking and other forms of exploitation, especially those affecting women and children. The overall objective of this exercise is to confirm the importance of evaluation and assessment when it comes to a country's performance in dealing with trafficking—while at the same time emphasizing the dangers and limitations inherent in a unilateralist approach which is fundamentally limited in its ability to accurately capture the situation and is not necessarily grounded in established and accepted international rules.

THE U.S. TRAFFICKING IN PERSONS REPORT

Since 2001, the U.S. government has issued annual reports describing "the nature and extent of severe forms of trafficking in persons . . . in each foreign country" and assessing governmental efforts to combat such trafficking.[1] These reports are mandated by the 2000 Victims of Trafficking and Violence Prevention Act,[2] which set out minimum standards for the elimination of trafficking applicable to "the government of a country of origin, transit or destination."[3] In brief, these standards require governments to: (1) prohibit and appropriately punish severe forms of trafficking; and (2) make serious and sustained efforts to eliminate such trafficking. In evaluating governmental efforts in this latter regard, consideration is to be given to the following criteria: whether the government vigorously investigates and punishes acts of severe forms of trafficking; whether it protects victims and encourages their participation in the investigation and prosecution process; whether it has adopted prevention measures such as public education; whether it cooperates with other governments in investigations and prosecutions; whether it extradites (or is attempting to permit extradition of) traffickers; whether it monitors migration patterns for evidence of trafficking and responds to such evidence; and, finally, whether it investigates, prosecutes, and takes appropriate measures against the involvement of public officials in trafficking.

Under the Act, the United States will not, as a matter of policy, provide non-humanitarian, non–trade-related assistance to any government that does not comply with the minimum standards and that is not making significant efforts to bring itself into compliance.[4] In addition, such countries will also face U.S. opposition to their seeking and obtaining funds from multilateral financial institutions, including the World Bank and the IMF.[5] The annual reports are used as a basis for determining whether, and to what extent, sanctions are to be imposed.

The first TIP report instituted a system of grading based on three tiers. Tier One was for countries in full compliance with the required standards; Tier Two for countries making an effort but not yet fully compliant; and Tier Three for those countries who were not even trying or coming close. The Trafficking Victims Protection Reauthorization Act (December 2003) strengthened the minimum standards to be applied in determining an individual country's rating. These now include consideration of convictions and sentences (for traffickers and complicit officials) as well as investigations and prosecutions. Willingness to provide data on law enforcement action is now also a relevant consideration. The Act created a new category—a Special Watch List of countries to receive special scrutiny. The list includes countries that have [moved] down one tier from the previous report as well as "weak Tier 2 countries":[6] those which have a significant number of trafficking victims, and have not made increasing efforts over the past year, or have been provisionally exempted from Tier 3 status on the basis of commitments to progress.

The TIP report is highly controversial in Thailand but also extremely influential. Government agencies are very sensitive to the grading they are awarded and strive to provide positive information to those responsible for its compilation. Thailand has moved up and down several tiers over the past five years. It was originally in Tier 2, moved to the watch list in 2004, and moved back to Tier 2 in 2005. This most recent report justified the promotion with reference to the Government demonstrating that it was making a significant effort to comply with the minimum U.S. standards. In terms of prosecution, the report identified progress in the law enforcement response, including an increase in the prosecution and conviction rate. "Modest progress" was also noted in addressing widespread trafficking-related corruption within criminal justice agencies, although other information in the report did not seem to confirm this. Thailand scored highly in relation to victim protection. According to the report, identification procedures have improved markedly although there are indications that children are not always identified and treated correctly. The report noted that overseas missions provide support to Thai victims returning home. Prevention also ranked highly, with the report noting public information campaigns and government support to NGOs working with victims of trafficking.

It is inevitable in a report of this brevity that there will be many more questions than answers. The following are just a few that come to mind: to what extent can the prosecution figures and those related to action against official corruption (both provided by the police) be independently verified? What is the quality of investigations and prosecutions? To what extent do the practices and procedures related to investigation, prosecution, and punishment meet international criminal justice standards? How can identification of 108 victims in a country with a problem the size of Thailand's be considered adequate or even representative of a significant effort? What about the problem of long-term detention of victims in Thailand? How do official and community attitudes toward migrant workers and women in the sex industry impact on the trafficking phenomenon in Thailand and what is being done about this?

HUMAN TRAFFICKING IN INTERNATIONAL LAW

Human trafficking has been recognized as an international legal issue for well over a hundred years. A number of international legal treaties, focusing particularly on the movement of women and girls for sexual exploitation, were developed in the first half of the twentieth century. Today, at least two of the major contemporary human rights instruments (the Convention on the Rights of the Child and the Convention on the Elimination of Discrimination Against Women) prohibit trafficking and related exploitation.[7] However, the international legal landscape as it applies to trafficking changed forever in December 2000 when representatives from more than eighty countries adopted the Convention against Transnational Organized Crime and its associated Protocol to Prevent, Suppress and Punish Trafficking in Persons, Especially Women and Children.[8] One of the major achievements of the Protocol was the inclusion of a first-ever legal definition of trafficking. Thanks to this treaty, we now know that trafficking is the buying, selling, and movement of persons within or between countries through (in the case of adults) a range of means such as coercion and deception, for the express purpose of exploiting them.

The Trafficking Protocol did not just create a definition. It also set out, in considerable detail, the steps to be taken by State Parties in preventing and dealing with this crime. Some of these are couched in the language of legal obligation. Others, including most of those related to protecting the rights of victims, are more equivocal. Since its adoption, however, the Protocol has been supplemented by a range of international and regional agreements and instruments which, with only a few exceptions, add considerably to our understanding of the "wrong" of trafficking. These include a set of Principles and Guidelines on Human Rights and Human Trafficking introduced to the U.N. Economic and Social Council in 2002,[9] and a European Convention against trafficking adopted in May 2005.[10] Legal and sub-legal agreements have also been concluded at the bilateral and regional levels[11] and many individual countries have developed their own special laws on trafficking. While there is still considerable room for debate and discussion regarding the exact nature and content of the main rules, there can be no doubt as to their existence. International law clearly recognizes a core set of obligations on States in relation to human trafficking. These obligations include the following:

- An obligation to criminalize trafficking;
- An obligation to actively identify victims;
- An obligation to diligently investigate and prosecute trafficking;
- An obligation to protect, support, and provide remedies to victims;
- An obligation to provide special measures for child victims;
- An obligation to actively prevent trafficking; and
- An obligation to cooperate (bilaterally, regionally, and internationally).

The following sections examine the Thai response with a view to making a preliminary determination of the extent to which Thailand is moving toward meeting the international obligations set out above, including the key ones related to criminalization of trafficking and protection of victims. An effort is also made to identify areas where legislative, policy, or other changes could bring Thailand more closely in line with international standards and emerging best practice.

OVERVIEW OF THE THAI
SITUATION AND RECENT RESPONSES

Thailand is a country of origin, transit, and destination for trafficked persons. Thais, particularly women and older girls, are trafficked to Europe, Japan, North America, and Australia, mostly for sexual exploitation through debt bondage. Internal trafficking used to be a problem but today is much less so as Thailand's economic growth has ensured a steady supply of exploitable labor sourced from outside the country. Lao, Cambodian, Chinese, and Burmese nationals are trafficked to Thailand as well as through Thailand to places further afield, including Malaysia. End-purposes of trafficking into Thailand include sexual exploitation, begging, and forced and exploitative labor in factories, agriculture, and fisheries. There is considerable evidence of official complicity and involvement in trafficking to, from, and through Thailand—particularly within the lower levels of law enforcement and immigration control. However, senior Thai public officials, including politicians, police, and military, have also been identified as having commercial interests in the brothels and factories into which many victims are trafficked. Trafficking in and through Thailand is not highly organized and primarily involves loosely connected criminal networks. In the case of trafficking from Thailand, there are strong indications that Thai criminals collaborate closely with foreign criminal syndicates.

Thailand's first exposure to trafficking came in 1984 when five girls who had been trafficked from the north to the south of the country were found chained to steel window bars and burnt to death following a fire in a brothel.[12] The country has since been grappling with the problem of trafficking and has accumulated more experience in this area than many other nations. The first law against trafficking was passed in 1992 and was amended in 1997. A new law, based on the Trafficking Protocol, has been finalized and is expected to pass in late 2005. A network of other laws, including those related to money laundering, prostitution, and migrants' and workers' rights, have been developed to deal with trafficking and related crimes. While prosecutions have been sporadic they have indeed taken place and there is a perceptible trend toward increased and better-prepared cases making it to court. Perhaps more so than any other country of the region, Thailand has been active in identifying and responding to the vulnerabilities of victims, including those who are brought into the criminal justice process. There is a rudimentary system in place to identify victims of trafficking from the huge pools of illegal and undocumented migrants who come to the attention of national authorities. While there are significant gaps and weaknesses, the system does ensure that at least a percentage of victims of trafficking in Thailand are given immediate support and assistance in repatriation. Thailand has been less successful in utilizing victims to investigate and prosecute perpetrators, although it is possible that proposed structural and procedural changes within the relevant law enforcement agencies might improve this situation.

Cooperation and coordination between the myriad organizations working on trafficking in Thailand continue to be a problem here as elsewhere. Responsibilities have been allocated between government agencies on the one hand, and between those agencies and NGOs on the other, but implementation of these agreements remains a problem. The Government has recently begun to take seriously its role as a regional policy leader on the issue of trafficking. Agreements have been concluded with both Lao PDR and Cambodia on the issue of trafficking, focusing particularly on identification and repatriation of victims. Thailand initiated a high-level ministerial process involving all six countries of the Greater Mekong Sub-region (the COMMIT process) and saw it through to the adoption of a landmark Memorandum of Understanding (MOU). Thailand is also playing an important role in promoting and coordinating cooperation between law enforcement agencies within the sub-region. Thailand has signed but not yet ratified the Organized Crime Convention and Trafficking Protocol. It is party to a number of key international human rights instruments, including the Women's Convention, the Convention on the Rights of the Child, and the ILO Convention on the Worst Forms of Child Labor.

Thailand and the Obligation to Criminalize Trafficking

The obligation to criminalize trafficking, as defined above and when committed intentionally, is contained in Article 5 of the Trafficking Protocol. All other international and regional agreements echo this requirement.[13] However, it is also important that States criminalize certain offenses that are related to trafficking, such as debt bondage, forced labor, and child labor. The offense of trafficking will often be very difficult to prove and it is necessary to ensure that traffickers and their accomplices are held responsible for related offenses. Effective criminalization can involve the passing of a special law, but this does not need to be the case.

Thailand's long exposure to the trafficking phenomenon has resulted in a raft of legislative initiatives. A specific law on trafficking in women and children, repealing a 1992 law on the same subject, was passed in 1997 and remains today the main legislative basis for dealing with trafficking.[14] The law prohibits the selling, buying, luring, sending, receiving, procuring, and detaining of women and children to perform sexual acts. It (almost) decriminalizes prostitution and confirms that commercial sex with children under 18 is a crime. The law has two significant weaknesses: it does not cover trafficking in men and fails to recognize that trafficking in and involving Thailand takes place for a range of purposes beyond sexual exploitation.[15] In addition to its specialized law on trafficking, Thailand has criminalized a range of related offenses including slavery and forced labor, child labor, sexual exploitation of children, illegal adoption, forced marriage, forced prostitution, and deprivation of liberty. Many of these laws provide additional protections for children and for stronger penalties when the victim is less than eighteen years of age. Thailand's anti-money-laundering laws allow the relevant agency to trace and seize profits from the crime of trafficking.[16]

On balance, Thailand's legislative framework in relation to criminalization of trafficking and related offences is generally in conformity with international requirements save for the weaknesses identified above. A revised law has been prepared to address these shortcomings and to more generally bring Thailand in line with the requirements of the Trafficking Protocol. This draft is currently under review and is expected to be adopted in late 2005.[17]

Thailand and the Obligation to Actively Identify Victims of Trafficking

The obligation to actively identify victims of trafficking is the foundation upon which all other obligations with respect to victims rests. It is also essential when it comes to investigation and prosecution of traffickers because of the necessarily heavy reliance on victim cooperation and testimony.[18] The obligation is not contained within the Trafficking Protocol but is reflected in both the

European Convention,[19] the Trafficking Principles and Guidelines,[20] and the COMMIT MOU.[21] The Principles and Guidelines explain very clearly why identification of victims is so important and why it is an obligation: "A failure to identify a trafficked person correctly is likely to result in a further denial of that person's rights. States are therefore under an obligation to ensure that such identification can and does take place."

Thailand's relatively longer experience with the trafficking phenomenon, coupled with its position as a major point of destination, could be presumed to be reflected in a relatively advanced approach to victim identification. Unfortunately, this is not always the case. Victims of trafficking in Thailand are most often identified by the non-governmental organizations trawling the major immigration detention centers. The formation of multi-disciplinary counter-trafficking teams in some parts of the country and the development of common operational guidelines for NGOs and government agencies (see section below) has increased official identification rates in some cases. Overall, however, identification of victims of trafficking is rarely the result of any concerted government action or strategy. It is often up to the victim (or her advocate) to prove she was trafficked, and investigative resources are almost never deployed to this end. A similar picture emerges in relation to Thai victims of trafficking abroad. Most of these cases are brought to the attention of the Government through Thai and local victim support agencies that have come across suspected victims in immigration detention. Thai diplomatic missions do not appear to have a proactive approach toward identifying trafficked nationals.

According to the TIP report, 108 new victims of trafficking were identified in 2004. If this figure is correct (and it seems incredibly low) then it is certain that only a very small percentage of total victims in Thailand have been identified. Certainly there is strong anecdotal evidence of individuals exhibiting all the characteristics associated with trafficking being regularly arrested, charged, and quickly deported. Conversely, individuals who do not appear to be victims of trafficking are occasionally "rescued."[22] These problems are no doubt due, at least in part, to a widespread lack of understanding about trafficking (including conflation of trafficking with prostitution and an unwillingness to recognize that trafficking is associated with labor exploitation at least as much as with sexual exploitation). Very few of Thailand's frontline law enforcement agencies most likely to be the first point of contact for a victim of trafficking have received special training in identification and treatment of victims. Criteria or guidelines for determining victim status are being developed but are not yet available.[23]

Thailand and the Obligation to Diligently Investigate and Prosecute Trafficking Cases

The Trafficking Principles and Guidelines declare unequivocally that: "States have a responsibility under international law to act with due diligence to . . .

investigate and prosecute traffickers."[24] This is a reiteration of a basic principle of international law relating to state responsibility for violations of human rights.[25] How does one measure whether a State is taking seriously its obligation to investigate and prosecute? The worst case will naturally be the easiest to decide. A State which doesn't even bother to have a law against trafficking; which fails to investigate *any* cases of trafficking; which fails to protect *any* victims or to prosecute *any* perpetrators when there is reliable evidence available of the existence of a trafficking problem, will clearly not pass the due diligence test. In less egregious cases, it is necessary to evaluate whether the steps taken evidence a seriousness on the part of the State investigate and prosecute trafficking.

Evaluating Thailand's criminal justice response to trafficking is complicated by the fact of it being a country of origin, transit and destination. The way in which Thailand deals with trafficking of its own nationals abroad is significantly different from the manner in which it responds to trafficking and related exploitation of foreigners within its own borders. In relation to trafficking *from* Thailand, investigations are very rarely commenced on the Thai side. Typically, Thai police will respond to requests for information and assistance from foreign governments attempting to investigate cases of trafficking of Thai citizens into their own countries. The consensus view is that such responses are generally adequate, although the vagaries of the Thai criminal justice system will often operate to frustrate operational cooperation on trafficking cases.[26] Trafficking *within* and *into* Thailand is generally not investigated or prosecuted in any systematic or particularly effective way. The Royal Thai Police, with primary responsibility in this area, will usually only act in response to a specific complaint, and the avenue through which the complaint is channeled will generally determine the speed and depth of any subsequent investigation. Cases that are being pushed by the media or by local and international NGO tend to be dealt with quicker and more effectively. High levels of public sector complicity and a general distrust of law enforcement mean that victims are often reluctant to lodge complaints, particularly if they are foreign, illegally present in Thailand, and/or have suffered exploitation in the sex industry.

While rates of victim identification and rescue are improving, Thai authorities seem to find the task of arresting traffickers and their accomplices much more daunting. Police do, however, occasionally arrest exploiters although they have a hard time linking even the worst cases of labor exploitation involving foreign workers to trafficking. The investigation/arrest/ prosecution/conviction ratio, such as it can be relied on, indicates that problems exist throughout the system, including at the level of the prosecutors office and the judiciary.[27] Some innovative structures (such as multi-disciplinary teams comprising police, prosecutors, and health care workers) have been developed to formalize operational level cooperation between different criminal justice and victim support agencies. As noted above, these have resulted in increased identification and rescue of victims. However, they do not seem to have had much impact on prosecutions. In summary, there are relatively few prosecutions given the large number of known and suspected cases and only a small percentage of them result in a conviction. The U.S. TIP report characterization of 307 arrests resulting in 12 convictions during 2004 as being indicative of an improvement in the criminal justice response would seem, on balance, a very kind reading of the situation.

In terms of its task organization, training, and understanding of trafficking, the Thai criminal justice system has a mixed record. Until recently, very little has been done at the level of the prosecutor's office or the judiciary.[28] Thai law enforcement is moving ahead, albeit slowly. A recent restructuring of the RTP has given the go-ahead for the establishment of a specialist trafficking unit within the Crime Suppression Division which will replace the temporary unit currently responsible for dealing with issues relating to women and children. The unit will operate at both central and provincial level and is expected to receive both basic awareness training about trafficking as well as more specialized training in investigative techniques appropriate to this crime. It is likely the establishment of the new unit will give a significant boost to Thailand's current investigative capacities in the area of human trafficking. A final determination on whether Thailand is meeting its obligations in this area will depend heavily on the extent to which this unit is adequately empowered and resourced; whether similar steps are taken in other criminal justice agencies to improve capacities; and whether serious action is taken to fight trafficking-related corruption, especially within criminal justice agencies.

Thailand and the Obligation to Provide Support,
Protection, and Remedies to Victims of Trafficking

The Trafficking Principles and Guidelines require States to: "[E]nsure that trafficked persons are protected from further exploitation and harm and have access to adequate physical and psychological care [which] shall not be made conditional on the capacity or willingness of trafficked persons to cooperate in legal proceedings."[29]

The Trafficking Protocol acknowledges the importance of victim support and assistance, encouraging (but not requiring) States to help victims of trafficking. However, other international, regional, and bilateral agreements on trafficking are much more specific when it comes to obligations toward victims. It is also relevant to note that international law more generally is increasingly recognizing and articulating the rights of victims, particularly those who have been subject to serious violation of their rights.[30] On the basis of this, the following core obligations are proposed as applicable to the State in its dealings with victims of trafficking: (1) protection from further harm; (2) provision of emergency shelter, primary health care, and counseling; (3) assistance with legal proceedings; (4) safe and, where possible, voluntary return; and (5) access to remedies.

Thailand's main trafficking law mandates that victims are not treated as criminals. However, the law is quite vague when it comes to the provision of assistance, protection, and support. Senior police or administrative officials involved in the case are to use their discretion in giving "appropriate assistance" including food, shelter, and repatriation.[31] Internal MOUs and other sub-legal agreements on trafficking confirm the right of victims to immediate assistance and protection.[32] In practice, foreign victims in Thailand (once identified as such) are separated from irregular migrants and sent to one of six designated shelters. These shelters are operated by the Ministry of Social Welfare and generally provide an adequate standard of treatment and care for victims including medical assistance and psychological support. Victims are generally required to remain in the shelter until their case is resolved (i.e., a decision taken on how they are to be sent home). During this time they may be offered the chance to participate in training activities, which aim to equip them with skills that will make reintegration easier and help to prevent re-trafficking.[33] However, it is starting to become apparent that many victims of trafficking in Thailand, especially adult women, are reluctant to use this system, preferring to be identified as legal migrants and quickly deported.[34]

Thai law grants witnesses in criminal cases the right to protection, appropriate treatment, and remuneration.[35] Temporary residency permits are not available in Thailand although victims agreeing to testify can be permitted to remain in the country through a provision of the Immigration Law.[36] There is no possibility for trafficked persons to remain in Thailand once court proceedings are over.[37] In theory, victim identity can be protected and victims have the right to free legal counsel.[38] In practice, criminal justice agencies evidence a disregard for victims' right to privacy, and legal counsel is only ever available through NGOs. Thailand does not have a system for protection of witnesses, and victims of trafficking who agree to cooperate with authorities are often subject to intimidation and reprisals. In such cases, police seem to be both unable and unwilling to provide even basic protection.[39]

Thailand has made some effort to ensure the humane repatriation of victims. A family tracing and assessment procedure is in place and, in theory, should go some considerable way to ensuring safety in the return process. In practice, however, there are few resources and much of this work is left to international organizations and NGOs. Victims languish many months in "shelters" (which they are not allowed to leave) because the tracing and assessment procedures have not been completed.[40] Sometimes mass repatriations occur without any attention to the needs of the victims or the strong possibility of re-victimization.[41] Formal and informal repatriation programs have been concluded with Cambodia, Lao PDR and Myanmar. These work some of the time but are mostly slow, cumbersome and heavily reliant on individual contacts. In a country such as Myanmar, a major point of origin for many victims of trafficking in Thailand, such contacts are extremely difficult to establish and maintain.

In Thailand, victims have the right to sue for compensation from traffickers and exploiters but there is no possibility for a victim of trafficking to link a civil claim for damages to this criminal action. This means that actions for compensation are only possible *after* conviction in a criminal court.[42] A criminal compensation fund exists, but it is small and does not seem to have ever been used for a trafficking case.[43] Both governmental and non-governmental victim support agencies provide legal assistance for recovery of unpaid wages.[44] However, it is not surprising to learn that very few of the already small group of victims who have managed to endure a successful criminal action are willing to stick around even longer to pursue civil compensation claims. Nevertheless, a number of such cases have been successfully concluded over the past few years, although it is not clear whether the legal victory resulted in the repayments ordered by the court actually being made.[45] Another possibility for victims of trafficking is to sue for unpaid wages in the Labor Court. Such actions do not require prior completion of criminal proceedings and have resulted in awards being made to trafficked persons in several cases.[46] Thailand has not been active in pursuing justice for Thai victims who have been trafficked to countries such as Japan and Australia. While the Government will facilitate repatriation in such circumstances, it does not offer legal or other assistance.[47]

Thailand and the Obligation to Provide Special Measures for Child Victims

Children are naturally included in all of the protection and assistance rules and standards set out above. However, it is widely accepted that the particular physical, psychological and psychosocial harm suffered by trafficked children and their increased vulnerability to exploitation requires that they be dealt with separately from adult trafficked persons in terms of laws, policies and programs. This approach is validated by international human rights law, which explicitly recognizes the special position of children and thereby accords them special rights.

What are States required to do as a matter of law when it comes to child victims of trafficking? The core rule is derived from the obligations contained in the Convention on the Rights of the Child to which Thailand is party: in dealing with child victims of trafficking, the best interests of the child (including the specific right to physical and psychological recovery and social integration) are to be at all times paramount.[48] This position, affirmed by the Trafficking Principles and Guidelines, means that States cannot privilege other considerations, such as those related to immigration control or public order, over the best interests of the child victim of trafficking.[49] In addition, because of the applicability of the Convention on the Rights of the Child to all children under the jurisdiction or control of a State, child victims of trafficking are entitled to the same protection as nationals of the receiving State in all matters, including those related to protection of their privacy and physical and moral integrity.

Thailand's efforts in the area of child trafficking have focused on: (1) providing special care and support for child victims of trafficking; (2) preventing trafficking in children; and (3) facilitating the non-harmful involvement of children as witnesses in criminal actions against traffickers. In relation to the first area, child victims of trafficking receive a higher standard of treatment than adults. They are more quickly identified, especially in relation to trafficking for sexual exploitation, due to the lack of any need to prove deception, coercion, or other means. This, coupled with a generally lower level of criminalization, means that child victims of trafficking are brought into the protective ambit of the State much more rapidly. Thailand has developed an impressive array of prevention measures and strategies (see next section) that generally single out child victims for special attention. The legislative framework protecting children is strong with laws prohibiting commercial sex with anyone under 18; child labor; and all trafficking related actions including the buying, selling, movement, and exploitation of children. In relation to the third area, a 1999 amendment to the Thai Criminal Procedure Act provides for a range of measures to protect the rights of children in the criminal justice matters whether as offenders, victims or witnesses.[50] These measures aim to create an environment that is sensitive to the special needs and rights of children. Measures mandated in the Act include the use of video to record statements and deliver testimony; separation of the child from the accused; and the provision of support services to children through a social worker or psychologist. The Act also institutes an "early deposition" procedure permitting the child victim or witness to give immediate testimony even before an arrest has been made. This procedure is claimed to reduce the trauma of court testimony for children and lessen the possibility of corruption (in relation to public officials) and intimidation (in relation to the child and his/her family).[51]

Despite these significant achievements, many trafficked and exploited children still fall through the safety net. Child victims are not always identified as such but are sometimes rounded up in immigration raids and deported before mandated protection and assistance measures can be implemented. Child beggars, most of whom have been trafficked from Cambodia, are a common sight on the streets of Bangkok. While the child sex industry seems to have diminished (or moved far underground), its continuing existence is not denied by Thai authorities. Children who are identified as having been trafficked into Thailand are often detained in government shelters for long periods of time. The length of such detention seems to be related more to administrative and other inadequacies than to the immediate protection and well-being of the child. While the standard of care is usually sufficient, these children do not receive access to education or other benefits on the same basis as Thai nationals as is required under international law.

Thailand and the Obligation to Prevent Trafficking

International law recognizes an obligation of "reasonable and appropriate" prevention on the State in relation to trafficking. The obligation is a consequence of the recognition of trafficking as a violation of human rights law. The obligation of prevention when it comes to trafficking can also be found in all the principal international instruments on trafficking, including the Trafficking Protocol, the European Convention, and the Trafficking Principles and Guidelines.[52] A determination of whether or not a State has met the "reasonable and appropriate" standard of prevention will depend on its individual circumstances and its place in the trafficking chain. A poor country of origin will not need to meet the same standard as a developed country of destination. However, in relation to any State, failure to take known preventive measures when this is both possible and practical should be considered sufficient grounds for establishing a violation of the obligation of prevention.

There is much to criticize about Thailand's response to trafficking when it comes to prevention. Despite being one of the most active and experienced of all countries in this area, Thailand has done very little to address some of the most glaring causes of trafficking. For example, Thailand has failed to provide citizenship and birth registration to ethnic minorities living in the north of the country. This failure greatly increases vulnerability of these minority groups to trafficking and related exploitation.[53] Another example of failure to prevent is Thailand's apparent inability to deal with the issue of trafficked street beggars despite the very public nature of this phenomenon and despite repeated pressure from international agencies and the non-governmental community. Perhaps most important is Thailand's apparent inability to deal with the impact of corruption on trafficking in, through, and from the country, as well as its refusal to acknowledge and explore the implications of high-level public sector involvement in the very lucrative Thai sex industry. While prosecutions for complicity in trafficking and trafficking-related corruption have occurred, these are still rare and tend to target only the minor players. This is a failure in prevention because a properly waged "war on corruption," especially within the police and especially related to the sex industry, would probably do more to prevent trafficking in and through Thailand than anything else.[54] It is also relevant to mention the fact that Thailand has done very little to address the various factors which create and sustain demand for the dirt-cheap labor and highly exploitative sex which in turn drives and sustains trafficking into this country.

In terms of more generic and programmatic prevention measures, Thailand fares much better, not least because of its capacity to promulgate (but not necessarily implement) thoughtful and high-quality policies. A strong policy framework has been developed through a series of national Action Plans (1996, 2003) and three very detailed internal memoranda of understanding (MOUs), which set out common operational guidelines and allocate roles and responsibilities for all aspects of the national trafficking response. The first MOU is for all government agencies and covers procedures for rescue, investigation, and support to victims, as well as the roles of specific departments, ministries, and other entities such as embassies and the police. The second MOU outlines procedures for cooperation between the government and NGOs. The third MOU is between government agencies, intergovernmental organizations, and NGOs and deals with cooperation to combat trafficking in the northern border regions of Thailand. Unfortunately, the conclusion of the MOUs was seen as a victory in itself and the Government is not closely monitoring their implementation. A dedicated bureau has been established within the Social Welfare Ministry to act as focal point for trafficking prevention and victim assistance activities in Thailand. The bureau coordinates a range of prevention activities for Thai women and girls considered at risk of: "being lured into the sex trade."[55] Some work has been done with diplomatic missions in countries where there are suspected to be large numbers of Thai victims of trafficking.[56] On balance, it can be said that Thailand is moving toward but not yet meeting its obligation to prevent trafficking. Much more work needs to go into making sure the fine policies which have been developed are actually put into place. Thailand also needs to accept responsibility for reducing the demand for trafficking—for example, by criminalizing the knowing or reckless use of the services of a victim and by dealing with the corruption which facilitates trafficking into factories and brothels. Thailand also needs to be careful to ensure that its efforts to appear to be doing something about trafficking do not violate the rights of accused persons to a fair trial and to an appropriate sentence if found guilty.[57]

Thailand and the Obligation of Cooperation

In most cases, successful investigation and prosecution of international trafficking cases requires cooperation between national criminal justice authorities. The lack of a tradition of criminal justice cooperation between countries, even those sharing a common border, has been identified in the Trafficking Principles and Guidelines, as a key obstacle to the development of meaningful, effective responses to trafficking. Thus, the obligation to cooperation is directly linked to the obligation to investigate and prosecute trafficking with due diligence—if cooperation does not occur, investigation and prosecution will, in turn, be severely compromised.[58]

Cultural, linguistic, and political differences often work to prevent the development of a habit of cooperation. Even in situations where contacts at the highest levels of government are both frequent and substantive, operational links between governmental agencies (e.g., between national police forces or other parts of the national criminal justice process) tend to be much less developed. Traditional cooperation mechanisms such as mutual legal assistance arrangements, where they do exist, are generally unsuited to the type and quality of collaboration required for successful investigation of trafficking cases. All key legal agreements and policy documents on trafficking recognize the critical importance of international cooperation.[59]

Thailand is at the forefront when it comes to international engagement and cooperation on the issue of human trafficking. Thailand's relatively advanced position reflects, once again, its long-term attention to the trafficking issue as well as an early realization that to be successful, counter-trafficking efforts require substantive engagement with other countries in the region. Thailand has hosted and participated in numerous meetings, workshops, and conferences on trafficking over the past decade. It has developed strong relationships with intergovernmental and international non-governmental organizations working on the issue. It has convinced its neighbors of the value of working together in the identification and safe repatriation of victims. Thai law enforcement agencies have a long history of cooperation with their foreign counterparts. This has recently evolved to include the establishment of operational contacts at both bilateral and sub-regional levels with specialist police units in neighboring countries including Cambodia, Myanmar, and Lao PDR. Mutual legal assistance arrangements in Thailand allow for any country to request assistance in criminal matters from Thailand through diplomatic channels on the basis of reciprocity.[60] As with most other countries, these arrangements with their inevitable delays and complicated administrative requirements do not appear especially geared to the particularities of the crime of trafficking and are reportedly only rarely used in such cases.

Two other achievements stand out. The first is Thailand's initiation of COMMIT. The decision of the Thai Government to lead a highly sensitive process designed to develop a common policy on and approach to trafficking within the six countries of the Greater Mekong Sub-region could not have been an easy one to make. The second achievement is in securing detailed agreements with both Cambodia (2003) and Lao PDR (2005).[61] At the time of its adoption, the MOU with Cambodia was a world-first when it came to bilateral cooperation on the issue of trafficking. Both MOUs allocate responsibilities and establish detailed arrangements on a range of issues in particular related to the treatment and repatriation of victims. They also establish common frameworks of understanding between the two countries by defining key concepts and reinforce an approach to trafficking that emphasizes respect for human rights. While it is too early to provide even a preliminary view on the success of the agreement with Lao PDR, implementation of the Cambodia MOU has, unfortunately, been less than spectacular. Thai authorities have publicly acknowledged the need for awareness raising about the agreement on both sides of the border as well as the development of procedures and practices that are in line with its provisions.[62]

CONCLUSION

In order to determine whether a State is responsible for trafficking taking place within its territory or involving its citizens, it is necessary to evaluate whether all reasonable measures have been taken by that State to prevent and deal with trafficking. From this perspective, the record of Thailand is a mixed one. Certainly, the Government has made some genuine efforts to criminalize trafficking and related exploitation, to investigate and prosecute perpetrators, and to help and protect victims. It has also undertaken a range of prevention measures and has taken the lead in promoting common standards and regional policy development on trafficking. Ultimately, however, much more can be expected from Thailand. An opportunistic and profit-at-all-costs approach to economic development has led to a situation whereby exploited foreign labor and a burgeoning sex industry built on corruption and exploitation are entrenched and, to some degree at least, accepted. The racism and sexism that permit and facilitate this situation often go unchallenged at all levels of government and in most sectors of society. Despite considerable legislative and technical capacity, the Thai criminal justice system has not done enough to prosecute perpetrators, to protect victims, or to uphold their right to a remedy.

These conclusions have been reached through the application of international legal standards that have been accepted by Thailand and, in most cases, developed with its direct input. It is to these standards that Thailand must be held accountable. The assessments of individual countries, even powerful ones, may be important for political and other reasons. They might even push a government to do something that it might not otherwise have bothered with. Ultimately however, lasting change must come from within. Such assessments will therefore never be as significant or as legitimate as a judgment made on the basis of standards to which Thailand itself has voluntarily committed. This is the value and the strength of international law.

NOTES

This paper has been written in the author's private capacity. The views expressed herein are strictly her own. The analysis builds on a model of responsibilities and obligations created by the author in the context of her PhD dissertation at the University of Utrecht. A similar study, of Australia's response to trafficking, has been published as Anne Gallagher, "Human Rights and Human Trafficking: A Preliminary Review of Australia's Response," in *Human Rights 2004: The Year in Review*, ed. Marius Smith, Melbourne: The Castan Centre for Human Rights Law, Monash University, 2005. Another study, this time of Lao PDR's response, will be published in *The Asian and Pacific Migration Journal* in early 2006.

1. 146 Congressional Record, D1168 (Daily ed., November, 2000), [Hereafter: Trafficking Act] Sec.110. The Act also provides that the annual State Department Country Reports on Human Rights Practices are to include a section describing the nature and extent of severe forms of trafficking and, for countries of origin, transit, and destination, an assessment of governmental efforts to combat such trafficking, Sec. 104.

2. For a comprehensive summary of the Act and for citations of the major provisions set out below, see S. Feve and C. Finzel, "Trafficking of People," *Harvard Journal on Legislation* 38 (2001): 283–284.

3. Trafficking Act, Sec. 108.

4. Trafficking Act, Sec. 10(a) A determination to this effect is to be made by the President.

5. Trafficking Act, Sec.110 (d) (1) (B).

6. Committee on International Relations, U.S. House of Representatives, "Testimony of John R. Miller," June 24 2004, http://wwwc.house.gov/international_relations/108/mil062404.htm (11 July 2005).

7. For an overview of international legal developments relating to trafficking, see Anne Gallagher, *Consideration of the Issue of Trafficking: Background Paper* (Advisory

Council of Jurists, The Asia Pacific Forum, 2002), http://www.asiapacificforum.net/jurists/trafficking/background.pdf (11 July 2005).

8. United Nations Convention Against Transnational Organized Crime, adopted 15 November 2000, U.N. GAOR, 55th Sess., Annex 1, Agenda Item 105, at 25, U.N. Doc. A/55/383 (2000), entered into force 29 September 2003, [Hereafter Organized Crime Convention]; Protocol to Prevent, Suppress and Punish Trafficking in Persons, Especially Women and Children, supplementing the United Nations Convention against Transnational Organized Crime, adopted 15 November 2000, G.A. Res. 25, annex II, U.N. GAOR, 55th Sess., Supp. No. 49, at 60, U.N. Doc. A/45/49 (Vol. I) (2001), entered into force 25 December 2003, [Hereafter Trafficking Protocol].

9. Recommended Principles and Guidelines on Human Rights and Human Trafficking, Report of the High Commissioner for Human Rights to the Economic and Social Council, U.N. Doc. E/2002/68/Add.1. [Hereafter: Trafficking Principles and Guidelines].

10. Council of Europe, *Convention on Action Against Trafficking in Human Beings,* Council of Europe Treaty Series 197, 16.V.2005. [Hereafter: European Convention].

11. For example, the *SAARC Convention on Preventing and Combating Trafficking in Women and Children for Prostitution,* adopted by the South Asian Association for Regional Cooperation in January, 2002; and the *Memorandum of Understanding on Cooperation against Trafficking in Persons in the Greater Mekong Sub-region,* adopted on 29 October 2004 by ministerial representatives from Cambodia, China, Lao PDR, Myanmar, Thailand, and Vietnam [Hereafter COMMIT MOU]. This MOU was created through the Coordinated Mekong Ministerial Initiative against Trafficking, known as the COMMIT process. Hence the MOU is referred to as the COMMIT MOU.

12. Saisuree Chutikul and Phil Marshall, *Thailand Country Report on Trafficking in Persons* (Bangkok: Office of the Permanent Secretary, Office of the Prime Minister, Ministry of Social Development and Human Security, 2004), 5. [Hereafter: Thailand Country report].

13. For example, The European Convention, Article 18 and the Trafficking Principles and Guidelines, Principles 12—17 and Guideline 4.

14. "The Measures in Prevention and Suppression of Trafficking in Women and Children Act (1997)" [Hereafter Thai Trafficking Law 1997]. Reproduced in: *Laws Relating to Prevention and Combating Commercial Sexual Exploitation and Trafficking in Women and Children* (undated compilation published by the Bureau of Anti-Trafficking in Women and Children, Department of Social Development and Welfare, Ministry of Social Development and Human Security) [Hereafter Thai Law Compilation].

15. This problem is ameliorated, at least in part, by Sections 282–283 of the Thai Penal Code (reproduced in the Thai Law Compilation, 30–31), which prohibits a range of sexually exploitative acts against men, women, and children. The remaining lacunae therefore relate to trafficking of all persons for purposes other than sexual exploitation.

16. Relevant laws are reproduced in the Thai Law Compilation. See also Thailand Country Report, 12–13.

17. Information obtained by the author from Thai authorities, June 2005.

18. Further on this, see Anne Gallagher, "Strengthening National Responses to the Crime of Trafficking: Obstacles, Responsibilities, and Opportunities," *Development Bulletin,* no. 66 (December 2004).

19. Article 10 of the European Convention requires State parties to make available persons who are trained and qualified in preventing and combating trafficking and to ensure that there is collaboration between different agencies "*with a view to enabling an identification of victims*" (Art. 10.1. emphasis added). The draft Convention also places certain obligations on State parties if there are reasonable grounds to believe that a person has been a victim of trafficking (Art 10.2.). If there are reasons to believe that the victim is a child then there is to be a presumption that the victim is indeed a child (Art. 10.3.).

20. Trafficking Principles and Guidelines, Guideline 2; see also Guideline 11.5.

21. Signatories to the COMMIT MOU commit themselves to: "*Adopting appropriate guidelines and providing training for relevant officials to permit the rapid and accurate identification of trafficked persons*" (COMMIT MOU, para. 8).

22. See: Simon Montlake, "In Thailand: a struggle to halt human trafficking," *Christian Science Monitor* (August 29, 2003) (reporting on raids on brothels in Northern Thailand netting women who rejected identification as victims of trafficking). See also another analysis of the same raids, this time by an NGO working with and for sex workers in Northern Thailand: Empower Chiang Mai, *A report by Empower Chiang Mai on the human rights violations women are subjected to when "rescued" by anti-trafficking groups who employ methods using deception, force and coercion* (Chiang Mai: Empower Chiang Mai, 2003).

23. The Royal Thai Police is currently chairing a working group to develop such criteria: a checklist which can be used by front-line officers and their superiors to determine whether an individual can be provisionally identified as a victim of trafficking and therefore to be placed in a separate stream from the thousands of illegal migrants who are detained and repatriated by Thailand every week.

24. Trafficking Principles and Guidelines, Principle 2, Guideline 2; see also Guideline 11.5.

25. The due diligence standard as it relates to investigation and prosecution is well established in cases of human rights violations. The duty to investigate and prosecute is applicable when there is an allegation of violation by state officials *and* when the alleged perpetrator is a non-State actor.

26. An example is provided by an investigation of a case of trafficking of Thai women to Australia. In 2004, using information and resources provided by the Australian authorities, Thai police arrested a group of suspected traffickers operating out of Bangkok. Those arrested were, however, very quickly granted bail and, at the time of writing (June 2005), are yet to face prosecution.

27. In 2002 there were 504 trafficking-related arrests recorded. These led to 42 prosecutions, 21 of which resulted in a successful conviction with a custodial sentence (Thailand Country report, 14). In 2004, according to the 2005 U.S. TIP Report, the government reported 307 trafficking-related arrests, 66 prosecutions, and 12 convictions. See also, Elaine Pearson, *Human Traffic, Human Rights: Redefining Victim Protection* (London: Anti-Slavery International, 2002), 175–176 (discussing the results of an NGO study into trafficking-related prosecutions during the period 1999–2001 [Hereafter: ASI Victim Protection Study]. Note that one major obstacle to successful prosecution is the release of offenders on bail who subsequently abscond. ASI Victim Protection Study, 176.

28. Although a special office to deal with trafficking and sexual exploitation was recently established within the Office of the Attorney General and the Department of Special Investigations, the new "Thai FBI" has decided to take up high-profile trafficking cases involving a strong transnational element.

29. Trafficking Principles and Guidelines, Guideline 8.

30. Article 68 of the Statute of the International Criminal Court, for example, requires the court to "protect the safety, physical and psychological well-being, dignity and privacy of victims" as well as to permit the participation of victims at all stages of the proceedings as determined to be appropriate. The Statute also includes provisions on reparation, including restitution, compensation, and rehabilitation. The Rome Statute of the International Criminal Court, signed 17th day of July 1998, U.N. Doc. A/CONF.183/9, entered into force 1 July 2002. In April 2005, the U.N. Commission on Human Rights adopted a set of Principles and Guidelines which set out the entitlements of victims of gross human rights violations and serious violations of international humanitarian law to remedies and reparation, the *Basic principles and guidelines on the right to a remedy and reparation for victims of gross violations of international human rights law and serious violations of international humanitarian law*, C.H.R. res. 2005/35, U.N. Doc. E/CN.4/2005/ L.10/Add.11 (19 April 2005).

31. Thai Trafficking Law 1997, Sections 11, 14.

32. For example, the *Memorandum of Understanding (2003) on Common Operational Guidelines for Government Agencies Engaged in Addressing Trafficking in Women and Children*; and the *Memorandum of Understanding (2003) on Operations Between State Agencies and Non-Governmental Organizations Engaged in Addressing Trafficking in Women and Children*.

33. For a more detailed description of the services offered to victims of trafficking in Thailand, see Thailand Country Report, 14–15.

34. "Most [victims] did not [consent to receive recovery services in shelters] because the recovery process took a very long time, as well as the limited nature of the recovery skills, especially psychological recovery. Moreover, the process focused more on children than adult victims and tended to treat women in the same way as children, even though they have different needs for services." Siriporn Skrobanek, "Remarks by Siriporn Skrobanek, Chairperson of the Foundation for Women," *Proceedings from the Chiang Rai Workshop on Human Trafficking, 13–14 May 2004*, (2004) [Hereafter Skrobanek].

35. Constitution of the Kingdom of Thailand (1997), Article 244; Criminal Cases Act (2003), Articles 6,8,10,13,15,17. For an overview of victim and witness protection in Thailand, see *Thailand Country Report to the Eleventh United Nations Congress on Crime Prevention and Criminal Justice, 18–25 April 2005* (2005), 275–276 [Hereafter: Thailand Criminal Justice Report].

36. Thailand Country Report, 15. Note that the Trafficking Act (Section 12) enables victims to provide a preliminary deposition to a prosecutor even if no trafficker has been arrested. This testimony can be used as evidence in a later trial.

37. ASI Victim Protection Study, 178.

38. Thailand Country Report, 15.

39. ASI Victim Protection Study, 179.

40. See further Skrobanek.

41. A recent example is the mass rounding-up and repatriation of roughly 900 Cambodian beggars, the number of whom that were trafficked is unknown (though is likely to have been considerable), which took place in 2003 as part of the Thai Government's clean-up of Bangkok prior to the APEC Summit. See Samantha Brown, "Thailand's capital transformed to impress world leaders at APEC," *AFP*, 13 October 2003; Kate McGeown, "Thailand's Mass APEC Clean-up," *BBC News Online*, 16 October 2003 http://news.bbc.co.uk/1/hi/world/asia-pacific/3182184.stm (08 July 2005).

42. There has been a bill before Parliament for at least three years, which would expand the ability to claim damages through criminal proceedings. Thai Criminal Justice Report, 274 (written and published in 2005) and ASI Victim Protection Study, 181 (published 2002).

43. Further on this fund, see Thailand Criminal Justice Report, 275.

44. Thailand Country Report, 15.

45. See ASI Victim Protection Study, 182.

46. ASI Victim Protection Study, 182

47. Information obtained from non-governmental organizations working with Thai victims of trafficking in Malaysia and Australia. See also, Kinsey Alden Dinan, "Trafficking in Women from Thailand to Japan, the Role of Organised Crime and Governmental Response," *Harvard Asia Quarterly* (Summer, 2002). http://www.fas.harvard.edu (16 June 2005).

48. Convention on the Rights of the Child, G.A. res. 44/25, annex, 44 U.N. GAOR Supp. (No. 49) at 167, U.N. Doc. A/44/49 (1989), entered into force Sept. 2, 1990, Articles 32–39.

49. Principle 10 states, in relation to child victims, that: "[t]heir best interests shall be considered paramount at all times. Child victims of trafficking shall be provided with appropriate assistance and protection. Full account shall be taken of their special vulnerabilities, rights and needs."

50. The Criminal Procedure Amendment Act (No.20) B.E. 2542 (1999). Reproduced in Thai Law Compilation, 33.

51. Sirisak Tiyapan, "Thailand's Experiences in Dealing with Human Trafficking" (paper delivered to the Seventh Annual Conference of the International Association of Prosecutors, London, 8–12 September 2000).

52. Prevention is one of the main purposes of both the Trafficking Protocol (Article 2.1.) and the European Convention, Article 1.1.). The Protocol also contains detailed mandatory provisions on prevention (Articles 9, 11. 12) as does the European Convention (Articles 29, 32). Prevention of trafficking is a strong theme of the Trafficking Principles and Guidelines (Principles 2, 4–6, Guideline 7).

53. Further on the connection between lack of citizenship and trafficking, see Physicians for Human Rights, *No Status: Migration, Trafficking and Exploitation of Women in Thailand: Health and HIV/AIDS Risks for Burmese and Hill Tribe Women and Girls* (Boston: Physicians for Human Rights, 2004).

54. The Thai Government has instituted numerous measures to deal with corruption including laws, policies, new institutions, and programs. For a very detailed overview of these, see Thailand Criminal Justice Report, 118–196.

55. Thailand Country report, 9.

56. Thailand Country report, 9.

57. Thai courts recently (May 2005) found a Cambodian woman guilty of trafficking related offences and sentenced her to 85 years in jail. It is justifiable to question whether this offense was proportionate to the circumstances of the case. This is especially relevant given the fact that the sentence was imposed on a female non-national who was clearly not the major financial beneficiary of the exploitation.

58. Of course, cooperation is crucial in all areas of counter-trafficking, not just in the criminal justice response to trafficking.

59. Trafficking Protocol, Articles 2, 9, 10, 13, Organized Crime Convention, Articles 16 and 18; European Convention, Articles 18, 33, 34; Trafficking Principles and Guidelines, Guideline 11.

60. The basic legal framework is provided by the Act on Mutual Assistance in Criminal Matters B.E. 2535 (1992). Thailand has also concluded bilateral mutual legal assistance treaties with 10 countries. For a detailed analysis of mutual legal assistance arrangements and practices in Thailand, see Thailand Criminal Justice Report, 50–63.

61. The text of both MOUs is available from www.arcppt.org

62. See, for example, Saisuree Chutikul, "The Domestic MOUs and the MOU between Thailand and Cambodia," *Proceedings from the Chiang Rai Workshop on Human Trafficking, 13–14 May 2004* (Thailand, 2004), 240.

BIBLIOGRAPHY

Brown, Samantha. "Thailand's Capital Transformed to Impress World Leaders at APEC." *AFP*, 13 October 2003.

Governments of Cambodia, China, Lao PDR, Myanmar, Thailand and Vietnam. *Memorandum of Understanding on Cooperation against Trafficking in Persons in the Greater Mekong Sub-region*, 2004.

Chutikul, Saisuree, The Domestic MOUs and the MOU between Thailand and Cambodia. Proceedings from the Chiang Rai Workshop on Human Trafficking, 13–14 May 2004 (Thailand, 2004).

Chutikul, Saisuree and Phil Marshall. *Thailand Country Report on Trafficking in Persons.* Bangkok: Office of the Permanent Secretary, Office of the Prime Minister, Ministry of Social Development and Human Security, 2004.

Committee on International Relations, U.S. House of Representatives. "Testimony of John R. Miller, June 24 2004." 2004. http://wwwc.house.gov/international _relations/108/mil062404.htm (11 July 2005).

Council of Europe. *Convention on Action against Trafficking in Human Beings.* Council of Europe Treaty Series 197, 16.V.2005.

Dinan, Kinsey Alden. "Trafficking in Women from Thailand to Japan, the Role of Organised Crime and Governmental Response." *Harvard Asia Quarterly* (Summer 2002). http://www.fas.harvard.edu/ (16 June 2005).

Empower Chiang Mai. A report by Empower Chiang Mai on the human rights violations women are subjected to when "'rescued" by anti-trafficking groups who employ methods using deception, force and coercion. Chiang Mai: Empower Chiang Mai, 2003.

Feve, S., and C. Finzel. "Trafficking of People." *Harvard Journal on Legislation* 38 (2001).

Gallagher, Anne. "Consideration of the Issue of Trafficking: Background Paper." (Advisory Council of Jurists, The Asia Pacific Forum, 2002). http://www.asiapacific forum.net/jurists/trafficking/background.pdf (11 July 2005).

——. "Strengthening National Responses to the Crime of Trafficking: Obstacles, Responsibilities and Opportunities." *Development Bulletin*, No. 66 (December 2004).

——. "Human Rights and Human Trafficking: A Preliminary Review of Australia's Response" *Human Rights 2004: The Year in Review*, ed. Marius Smith. Melbourne: The Castan Centre for Human Rights Law, Monash University, 2005.

McGeown, Kate. "Thailand's Mass APEC Clean-up." *BBC News Online*, 16 October 2003, http://news.bbc.co.uk/1/hi/world/asia-pacific/3182184.stm (8 July 2005).

Montlake, Simon. "In Thailand: A Struggle to Halt Human Trafficking." *Christian Science Monitor* (August 29, 2003).

Pearson, Elaine. *Human Traffic, Human Rights: Redefining Victim Protection*. London: Anti-Slavery International, 2002.

Physicians for Human Rights. *No Status: Migration, Trafficking and Exploitation of Women in Thailand: Health and HIV/AIDS Risks for Burmese and Hill Tribe Women and Girls*. Boston: Physicians for Human Rights, 2004.

Skrobanek, Siriporn. "Remarks by Siriporn Skrobanek, Chairperson of the Foundation for Women." Proceedings from the Chiang Rai Workshop on Human Trafficking, 13–14 May 2004 (Thailand, 2004).

South Asian Association for Regional Cooperation. SAARC Convention on Preventing and Combating Trafficking in Women and Children for Prostitution. 2002.

Government of Thailand. "The Criminal Procedure Amendment Act (No.20) B.E. 2542 (1999)." *Laws Relating to Prevention and Combating Commercial Sexual Exploitation and Trafficking in Women and Children*. Bureau of Anti-Trafficking in Women and Children, Department of Social Development and Welfare, Ministry of Social Development and Human Security, undated.

——. "Measures in Prevention and Suppression of Trafficking in Women and Children Act (1997)" in *Laws Relating to Prevention and Combating Commercial Sexual Exploitation and Trafficking in Women and Children*. Bureau of Anti-Trafficking in Women and Children, Department of Social Development and Welfare, Ministry of Social Development and Human Security, undated.

——. "Penal Code 1956." in *Laws Relating to Prevention and Combating Commercial Sexual Exploitation and Trafficking in Women and Children*. Bureau of Anti-Trafficking in Women and Children, Department of Social Development and Welfare, Ministry of Social Development and Human Security, undated.

——. Thailand Country Report to the Eleventh United Nations Congress on Crime Prevention and Criminal Justice, 18–25 April 2005.

——. Criminal Cases Act. 2003.

——. Memorandum of Understanding (2003) on Common Operational Guidelines for Government Agencies Engaged in Addressing Trafficking in Women and Children. 2003.

——. Memorandum of Understanding (2003) on Operations Between State Agencies and Non-Governmental Organizations Engaged in Addressing Trafficking in Women and Children. 2003.

————. Constitution of the Kingdom of Thailand. 1997.

————. Act on Mutual Assistance in Criminal Matters B.E. 2535. 1992.

Tiyapan, Sirisak. "Thailand's Experiences in Dealing with Human Trafficking." Paper delivered to the Seventh Annual Conference of the International Association of Prosecutors, London, 8–12 September 2000.

United Nations. *The Rome Statute of the International Criminal Court*, signed 17th day of July 1998, U.N. Doc. A/CONF.183/9, entered into force 1 July 2002.

United Nations Commission on Human Rights. Basic principles and guidelines on the right to a remedy and reparation for victims of gross violations of international human rights law and serious violations of international humanitarian law, C.H.R. res. 2005/35, U.N. Doc. E/CN.4/2005/ L.10/Add.11 (19 April 2005).

United Nations Economic and Social Council. Recommended Principles and Guidelines on Human Rights and Human Trafficking. Report of the High Commissioner for Human Rights to the Economic and Social Council, U.N. Doc. E/2002/68/Add.1.

United Nations General Assembly. Convention on the Rights of the Child, G.A. res. 44/25, annex, 44 U.N. GAOR Supp. (No. 49) at 167, U.N. Doc. A/44/49 (1989), entered into force 2 September 1990.

————. *United Nations Convention Against Transnational Organized Crime*, adopted 15 November 2000, U.N. GAOR, 55th Sess., Annex 1, Agenda Item 105, at 25, U.N. Doc. A/55/383 (2000), entered into force 29 September 2003.

————. *Protocol to Prevent, Suppress and Punish Trafficking in Persons, Especially Women and Children, supplementing the United Nations Convention against Transnational Organized Crime*, adopted 15 November 2000, G.A. Res. 25, annex II, U.N. GAOR, 55th Sess., Supp. No. 49, at 60, U.N. Doc. A/45/49 (Vol. I) (2001), entered into force 25 December 2003.

Victims of Trafficking and Violence Prevention Act. 146 Congressional Record, D1168 (Daily ed., November 2000).

From Home to Hell:
The Telling Story of an African
Woman's Journey and Stay in Europe

William A. E. Ejalu

> I believe the trafficking of persons, particularly women and children, for forced and exploitative labor, including for sexual exploitation, is one of the most egregious violations of human rights.
>
> —Kofi Annan, United Nations Secretary General

*G*lobalization influences all societies in various ways and stages and one of the effects for many countries is the internationalizing of crimes and criminal networks. Human trafficking is one of the transnational crimes showing a drastic increase by taking advantage of this globalization.

The central theme of this paper is the trafficking of women and children from West Africa to Europe. This is of vital importance because few scholars, organizations, and institutions in Europe consider the trend of trafficking people from Africa and the plight of African victims in Europe in their prevention, assistance, or prosecution discussions. Most of the attention is directed toward the victims from Europe, especially Eastern and Central Europe. Victims of trafficking from Africa or Asia are regarded as illegal migrants rather than victims of trafficking. The use of the African woman's journey to Europe is symbolic of all victims within and/or coming from the continent.

Trafficking in humans is modern-day slave trade that exists within Africa, both internal (within a country's borders) and external (within Africa), meaning that as well as a being a continent of origin, Africa is also a place of transit and destination. Manipulative methods such as violence, coercion, and deception are common practices used to lure victims into prostitution, pornography, and various forms of forced labor, and recently, unknowing to parents, children end up being sacrificial lambs in centuries-old primitive voodoo practices, while babies are meant for adoption.

The failure to curtail this trade could be attributed to political, social, economic, cultural, and legal attitudes in the countries involved. Most communities do not openly consider this a problem due to existing taboos, social stigma attached to prostitution, and social roles of women and children. It is important to note that although international law does protect women and children from exploitation, this issue is more than a legal problem. It is a political, social, economic, cultural, environmental, educational, and developmental phenomenon.

International conventions make the trafficking of humans unlawful and punishable; however, these conventions are difficult to implement and monitor. While governments are able to ratify these conventions, they are not required to have any national laws relating to specific legislation.[1] It is a shame to humanity itself that, in the new era of human rights ushered in immediately after World War II, we still have to contend with such flagrant disregard of the prescribed rights. Unfortunately, few countries have the political will, national legislation, and/or well-developed and effective legal structure and institutions to combat the trade, thereby making it an uphill task to prosecute the trafficker/s and eradicate this horrendous crime. Ibolya David, former Minister of Justice in Hungary between 1998 and 2002, expressed her disappointment, stating, "The common man would be surprised, that, today, at the end of the twentieth century, 73 years after the Treaty Abolishing Slave Trade was signed, we in the middle of Europe still talk of trafficking in women, a modern type of slave trade."[2]

Most trafficking victims are not aware that they have legal protections through the existence of these conventions and laws. But, trafficking will not be eradicated by simply passing legal instruments; respect for human rights is paramount in the struggle to end trafficking of humans between countries by promoting improved attitudes toward humanity and higher standards of living.

THE BUSINESS

Trafficking in humans is widely spread and very lucrative through an illicit business that gives a higher tax-free income to the perpetrators. The proceeds are diverted to other illegal and/or legitimate ventures (money laundering). To the innocent victim, it is a very dangerous and life-threatening experience. Victims of trafficking forced into prostitution and other forms of forced labor usually are not protected by national laws of the countries they find themselves residing in, as they are living illegally in that country and the fear or threat of deportation or imprisonment prevents them from going to the authorities for assistance. At times, when they do approach the authorities for help, law enforcement appears eager to consider them as illegal aliens rather than victims of trafficking.

According to Human Rights Watch, local officials often ignore or are complicit in trafficking. It is commonplace for government officials in some countries to accept bribes from traffickers, help provide false documentation, and patronize brothels linked to trafficking rings, at times being directly involved in the trade.

Some corrupt policemen and border guards have been known to facilitate the smooth movement of human cargo within the borders and at the border crossings of the transit countries in collaboration with the traffickers and/or contacts. This is attributed mainly to low salaries and lack of morale, and, in addition, local police often fear reprisals from criminal gangs.

Most cases of trafficking in persons are usually coordinated by organized crime rings or networks of criminals made up of family and associates. These are well-organized hierarchical groups with the money and resources to enable them to bribe, corrupt, and/or intimidate border guards, police, etc. They have representatives or contacts in various areas and countries and include the Chinese and other Asians, and Mexican, Central American, Russian, and former Soviet Union gangs. The United Nations has identified Albanian gangs involved in trafficking as being "particularly ferocious."

Although large crime rings are common, a single person or a few persons may also orchestrate a trafficking operation. There is also growing evidence that small groups of individuals, friends, asylum seekers and refugees, coordinating with one another, are deeply involved in the moving and transporting of women and children from West Africa to Europe. During the course of my research, I found the majority of these people either failed to get employment or were stranded in 'transit' countries of Central and Eastern Europe (i.e., Hungary, Romania, Ukraine, and Russia) and forced to engage in illegal activities to sustain themselves. They contact persons in their countries of origin, convincing them to embark on a journey to the unknown with grandiose stories of "Europe, a land of opportunity," with an understanding that a fee is to be paid for their assistance. Human rights organizations and human rights activists, generally those founded by native Africans, former asylum seekers themselves, are also involved in the trafficking of women from Africa. A majority of the women being trafficked by fellow Africans illegally enter Hungary or any other transit country. If or when they are arrested, these organizations are contacted and paid a fee for their assistance by the traffickers or their contacts to get the women released from detention. After their release, the women continue their journey to Italy, Germany, or The Netherlands.

A UNICEF report states that intermediaries may include recruiters, transporters, hotel clerks, police officers, government officials, brothel owners, pimps, neighbors, and relatives, including mothers and fathers. Family members will take all the necessary measures to have their next of kin and relatives join them in Europe including the paying of smugglers or traffickers to help them achieve this goal.

Some citizens unaware of trafficking innocently issue, assist, or help acquire official invitation letters to help African friends whom they have met in Hungary, not knowing that some of these people are not inviting relatives but generating an income for themselves from slave labor. Still others—international train and bus drivers who assist in the secret transporting of the victims and university employees who admit a large number of applicants for a basic fee, knowing that the applicants will not attend the school but will use the opportunity to acquire a visa to one of the transit countries before continuing on to West Europe illegally—are fully aware of that they are involved with traffickers.

Traffickers have found a multitude of ways to smuggle their victims into a country. While many enter on foot, a number of the cases have their travel abroad facilitated by the traffickers who provide visas, passports (often forged), and airfare. In making these arrangements, traffickers force a commitment that obligates victims to a "contract" or bondage. Often, the victims have paid a fee to travel and know that they are entering countries illegally but believe that they will be free once they arrive. Other traffickers obtain valid visas for their victims who then overstay the given time of stay.

Upon arriving in the destination country, traffickers typically confiscate their victims' documents and force their victims to remain in servitude until their contract—which can be tens of thousands of dollars—is paid off. During such servitude, victims often incur more debt because traffickers will frequently charge them for necessary expenses like food, rent, and visits to the doctor. Thus begins an endless cycle of debt and bondage.

FORMS OF RECRUITMENT

The most common form of recruitment for the majority of the victims in West Africa is the personal approach: recruiters and traffickers take advantage of the trust bestowed on them to impress and manipulate a person known to them such as a family member, neighbor, former schoolmate, or boyfriend. In the case of children, the person is always well known to the family. The promises include providing a better future for the child by paying for school tuition and remitting some money to the family at home. For children without families, such as the former child soldiers in war-torn countries already experiencing problems leading a normal life, the promises are levied directly to the child.

Many times unsuspecting victims are approached by a stranger at a public place, either a disco or any other communal gathering place. A friendship is created and the stranger is always kind and helpful and ultimately catches the future victim unaware by offering help in securing a job and a chance for better opportunities abroad. To most of the future victims, this is a dream come true.

Advertisements aimed at young and desperate women in local newspapers, on the radio, and the Internet are common. While the Internet is fast becoming widely used for trafficking, the radio is still an effective tool of communication in Africa due to its nationwide audience. A contact address and/or telephone number is given to those who might be interested in working overseas as domestic servants, baby sitters, and other similar jobs. A disadvantage of the technological age is that after contact is made between the recruiter/traffickers and the victim, it is difficult to provide evidence against such a contact because they have never met in person and e-mail addresses may be changed to prevent being tracked by law enforcement.

TARGET GROUPS

Trafficking in humans is a heinous crime and the ever-increasing involvement of women and children, who are the most vulnerable because they can be easily threatened, coerced, and manipulated, should be condemned. According to Rima Salah, the UNICEF Regional Director for West and Central Africa, children and women trafficking in Africa is very complex. This reality goes beyond the abuse of traditional deployments or migration for labor. It represents a major paradox of our time, especially for children, where our society agrees that children are the most valuable natural resource, yet they are being plundered through exploitative labor and trafficking; where adults agree that children should be given first priority but most economic and political decisions are made without childhood in mind; and where most families believe those children must be given the best start in life, but children are at a greater risk for poverty than any other societal group.[3]

Victims of trafficking can be either gender. However, the overwhelming majority of victims are female and children. Gender discrimination, poverty, war, and/or abuse drive millions of women and girls to migrate for work, marriage, or to escape untenable situations.[4] Europol has identified the three types of women who are recruited into the sex industry each year:

- Exploited women who have a low level of education, previously worked in the sex industry in their home country, and have been recruited for similar work in a EU country. These women have often approached the traffickers to arrange travel and are aware that they will be working in the sex industry. However, on their arrival, the exploitation begins when they discover they have been deceived into working under slave-like conditions with little chance of keeping the money they earn.

- Those who have been deceived. These women have been recruited to work in the service/entertainment industry through seemingly legitimate employment agencies, advertisements in the media or on the Internet. These women have more ambition and education than the first group of women, so they are willing to take the risk to travel to an unknown country in order to escape the lack of opportunity back home. These women have absolutely no idea that they will be working in the sex industry.

- Those who have been kidnapped, who form the smallest group. These women may have already been working in the sex industry but have no intention of going abroad. Europol reported that this last group of women "remain the chattels of their owners and are often sold amongst networks or individual pimps—sex slaves in the truest sense of the word." In addition, there are alarming reports of young women kidnapped from Kosovan refugee camps and trafficked to the West.[5]

CAUSES FOR TRADE IN HUMANS

Causes for this inhumane trade for sexual and labor exploitation must be determined to create effective and efficient solutions. Attention should not, however, be directed only at the perpetrators, as in more than 50 percent of the cases, the victim plays a vital and conscious role, not only in her own case, but in convincing more people from her home area to embark on the journey while being fully aware of what conditions await the new victims.

Poverty

Poverty is acclaimed to be the major incentive in forcing people to move to other countries in search of employment and to better their lives. The belief that urban areas and certain countries offer better economic opportunities is a vital convincing point when it comes to making the decision to embark on the journey to the unknown. During the colonial era, the imperialist countries managed to successfully implant on the African masses that Europe was better than Africa and offered more opportunities. Unfortunately, many people deep in the African countryside are still influenced by this belief. This misconception of Europe and the white world leads uninformed and misinformed persons to partake this grueling journey in hopes of a better life and more money. Many times, without any skills, knowledge of languages, or education, they fall into an environment facing massive unemployment. It would be an understatement and a misrepresentation of the facts, if one stated that poverty alone is responsible for trafficking of women and children.

A UNCHCR Report on the Sale of Children, Child Prostitution and Child Pornography submitted by Mr. Vitit Muntarbhorn, Special Rapporteur, in accordance with Commission on Human Rights Resolution 1993/82, had the following findings: poverty was cited by many sources during the year as a key cause of the exploitation of children. While this is true to some extent, in the opinion of the Special Rapporteur, "poverty cannot be accepted as a pretext and justification for the exploitation of children, which may damage children physically and mentally. Moreover, the poverty argument fails to take into account other elements, which lead to the sale of children, child prostitution and pornography." Poverty relates to the supply side of the problem but it does not explain the huge global demand of customers from rich countries that circumvent their national laws to exploit children in other countries. Sex tourism has spread to all parts of the globe and is compounded by the criminal networks that benefit from the trade in children, and, by collusion and corruption in many national settings. Thus, poverty alone does not lead to the exploitation of children; other factors, such as the role of customers and criminality help facilitate the demand.

The strain of economic development policies on the population also contributes to this trade in humans. In many developing and transition countries, new development policies being enacted by the governments have led to mass unemployment and rising costs of living, and a drop in purchasing power is forcing people to move abroad in search of a better life. Many of these persons end up in the hands of smugglers or traffickers. With "increasing economic hardship, particularly in developing and transitional countries, onerous obstacles to legal migration and serious armed conflict have coincided with a rise in the number of trafficking cases as well as a spreading of the problem to areas which were previously less affected."[6]

Lack of Education

Lack of education plays a vital role in this trade in humans. The uneducated and illiterate are a very vulnerable group, easily convinced, and believe the only way to better their lives and those of their families is to look for employment in urban areas and in other countries. The majority of the women from West Africa that I have had the opportunity to talk to during the course of my research are illiterates and can only communicate in their native languages and at times in colloquial/broken English, a common language in most parts of West Africa. Those who can communicate in English have only elementary skills. Most of the time, the victims proved to be very uncooperative due to threats and manipulation by traffickers.

Urbanization and Centralization of Educational and Employment Opportunities

Often due to lack of educational facilities in the rural areas, parents are forced to send their children to relatives and friends in the towns and cities, so that they may have the opportunity to attend school there. At times, these children are sent to work as domestic servants, with the promise that besides the parents getting a monthly remuneration for parents, the child would be sent to school. This behavior is based on a common tradition in many African societies under which financially incapable parents entrust the welfare of their children to wealthier relatives and friends. On the other hand, the difficulty in securing employment in the rural areas forces many women to move to urban areas in search of jobs, which also makes them vulnerable to trafficking.

Cultural Thinking and Attitude

Societies exist, especially in Nigeria, where ownership of money, property, and wealth is deemed to be of the highest importance. Success and prestige in such localities is measured in terms of possessions, regardless of how such possessions are acquired. With promises of wealth, most families send at least one member of the family abroad to work so that in return he/she can help the family. In such areas, what one does for a living is not an issue, but rather how much the families' wealth is compared to that of their neighbors/friends.

Traditional Practices

Age-old traditional practices such as forced and early marriages to elder persons that violate the rights of women have forced young girls to flee from their villages without any means to support themselves and make them extremely vulnerable to traffickers. On meeting with traffickers or their emissaries, these desperate girls are easily tricked into believing they are being offered legal and decent employment. According to the 2003 Report on Trafficking in Human Beings, Especially Women and Children, by the United Nations Children's Fund (UNICEF), it is estimated that 49 percent of the girls were married under the age of 19 years in West Africa. The average age of a first marriage in Niger is 15 years and is 17 years in Nigeria.

Domestic Violence

Domestic violence against women and children is very common in African societies. This also forces the victims to escape to the urban areas, hence making them vulnerable to manipulation by traffickers.

Corruption

Corruption is a contributing factor to the influx in this trade leading to an increase in moral decay and has promoted two major financial fraud crimes in Nigeria, locally referred to as "419," "Black Money,"[7] and human trafficking and smuggling. Decades of military rule, government mismanagement, and unbalanced regional development have also played a major role in human trafficking.

Conflicts

Civil, tribal, and religious conflicts force people to move from their homes, creating thousands of refugees and displaced people. Many are forced to participate in dubious work in order to earn a living. The uncertainty caused by the forced movements, along with the previous mentioned causes, contributes greatly to the raise in the number of potential victims of trafficking in women and children. For example, in post-conflict areas such as Sierra Leone and Liberia, where the number of child victims is on the increase, former child soldiers can easily be influenced with the promises of a better life in another country. In Nigeria, this is evident in territories facing religious skirmishes, forcing parents to send their children away to safety, increasing the chances of the children being preyed upon by traffickers.

Difficulty in Acquiring Visas

The difficulty in acquiring visas to developed countries has helped create a fertile environment for those already resident in Europe to profit from the situation of those wanting to travel and willing to pay large sums of money to acquire fake documents, use another person's documents, or obtain an invitation letter. Tightened border controls and the difficulty in migrating legally force the victims to turn to traffickers.

ROUTES

The choice of the routes to be used depends on how easy it is to enter a given country due to lack of complications in securing a visa, laxity in security at the port of departure, cost of the air tickets, the ability to bribe airline employees, and the effectiveness of monitoring and border control. Great Britain, Italy, The Netherlands and Germany are the main destinations for children and babies who travel directly to the country of destination with women who have the names of children included in their passports and made easier due to the fact that the passports do not contain children's photos. A majority of the women travel to Europe via Russia, Serbia, and Ukraine using valid visas and then are transported illegally through Romania directly to Hungary. If they are not apprehended while trying to reach Hungary and travel arrangements can be made quickly, they are then transported to the main European Union destination countries such as Italy via Slovenia or Austria.

CASE STUDIES

The following cases illustrate how the trade is conducted. The names used are not the true names of the victims, to hide their identity:

Mary

Mary was a resident of a small trading center in Nigeria who wanted a better life but was illiterate with no formal education. Following a couple of cordial meetings with an acquaintance she met from the city, where they exchanged views and experiences about life, the acquaintance told Mary that she would be able to help her get a job as a baby-sitter or domestic servant through a very good friend in Europe. This sounded like a dream come true for Mary and she would be able to assist her family at home. The acquaintance proved to be someone she could trust and very helpful, even lending Mary the money needed to acquire a passport. On getting the passport, the passport number and Mary's personal details were sent to a contact in Budapest, Hungary, who procured an official invitation as a tourist for Mary. The invitation letter was forwarded to the contact in Nigeria via DHL (this is a commonly used media) who, after receiving it, escorted Mary to the Hungarian Embassy to apply for the visa. The acquaintance helped Mary pay part of the airfare and members of the family loaned her the rest. Three months after their first meeting, Mary flew to Hungary via Bucharest, Romania, and was met by another contact person who happened to be a Nigerian. After warning her to be careful when talking to strangers, he requested her passport on the pretext that he was going to get her a visa to Italy, which she had been told was the destination country where a job had been secured for her. After three days, she was told that she could not get a visa because she is not a resident in Hungary, but the contact said that he had solved the problem and someone would take her to Italy via Slovenia. He added that he was doing this because of his good friendship with the contact in Nigeria and considering a lot of money had already been spent, they would do anything to help a sister in need. The following night she was handed over to two persons and told that she would receive her passport when she arrived in Italy. A week later in Italy, Mary's dream did not come true. Instead, she found the beginning of a tragic experience and fear of the shame it would bring to the family. She knows no one would believe her story, for the acquaintance is well respected and a very helpful person in his community. With nowhere to go and no documentation, she waits for a miracle to save her.

Jane

Jane's story more or less follows the same pattern except that, in her case, she knew that she was going to work as a prostitute. What she did not know was that any income she made would not be for her but was going to benefit someone else. With the help of her contacts, she managed to get a visa to Ukraine and from there she was taken illegally to Hungary where she was arrested after crossing the border with a couple of other people. On the advice of the handlers, she applied for asylum. During this process, she was transferred to a center in Debrecen in Hungary. She contacted the traffickers and was taken to Italy via Slovenia. On arriving, she found herself burdened with debts and forced to work as a prostitute for a Nigerian "madam." She faces constant beatings and is treated as a slave.

Brenda

Brenda's story is different in that she left willingly to better her chances in life and was promised a job as a baby-sitter. She also went through Ukraine and Hungary and underwent the same experiences. A major difference is that although she paid smugglers with her own money, she never realized until she got to Italy that the smugglers had discreetly sold her off to a gang involved in prostitution and drug trafficking. In Hungary, she left the detention center on medical grounds with the help of a human rights activist who had been contacted earlier and paid for his services by the traffickers. She spent a couple of nights with the activist before being picked up by the traffickers. She never knew the activist had been paid by the traffickers and said she was even forced into having sex with him in order to show her gratitude. Arriving in Italy, she realized she had been deceived and had two choices, work as a prostitute or pay back the money paid for her with interest. Since then she is trying to pay back the money with her body.

THE LAW

International Law

Trafficking in human beings is an infringement of various specific rights besides general human rights as embodied in the Universal Declaration of

Human Rights. It abrogates the rights of women, children, and workers to mention a few. International law portrays the willingness of the international community to safeguard and protect human rights, both general and specific. The Preamble of the Universal Declaration of Human Rights refers to "recognition of the inherent dignity and of equal and inalienable rights of all members of the human family" as "the foundation of freedom, justice and peace in the world." However, the international community needs the co-operation of States to realize its goals *vis-à-vis* the protection and promotion of the various rights.

International conventions make the trafficking of human beings unlawful; however, these conventions are difficult to implement and monitor. Governments are able to ratify conventions but are not required to have any national laws relating to specific legislation.[8] Trafficking of humans is at times referred to as modern-day slavery, and recently, the Statute of the International Criminal Court included enslavement as a crime against humanity[9] as defined in Article 7(2c).[10]

The implementation and monitoring of international conventions is problematic and inefficient since, although the majority of the State Parties have signed and ratified the instruments, they do not have national legislation criminalizing and combating the trafficking in persons. Article 35[11] of the Convention on the Rights of the Child (1989) leaves the responsibilities of creating measures to the State Parties. In most of the countries, trafficking in persons is not considered as a separate crime. Under existing German law, only trafficking for sexual exploitation is deemed as "trafficking" under Articles 180b and 181 of the German Penal Code. Other forms of exploitation linked to trafficking, such as forced labor, are not considered in these articles but are penalized under other regulations.[12]

As far as forced labor and inhumane working conditions, especially where children are concerned, the International Labor Organization has played a fundamental role in spearheading the protection of children. The Organization in its Declaration on Fundamental Principles and Rights at Work calls for the elimination of forced and compulsory labor and the complete abolition of child labor. These prohibitions can be found in many other international and regional human rights instruments.

Human trafficking is a transnational crime; therefore, to eliminate the trade, there has to be cooperation across borders among the various national enforcement agencies. The Protocol to Prevent, Suppress and Punish Trafficking in Persons, Especially Women and Children is a wide-ranging international agreement to address the crime of trafficking in persons, especially women and children, on a transnational level. It creates a global language and legislation to define trafficking in persons, assist victims of trafficking, and prevent trafficking in persons. The trafficking in persons protocol also establishes the parameters of judicial cooperation and exchanges of information among countries and is intended to jumpstart national laws and harmonize regional legislation against the trafficking in women and children.[13] At the moment, national law enforcement agencies do not have jurisdiction beyond their borders. Although human trafficking is a widespread problem, unfortunately, there is no international instrument specifically dealing with that crime and most of the time it is intertwined with organized crime and other crimes like prostitution and child prostitution.

The following Article illustrates that although the title of the concerned convention mentions trafficking, it was aiming at eradicating prostitution and other connected crimes in conjunction with trafficking of humans:

> The Parties to the present Convention agree to punish any person who, to gratify the passions of another: Procures, entices or leads away, for purposes of prostitution, another person, even with the consent of that person; Exploits the prostitutions of another person, even with the consent of that person.[14]

The failure of the international community, at that time, to draft a treaty specifically on human trafficking shows the lack of recognition or understanding that it is a separate crime deserving special attention. The attachment of trafficking of humans to other crimes makes it difficult to punish the perpetrators, as it basically means that separate treaties must be drawn up for the different aims of trafficking. The 1949 Convention for the Suppression of the Traffic in Persons and the Exploitation of the Prostitution of Others, a consolidation of four[15] earlier treaties, does not define trafficking but aims solely at trafficking for the purpose of prostitution as found in its Article 1.[16]

Trafficking in children is a global problem affecting a large number of children. Some estimates indicate as many as 1.2 million children being trafficked every year for cheap labor and sexual exploitation. Italy is a common destination for trafficked women and children from Nigeria. Between 60 percent and 80 percent of girls involved in the sex trade in Italy are Nigerian children with an average age of 15.[17] Children and their families are often unaware of the dangers of trafficking, believing that better employment and lives exist in another country.[18] Specific prohibition in trafficking of children is found under several international conventions: The 1956 Supplementary Convention on the Abolition of Slavery, the Slave Trade and of Institutions and Practices Similar to Slavery; the 1989 Convention the Rights of a Child; the Optional Protocol to the Convention on the Rights of the Child on the Sale of Children, Child Prostitution and Child Pornography; the Organization of African Unity's African Charter on the Rights and Welfare of the Child; the International Labor Organization Convention C182 on the Worst Forms of Child

Labor of 1999; and the Protocol to Prevent, Suppress and Punish Trafficking in Persons, Especially Women and Children, supplementing the UN Convention against Transnational Organized Crime.

The Convention on the Rights of a Child, Article 34,[19] pays attention to the protection of children from this inhuman and degrading treatment. A number of countries have directly adapted the convention in their national legislation. To widen the scope of protections for the children, the international community in 2000 introduced an Optional Protocol to the Convention on the Rights of the Child on the Sale of Children, Child Prostitution and Child Pornography. This Optional Protocol is not yet in force; however, it shows the willingness of the United Nations and its Member States to put an end to the exploitation of children. The Protocol diverts from the Convention by explicitly requesting member states to partake the given responsibilities.[20] In the Convention, the states "undertake" to protect—which is a promise to take the necessary measures possible and available to protect the rights embodied in the Convention. This crime does lead to the infringement of various specific rights, most notably, the rights of women and children. Children,[21] by reason of their physical and mental immaturity, need special safeguards and care, including appropriate legal protection, before as well as after birth.[22] In Article 6 of the Convention on Elimination of Discrimination Against Women, the international community calls upon the State Parties to take all appropriate measures, including legislation, to suppress all forms of traffic in women and exploitation of women for prostitution, further evidence that special attention must be made to protect women and children.

The Convention on the Rights of the Child spells out basic human rights that children have without discrimination. These rights include: the right to survival; to develop to the fullest; to protection from harmful influences, abuse and exploitation; and to participate fully in family, cultural, and social life. Subsequently, the drafters of the Covenant of the League of Nations deemed trafficking of such significance that they included "general supervision over the execution of agreements with regard to the trafficking in women and children" within the League's mandate. Under the auspices of the League of Nations, both the 1921 Convention for the Suppression of Traffic in Women and Children and the 1933 International Convention for the Suppression of the Traffic in Women of Full Age, were included. The 1921 Convention called for the prosecution of persons who trafficked children, the licensing of employment agencies, and the protection of women and children who immigrate or emigrate. The 1933 Convention required States Parties to punish persons who trafficked women of full age, irrespective of the women's consent.[23]

In a comparison of the different regions of the world, Europe, under the auspices of the European Union and the Council of Europe, provides the most advanced legal protection system to the victims and has taken credible steps in stopping the illegal trade. This does not mean that enough has been achieved. A Communication from the Commission to the Council and the European Parliament: Combating Trafficking in Human Beings[24] was issued to strengthen the fight against the exploitation of persons. Article 2 of the Communication deems it irrelevant as to whether the victim give his/her consent or not. The same is stated in the Trafficking in Persons Protocol in its Article 3b.

The Southern Asian countries under the auspices of the Southern Asian Association for Regional Cooperation (SAARC) have taken steps forward by drafting a convention aimed at preventing and combating trafficking in women and children for prostitution. Under the convention, State Members emphasize the need to cooperate to eliminate this heinous crime and at the same time provide the necessary and needed assistance, rehabilitation, and repatriation for the victims, an objective also being promoted by and within the European Union.

A Council Directive on the short-term residence permit issued to victims of action to facilitate illegal immigration or trafficking in human beings who cooperate with the competent authorities was issued in 2002. This directive aims at curbing illegal immigration, especially in its two odious forms: the smuggling of and trafficking in human beings. It introduces a short-term residence permit to be issued to victims who are willing to cooperate with the relevant authorities to bring the perpetrators of these crimes to justice.[25] On 25 March 2003, the European Commission (EC) adopted a decision to set up an Experts Group on Trafficking in Human Beings, in accordance with the recommendations of the Brussels Declaration endorsed in September 2002 at the European Conference on Combating and Preventing Trafficking in Human Beings. This consultative body is to develop new trafficking policies, strategies, and initiatives in the field of protection, prevention, law enforcement, and judicial cooperation.

Trafficking in human beings as defined by EU law is not only a crime aimed at the sexual or labor exploitation of persons, but mainly at the sexual exploitation of women and children and a fundamental violation of human rights. The Charter of Fundamental Rights of the European Union declares: "Trafficking in human beings is prohibited."[26] Others view trafficking in humans as a modern type of slavery and slave trade whose definitions we find in Article 1 of the Slavery Convention of 1926.[27] Article 4 of the Universal Declaration of Human Rights prohibits the same[28] and so does Article 8(1)[29] of 1966 International Covenant on Civil and Political Rights, while the International Criminal Court Statute includes enslavement as one of the crimes against humanity in Article 7(1c). Article 4 of the European Convention on Human Rights prohibits slavery and forced labor.

Depending on the region, there are various reasons for the trafficking of women and children as previously discussed in this chapter, including sexual and labor exploitation, and for voodoo[30] and other related practices. In my research, I have not found an international legal instrument or national legislation penalizing someone for trafficking in humans for voodoo practices. Such crimes are always considered under the crime of murder, thus, the importance of elevating human trafficking to be a crime of its own.

Another problem faced is that, in most of the cases, trafficking is intertwined with illegal migration and prostitution. Most countries have legislation against human smuggling[31] but not on human trafficking. Some countries, such as Russia, lack the concept of human trafficking, so basically this means that trafficking is not punishable in these countries. In incidences where there is an arrest, the law enforcement authorities always refer to the alien's law, which is disadvantageous to the victims, considering that most of the times they entered the country illegally. Although Latvia provides for criminal responsibility for a person who violates the regulations on prostitution, it lacks specific measures against trafficking in women. Elements against trafficking in women can be found in sections of the Latvian criminal code aimed at forced prostitution, pimping, and incapacitation of a person's freedom.

Since the late 1990s, a majority of the European countries, under the auspices of the Council of Europe, have incorporated trafficking in humans as a criminal offence into the national criminal codes. Hungary incorporated the offence into its criminal code in 1998 and it came into force on 1 March 1999. According to this new law, Section 175/B (1),[32] the crime is now punishable with up to three years of imprisonment, and, in cases where a minor is the victim, the period of imprisonment is from one to five years. Paragraphs 2, 3, 4, 5, and 6 give the different levels under which imprisonment is longer. These include the age and situation of the victim, type of criminal act involved, and the organizational structure of the perpetrators. This does not necessarily mean that the enforcement institutional system has been overhauled to meet the new challenges and requirements, as there is a shortage of trained professional staffs to specifically handle such cases.

Unfortunately, the Hungarian legislation does not provide for assistance and integration for the victims as, for example, in Italy and Holland. Besides imposing penalties on the perpetrators, Italian legislation provides for assistance and integration of the victims, if and when they cooperate with the law enforcement authorities. This includes the issuing of a special six-month resident permit.[33] In accordance with this provision, a six-month permit that is renewable after one year is issued to foreigners who are victims of human trafficking if they contact the authorities and there is proof that they are subject to violence and/or experience severe exploitation. The mode of exploitation could be either sexual or labor. With this permit, the victims have access to assistance services, education, and the ability to be included on the employment lists and gain employment. This decree has the same purpose and goals as the Council Directive for the short-term residence permit issued to victims of action to facilitate illegal immigration or trafficking in human beings who cooperate with the competent authorities that was issued in 2002.

Although international and national attention is be reverted to women and children who are victims of trafficking, this is mainly for women from Europe, in particular Eastern Europe. In Hungary, there is no organization that is working with women trafficked from Africa and very little attention is paid to this group of victims. Considering that Hungary is a major transit country and slowly becoming a major destination, a change of attitude and understanding of the problem being faced by African women and children has to take place. This may be attributed to the difficulty such organizations have in acquiring funds for a project aimed at African women and children, especially with social and economic conditions being faced by the people of the region.

In October 2001, a joint Europe-Africa summit was held in Brussels where countries agreed to draw up a joint Action Plan Against Human Trafficking. Part of the collaborative efforts in the fight is the teaming up of the immigration authorities. Under the auspices of the Economic Community of the West African States (ECOWAS),[34] initiatives to combat human trafficking, especially the trafficking in women and children, have been undertaken. Although these are not yet well advanced, it is a step in the right direction, signifying that the governments of the region have recognized human trafficking as a serious hazard to humanity. In 2001, 15 ECOWAS member states agreed to an action plan committing their countries to take steps in the next two years toward eliminating human trafficking. This followed scandals involving trafficking child slaves within and outside the region. The plan calls for the countries of the Community, ECOWAS, to ratify and fully implement international instruments of ECOWAS and the United Nations that strengthen laws against human trafficking and protect victims of trafficking, especially women and children.

Nigeria, a country from which more than 105,000 people are trafficked annually, has gone further and introduced a specific law to eliminate the trafficking of persons, especially women and children. Under the new law, a life sentence is imposed on anyone found guilty of trading in humans.[35] The same law also levies a fine of 100,000 Nigerian Naira for any individual found guilty of trafficking in humans. The new law does not only levy harsher punishment and stringent fines on the perpetrators, but goes ahead to provide for the victims by offering assistance to them, enabling them to resettle and start a new and normal life. This is adhered to the same spirit being promoted in the European Union, where the aim of the legal initiatives provided is twofold: to eradicate this heinous trade by punishing the perpetrators, and, to provide assistance in all ways possible to those victims willing to aid the police by providing more information and evidence on the traffickers.

National Law: Hungary

Toward the end of the 1990s, a number of European countries took action to incorporate trafficking in humans as an offence, by amending or passing legislation adhered to this. Hungary incorporated human trafficking as a criminal offence in its criminal code in 1998 and it came into force on 1 March 1999.[36] Under this section[37] imprisonment of up to 16 years could be levied against any person found guilty of trafficking in people. At the same time, section 204 of the criminal code abolished prostitution as a crime but the exploitation of prostitution of others remained a crime, vis-à-vis the promotion of prostitution,[38] living on earnings of prostitution,[39] and pandering.[40] Other prohibitions[41] are found in Act LXIX of 1999 on Violation of Administrative Rules.

A new law[42] to prevent and control prostitution was enacted where zones of prohibition and tolerance were introduced. The responsibility of creating tolerance zones in which prostitution would be allowed is left to the local governments. Due to public pressure, none of the local governments have yet been able to designate tolerance zones, thus forcing prostitutes to operate from wherever they can, an offence in itself leading to a fine of HUF 100,000. Unfortunately, the Hungarian legislation does not provide for assistance and integration of the victims as it does in Italy and Holland.

CONCLUSION

This research, while not exhaustive, will hopefully provoke further discussion on the issue of trafficking of humans, especially women and children, from the continent of Africa. In order to effectively combat this heinous trade, all sources and forces from all sectors of society on all continents must cooperate and coordinate to promote the inherent rights of women and children and to effectively end this trade.

Some suggestions for the countries of origin could include: raise public awareness of human trafficking using the media to impart the necessary information to the masses; provide free and easily accessible universal education; support community programs and non-governmental organizations in the fight against this crime; promote and provide equitable economic development and access to employment in the country; and enact stringent legislation and levy heavy punishment for perpetrators and corrupt officials involved in trafficking to protect children, women, and other vulnerable groups.

Suggestions for transit and destination countries in Europe include publicly condemning the trafficking in African women and children by the politicians, which would draw more attention to the victims coming from outside the region. There also is a need to better train the enforcement forces in handling the non-European victims so they will not be treated as illegal entrants, unless necessity demands; improve the legal structure to allow for training of special personnel in courts and other legal institutions on how to handle such cases; enact stringent legislation protecting children, women, and other vulnerable groups; and levy heavy punishment for perpetrators of this crime and corrupt officials. They should also promote fair economic development in developing countries, provide job training for temporary accepted asylum seekers and refugees, and promote and support NGOs already working with victims outside Europe.

NOTES

1. The 1990 Trust Statement on the Human Trafficking of West African Children into the United Kingdom, October 2002.

2. Personal translation of the original Hungarian language text.

3. Rima Salah, "Child Trafficking in West and Central Africa: An Overview" (paper presented at the First Pan-African Congress on Human Trafficking, Abuja, Nigeria, February 19–21, 2001).

4. Resources and Contacts of Human Trafficking compiled by The Initiative Against Human Trafficking, The International Human Rights Law Group, December 2002. See http://www.hrlawgroup.org/initiatives/trafficking_persons/default.asp.

5. See http://www.townswomen.org.uk/traffickingbrief03.htm.

6. "The Race Dimensions of Trafficking in Persons—Especially Women and Children" in Backgrounder: World Conference Against Racism, Racial Discrimination, Xenophobia and Related Intolerance, Durban, South Africa, 31 August–7 September 2001.

7. See http://www.419fraud.com/ and also http://www.crimes-of-persuasion .com/Nigerian /marked_currency.htm.

8. The 1990 Trust Statement on the Human Trafficking of West African Children into the United Kingdom, October 2002.

9. Article 7(1c).

10. "Enslavement means the exercise of any or all of the powers attaching to the right of ownership over a person and includes the exercise of such power in the course of trafficking in persons, in particular women and children."

11. "States Parties shall take all appropriate national, bilateral and multilateral measures to prevent the abduction of, the sale of or traffic in children for any purpose or in any form."

12. See http://www.iom.int//DOCUMENTS/PUBLICATION/EN/tm_27 .pdf, 1.

13. Janice G. Raymond, "Guide To The New UN Trafficking Protocol: Protocol to Prevent, Suppress and Punish Trafficking in Persons, Especially Women and Children," Supplementing the United Nations Convention Against Transnational Organized Crime, co-published by CATW, MAPP, The European Women's Lobby, Article Premier (France) and AFEM, 2001.

14. Article 1 of Convention for the Suppression of the Traffic in Persons and of the Exploitation of the Prostitution of Others, 1949.

15. 1904 International Agreement for the Suppression of the White Slave Trade, 1910 International Convention for the Suppression of White Slave Traffic, 1921 Convention for the Suppression of Traffic in Women and Children, and 1933 International Convention for the Suppression of the Traffic in Women of Full Age.

16. Article 1:

Parties to the Convention agree to punish any person, to gratify the passions of another procures, entices or leads away, for purposes of prostitution, another person, even with the consent of that person; exploits the prostitution of another person, even with the consent of that person.

17. UNICEF. See http://www.unicef.org/protection/index_exploitation.html.

18. See http://www.unicef.org/protection/index_exploitation.html.

19.

States Parties undertake to protect the child from all forms of sexual exploitation and sexual abuse. For these purposes, States Parties shall in particular take all appropriate national, bilateral and multilateral measures to prevent: (a) The inducement or coercion of a child to engage in any unlawful sexual activity; (b) The exploitative use of children in prostitution or other unlawful sexual practices; (c) The exploitative use of children in pornographic performances and materials.

20. Article 1 of Protocol:

State Parties shall prohibit the sale of children, child prostitution and child pornography as provided by the present Protocol.

Article 3:

Each State Party shall ensure that, as a minimum, the following acts and activities are fully covered under its criminal or penal law whether these offences are committed domestically or transnationally or on an individual or organized basis: (a) In the context of sale of children as defined in article 2: (i) The offering, delivering or accepting, by whatever means, a child for the purpose of: (a) Sexual exploitation.

21. Children: In majority of international instruments and national legislation, these are persons who have not reached the age of 18; sometimes referred to as minors. In some countries, those who have not reached the age of 21, especially common law countries.

22. Preamble of the Declaration on the Rights of the Child (1959).

23. United Nations Economic and Social Council, Commission on Human Rights Fifty-Sixth Session: E/6CN.4/2000/68: Integration of The Human Rights of Women and The Gender Perspective: Violence Against Women: Report of the Special Rapporteur on violence against women, its causes and consequences, Ms. Radhika Coomaraswamy, on trafficking in women, women's migration and violence against women, submitted in accordance with Commission on Human Rights Resolution 1997/44.

24.

Article 1: Offences concerning trafficking in human beings for the purposes of labor exploitation or sexual exploitation: Each Member shall take the necessary measures to ensure that the following acts are punishable: the recruitment, transportation, transfer, harboring, subsequent reception of a person, including exchange or transfer of control over that person, when (a) use is made of coercion, force or threat, including abduction, or (b) use is made of deceit or fraud, or (c) there is an abuse of authority or of a position of vulnerability, which is such that the person has no real and acceptable alternatives but to submit to the abuse involved, or (d) payments or benefits are given or received to achieve the consent of a person having the control over another for the purpose of the exploitation of the prostitution of others or other forms of sexual exploitation including pornography.

25.

Article 1 of Council Directive 2002/0043: The purpose of this Directive is to introduce a short term residence permit for third-country nationals who are victims of offences constituted by the action to facilitate illegal immigration or trafficking in human beings (hereafter referred to as "victims") who cooperate in the fight against the perpetrators of these offences.

26. For EU legislation being adopted against trafficking in humans and the sexual exploitation of children, see http://europa.eu.int/comm/justice_home/doc_centre/crime/trafficking/doc_crime_human_trafficking_en.htm.

27.

(1) Slavery is the status or condition of a person over whom any or all of the powers attaching to the right of ownership are exercised. (2) The slave trade includes all acts involved in the capture, acquisition or disposal of a person with intent to reduce him to slavery; all acts of disposal by sale or exchange of a slave acquired with a view to being sold or exchanged, and, in general, every act of trade or transport in slaves.

28. "No one shall be held in slavery or servitude; slavery and the slave trade shall be prohibited in all their forms."

29. "No one shall be held in slavery; slavery and slave trade in all forms shall be prohibited."

30. See http://www.thisislondon.co.uk/news/articles/19328071?version=1; article by Richard Edwards Crime Reporter, *Evening Standard*, 16 June 2005.

31. Article 218 of Hungarian Criminal Code .

32. "Any person, who sells, purchases, conveys or receives another person or exchanges a person for another person, or appropriates one for such purpose for another party commits a felony and shall be punishable with imprisonment up to three years."

33. Legislative Decree No. 286 of 25 July 1998.

34. Benin, Burkina Faso, Cape Verde, Côte d'Ivoire, Gambia, Ghana, Guinea, Guinea-Bissau, Liberia, Mali, Niger, Nigeria, Senegal, Sierra Leone, and Togo.

35. "Any person who procures a girl or woman . . . to become a common prostitute either in Nigeria or elsewhere is liable for life imprisonment."

36. Section 175/B of the Hungarian Criminal Code.

37.

(1) Any person who sells, purchases, conveys or receives another person or exchanges a person for another person, in addition to any person who recruits others for the above purpose, or transports, hides or appropriates a person for another party, commits a felony offence and shall be punishable with imprisonment of up to 3 years.

(2) The punishment shall be imprisonment between 1 to 5 years if the criminal act is committed: a) against the person under the age of 18 years; b) against a person deprived of personal freedom; c) for the purpose of labor; d) for the purpose of sodomy or sexual intercourse; e) for an illegal use of the human body; f) as an organized criminal act, or g) in return for a payment.

(3) The punishment shall be imprisonment between 2 to 8 years if the criminal act is committed: a) against the person under the tutelage, guardianship, supervision or medical treatment of the perpetrator; b) as described in points c)-e) of paragraph 2) if the perpetrator uses: 1) violence or threatens, 2) deceives or 3) tortures a person.

(4) The punishment shall be imprisonment between 5 to 10 years if the criminal act is committed a) against a person described in points a)-b) of paragraph 2) or in a point a) of paragraph 3) for the purposes defined in points c)-e) of paragraph 2), and in a manner described in sub-points 1–3 of point b) paragraph 3), or b) for the purposes of making illegal pornographic pictures.

(5) The punishment shall be imprisonment between 5 to 15 years or life imprisonment if the criminal act is committed against person under the age of 12 for the purpose defined in points c)-e) of paragraph 2), or b) in a manner described in sub-points 1–3 of point b), paragraph 3), or c) for the purpose of making illegal pornographic pictures.

(6) Any person making preparations to engage in trafficking of human beings commits a misdemeanor offence and shall be punishable with imprisonment of up to 2 years.

38. Section 205 of the Hungarian Criminal Code.

39. Section 206 of the Hungarian Criminal Code.

40. Section 207 of the Hungarian Criminal Code.

41. Sections 143, 144, and 145.

42. Act LXXV of 1999 on The Modification of Regulations on the Fight Against Organized Crime and Related Offences.

IV

NATIONAL AND LOCAL INITIATIVES AND SERVICE MODELS

• 11 •

Migration and Trafficking of Women and Girls: A Brief Review of Some Effective Models in India and Thailand

Upala Devi Banerjee

$\mathcal{M}$igration has been a process in existence from time immemorial. However, it is only in the last three decades that there has been a consistent pattern of unprecedented growth in migration, and it is increasingly being linked to economic growth. According to an International Labor Organization (ILO) publication, *Workers Without Frontiers*, the total number of migrants around the world now surpasses 120 million—up from 75 million in 1965—and continues to grow. Globalization, as a macro factor, has a profound effect on international labor migration. As technological development witnesses unprecedented growth, there is a heightened movement of goods, services, and capital across international boundaries.

The revolution in information technology and the advancement in transport systems also mean that people have more access to information and the resultant opportunities to move. The numbers of those willing to migrate from rural areas into cities or countries where these industries are based will only increase as more and more multinationals shift their industries to less-developed nations. However, the downside to this is that while rich, developed countries are profiting from the *trade without boundaries* phenomenon, workers from poor nations—often the most illiterate and not very technically skilled—are being exploited in their own countries or as migrants in the industrialized countries. Peter Stalker says that "while governments do little to interfere with flows of trade and finance, it does little to take action when it comes to human beings."[1] This is one of the main reasons why migration patterns have become so complex in recent times and have spawned an entire industry of illegal trafficking. Although not all migration is a consequence of globalization, nor has the loss of livelihoods resulted in trafficking, there has been increasing instances of such migrants being trafficked both as a cause or consequence of these factors.

Trafficking of persons, especially of women and children, has reached endemic proportions around the globe, with an estimated 1 to 2 million people trafficked each year into sexual subjugation, coerced prostitution, domestic servitude, bonded sweatshop labor, and other slavery-like conditions. Although few countries in the world are unaffected, Southeast Asia is the source of nearly one-third of the global trafficking taking place. And recent research suggests that as trafficking in South Asia is rising, the average age of those being trafficked is falling.

Trafficking as an enterprise is highly lucrative. For instance, smuggling a person by boat from Morocco to Spain will cost $500, but a very travel-sophisticated package for an undocumented Chinese migrant to the United States can cost up to $30,000.[2] Trafficking is now believed to be the third largest source of income for organized crime—behind narcotics and firearms—and has become a source of funding for, or is otherwise connected with other criminal activities like forgery, visa fraud, money laundering, bribery of public officials, drug use, and gambling. There are reports that state that trafficking of undocumented migrants brings in US$5 billion to US$7 billion a year.

FOCUS OF THIS CHAPTER

Both India and Thailand have had to deal with huge volumes of trafficking and migration in the last few decades. Historically too, most of the countries in South and Southeast Asia have had a tradition of migration but this has increased in the last two decades due to a number of factors as identified above. The highest numbers of those who are trafficked are women and children from Nepal and Bangladesh into India and from India into Pakistan and then on to the Gulf countries. India, a vast country strategically located, copes with a large amount of internal trafficking, too. Thailand, like India, has witnessed enormous numbers of trafficked women and children from interior villages into towns and cities (like Bangkok, Chiang Rai, and Chiang Mai) and also from across its borders (from Burma, Cambodia, and Laos).

UNICEF statistics estimate that there are at least a million child prostitutes in Asia,[3] the highest numbers present in India, followed by Thailand, Taiwan, and the Philippines. India has one of the highest rates of sexual exploitation of children, mostly through prostitution. Most of these abuses are committed on the girl child. Studies reveal women and girls are brought with the lure of jobs into red-light areas of cities from primary source areas into particular areas within India. The borders along Nepal and Bangladesh have a similar story to tell. The increasing linkages with globalization that is occurring in many parts across these two regions fuel all these patterns.

Using my grassroots experiences and exposure to some of the initiatives in India and Thailand, I will attempt to examine globalization as a new emerging force that is affecting local livelihood patterns and contributing to migration. Civil society organizations in South and Southeast Asia—primarily nongovernmental organizations (NGOs)—have recognized the potential threats that such globalization patterns are bringing in its wake and are tackling this issue by trying to protect the rights of women and children, often in collaboration with public authorities (related government departments).

GLOBALIZATION AND ITS IMPACT ON MIGRATION AND TRAFFICKING OF WOMEN AND CHILDREN IN SOUTH AND SOUTHEAST ASIA

The accelerated pace of globalization associated with trade liberalization in the last decade has had far-reaching effects worldwide, and nowhere have the effects been more pronounced than in South and Southeast Asia. Loan conditions coupled with the structural adjustment program have rapidly disintegrated rural communities in South Asia, and the impact has been felt the most by vulnerable women and children. While privatization policies have been depriving people of their customary rights over common property resources, the green revolution technologies have been causing serious ecological damages and, in many countries of South Asia, have reached alarming stages of agricultural stagnation.

Global policies such as the Agreement on Agriculture of the World Trade Organization (WTO) have tremendous negative consequences in the rural areas and have further exacerbated inequities. Agreements like the Trade-Related Aspects of Intellectual Property Rights (TRIPS) and Trade-Related Investment Measures (TRIMS)[4] could rob women of control over seed and land and devalue their position in agriculture accelerating their commodification. Introduction of biotechnology and genetic engineering in agriculture, particularly food production, will destroy the farming communities and give control to the multinational corporations (MNCs). Already, many giant MNCs are gaining entry into the South Asian countries (in Southeast Asia, such a scenario has been in existence for almost two decades now) with assistance from respective governments.

Thus, livelihoods, especially among the rural communities, have been destroyed systematically by unregulated market forces and inefficient government polices. With the increase in poverty, food insecurity, and insecurity of livelihoods, people have been forced to migrate out of their villages into neighboring towns and cities. An increasing number of South and Southeast Asians are migrating, legally or illegally, both internally and to other countries in search of employment. In most cases, such forms of migration have crossed geographical boundaries and taken the form of trafficking, especially trafficking of women and girl children. Trafficking in women and children cannot, therefore, be separated from globalization and livelihood issues. As migration is often linked with economic gain or the expectation of economic gain, the same is true of trafficking. Thus, trafficking has been very pronounced in the entire South and Southeast Asian region.

An important feature in all of this is the numbers of women joining the workforce to the extent that a trend of feminization is emerging in the workforce.[5] The number of women migrants increases daily as they are compelled to take on more responsibility in financially supporting their families. Promises of better paid jobs, in some cases, even the promise of a new experience and exposure, act as "pull factors" in this process. Although not all migrant workers face difficulties, there are many instances of workers trapped in highly exploitative conditions—e.g., low salaries or nonpayment of salaries, unreasonably long hours of work, abusive employers, more or different work than was in a contract, broken contract or non-employment, and lack of leave. The migrant workers are not covered by, nor would they know how to access information on, such services as labor laws or social security in the labor receiving country. They can become powerless and trapped in their jobs, unable to leave, or upon leaving an abusive workplace situation become illegal migrant workers—subject to arrest, imprisonment, fines, or other punishment, and deportation. In these cases, workers become trafficked migrants.

The most commonly quoted definition of trafficking was provided by the "United Nations Protocol to Prevent, Suppress, and Punish Trafficking in Persons, Especially Women and Children" passed in November 2000:

> The recruitment, transportation, transfer, harboring or receipt of persons, by means of threat or use of force or other forms of coercion, of abduction, of fraud, of deception, of the abuse of power or of a position of vulnerability or of the giving or receiving of payments or benefits to achieve the consent of a person having control over another person, for the purpose of exploitation (in particular, labor and sexual exploitation). Exploitation shall include, at a minimum, the exploitation of the prostitution of others or other forms of sexual exploitation, forced labor or services, slavery or practices similar to slavery, servitude or the removal of organs.

Trafficked migrants are dependent on agents and employers and are extremely vulnerable to exploitation in an insecure and unfamiliar environment. They are prevented from escape by retention of passports and other travel documents, violence, or threat of violence. Exploitation can take not only an economic form but also sexual, psychosocial, and other forms of violations of the migrants' human rights. Contrary to the common belief that trafficking happens only in the case of irregular migrants, it can also happen to persons who initially are regular migrants but are later trapped in extremely exploitative jobs, misled about the purpose of their travel at the time of recruitment or when they become targets of traffickers while looking for employment upon arrival in the receiving country. Women workers employed in low-status and low-paid jobs in the unorganized sectors, including women who arrive on entertainment visas and are forced into commercial sex work, can be extremely vulnerable.

CHALLENGES AHEAD

Since globalization and its impacts will persist for some time to come, it is imperative that the governments of these countries take measures to reduce the vulnerability of women migrant workers. A welcome development in South Asia has been the recognition of trafficking as one of the worst violations of human rights for women and children in South Asia by the South Asian Association for Regional Cooperation countries (SAARC). At the last SAARC Summit in Katmandu,[6] SAARC member countries agreed to put in place appropriate mechanisms to address the issue of trafficking from the prevention and protection angles on a regional level. This is especially significant to ensure extradition of criminals to countries, bringing them to court and through agreements to facilitate return operations of victims to their country of origin.

However, it is a known fact that gaps between policies and practices have often been the norm in both South and Southeast Asia. In such a scenario, for instance, it remains a daunting challenge for civil society to actually lobby for implementation of the two recent SAARC Conventions. The challenge becomes even harder as it involves governments and citizens of not one or two but seven South Asian countries.

Most observers believe strongly that there is a direct link between trafficking in persons, particularly women and children, with the ongoing insecurity of food and livelihood crises (that is, the whole question of macroeconomic policies, globalization and agrarian policies). Hence, much of the focus should be on linking anti-trafficking programs at the macro level with intensive anti-poverty programs at the local/national level.

Given the increasing feminization of migration and the overwhelming presence of women among those who are trafficked, mostly for sexual exploitation, attention should also be directed toward ending gender discrimination which cuts across all South Asian countries. This is especially important considering the low status given to women in the social sphere and their lack of access and control over economic resources.

The international aspect of the problem rises out of inadequate vigilance being exercised on the land borders between India and Nepal, India and Bangladesh, and India and Pakistan in South Asia or between Burma and Thailand in Southeast Asia. In this context, the training of police personnel to handle this issue becomes imperative. Border patrols are needed in these countries to keep vigilance on the entry and exit of young girls who have questionable travel documents or who have persons accompanying them with whom the girls cannot prove any familial relationship. Effective coordination and cooperation between the governments and NGOs of all the countries in question are essential.

Arguments are given by leading practitioners regarding the regulation of migration for creating an atmosphere conducive to migrating, thus reducing the dangers of trafficking. Most of the victims of trafficking come from the low end of the skills spectrum. To provide them the opportunity to migrate legally, pre-departure training could significantly reduce the dangers of trafficking. And this is where the role of the civil society—NGOs, trade unions, lawyers, teachers, religious groups, and so forth—is required along with active cooperation and collaboration with the government in effecting change.

In the past, it was usually the civil society in South and Southeast Asia who was often the most active when it came to promoting and protecting the rights of marginalized or vulnerable groups. This held true even in the context of issues surrounding trafficking, migration, and rights (though the scenario is changing now with increasing cooperation witnessed among civil society organizations and host governments in tackling and combating trafficking-related issues with support forthcoming from bilateral and multilateral donors). In general, however, South and Southeast Asian Governments have not been able to effectively address the rehabilitation needs of victims or been able to prevent trafficking. In recognizing the systematic causes of prostitution, the onus of responsibility has been shifted from the women in prostitution to the social system and the controllers of prostitution. As the famous woman activist and writer, Kathleen Barry, says, "Pimping becomes the oldest profession and not prostitution."

SOME INNOVATIVE APPROACHES IN INDIA AND THAILAND TO COMBAT TRAFFICKING

In India

A growing number of efforts have been initiated by the Indian Government in collaboration with state government to address issues related to prevention (and rehabilitation) of trafficking and prostitution, such as strengthening the primary school system, economic development opportunities (i.e., training in various livelihood skills), initiation of social reforms and legislation, revamping of state-run homes, and using the media to raise public awareness. Realizing the role of electronic media to get the message to the public to bring about effective policy orientation and solutions to combat this evil, the media has been used for optimal impact in highlighting and combating trafficking. In Nepal, for instance, especially in the interior villages, which have been affected the most by vast exoduses of people migrating or trafficked, the community radio has played a major role in reducing vulnerabilities by educating and sensitizing people regarding the dangers of being trafficked.

However, many of the efforts have not been very effective for lack of proper coordination and implementation. Hence, government efforts are being complemented by various civil society efforts.

According to the "Situation Report on Trafficking of Children for Prostitution, UNIFEM India Today," there are more than 80 non-governmental organizations (NGOs) in the country working in approximately 10 states engaged in working with sex workers. India is a huge country, and to combat a problem of this magnitude, no one single model would work. Thus, while such numerous efforts are varied and are rooted in and respond to local contexts, a few stand out due to their success and innovation

For instance, in the southern Indian State of Andhra Pradesh, an NGO called *Abhyudaya Ashram* has been relentlessly fighting with the police from the neighboring state of Madhya Pradesh on one hand, and the social system on the other hand, to combat prostitution. Public Interest Litigations (PILs) have been filed in local courts to free girls illegally lodged in various state-run homes. These girls are then rehabilitated through the residential school (through education) system. The aims of the NGO are to secure a decent future for the girls when they finish their education. Another NGO in Andhra Pradesh—the *Society for Awareness through Learning and Training (SALT)*—has been instrumental in the formulation and enactment of the Andhra Pradesh *Devadasi* (Prohibition and Dedication) Act, 1988.[7]

In Kolkata, in the eastern Indian State of West Bengal, the NGO, *Sanlaap*, provides legal aid and consultation to women and girls working in the red-light areas of Calcutta. Such a provision empowers the girls and women to fight for their rights in case of harassment by local officials and the police. Moreover, *Sanlaap* also offers medical guidance and lobbies with the state government to fight for the rights of the workers. In short, their approach is not service-delivery oriented but follows more of a rights-based approach where empowerment is the key for the workers to live with dignity and self-respect. Another NGO in Calcutta—*Socio-Legal Research and Training Center (SLARTC)*—is also involved in providing training to sex workers on women's rights and legal protection. Much of the training and awareness is conducted with the vision of stopping the entry of children into prostitution.

While some other NGOs like *Prerna* (in Mumbai) and the *Joint Women's Programme* (in New Delhi) are involved in rehabilitation, they are also actively involved in networking on this issue to actively lobby and advocate with the state governments. *Prerna* works in the red-light area of Kamatipura in Mumbai targeting children of sex workers and inducting them into a school system; the *Joint Women's Programme* carries out much of the same genre of work in the red-light area of G.B Road in Delhi. Both NGOs also provide health and medical counseling on various issues with a major focus on HIV/AIDS and have been instrumental in lobbying on behalf of the workers at both the state and national level. The *Joint Women's Programme*, in collaboration with other NGOs, is also providing gender sensitization training for police personnel in order for these cadres to be more sensitive while dealing with women and girls who are victims of violence and trafficking.

Indian NGOs are also actively collaborating with like-minded NGOs in Nepal and Bangladesh on the issue of cross-country trafficking. Workshops, meetings, and "exposure visits" between NGO personnel from these countries have revealed ways to deal with the issue at the local, state, national, and regional level to workers from different countries. As a result, strong networks have been formed to put pressure on respective governments to combat trafficking and to rehabilitate women and girls. Thus, while NGOs (who often have a more popular mandate than the government) are working simultaneously on different levels—providing direct services, sensitizing and building up capacities of the communities in terms of changing mindsets, and acting as lobbyists for change—they are also working in tandem with the state bureaucracy to train their bureaucrats for reforming legal and regulatory frameworks, as well as the systems for implementing them. Public awareness and social mobilization through citizen/social action groups are necessary in effecting change. In some cities, such as Kolkata, there has been growth in the unionization of sex workers movement. These women are now actively involved in fighting for their own rights and the recognition of their work, and, more importantly, to be treated with dignity and respect.

In Thailand

I had the opportunity to evaluate, at length (as a consultant with Christian Aid—a UK-based charity organization),[8] the role *EMPOWER*, a national organization that works with women and girls being trafficked or who have migrated on their own will and are into various forms of sex work. Based in Bangkok with offices in Chiang Mai and Mae Sai (a border town in the northernmost tip of Thailand bordering Burma), *EMPOWER's* approach is a combination of both the needs- and rights-based models. The needs-based approach provides service delivery to the sex workers through its various outreach programs such as training in various life skills and non-formal education and literacy classes and by providing counseling and health services. As part of its needs-based approach, *EMPOWER* does not discriminate between a Thai, a Burmese, or a Laotian but provides services to all those who need or ask for them.

The rights-based aspects are equally visible in its work operations and the ideology under which it functions. *EMPOWER* recognizes the right of all to work, irrespective of whether it is in sex work or any other form of occupation. The organization believes that the sex workers have the right to make their own informed choices in life and this includes their choice of vocation. They believe that sex workers, as human beings, have the right to demand and receive services. *EMPOWER* practices this approach in its daily functions and it is visible through the participation of all workers as equal partners in its various programs and services. Opinions of the workers are given due respect, and they are consulted in all aspects of the *EMPOWER* programs.

EMPOWER is very aware of the dimensions of the problem and that sex work is not the most desirable form of work. But, at the same time, it is also very conscious of the realities of poverty and the lack of and slow implementation of policies in regard to various social welfare, health, and labor schemes. Unless overall poverty and rights issues are urgently addressed, women and girls will continue to work in this profession at the risk of their own health, and at times, even their lives. Thus, while recognizing the right of the women to work, *EMPOWER* provides them with services that will not only help them counter various problems in the course of their work, but will also empower them to make more informed choices in terms of their career and other life choices.

Overall, I found the *EMPOWER* programs, especially in high-risk cities and towns like Bangkok, Chiang Mai, and Mae Sai, are not only visible but will have long-lasting impact on the lives of the workers. By working with the government officials and even enlisting the cooperation of the pimps and the brothel owners in their activities, it is ensuring that the impact of its activities are sustainable for the long run.

CONCLUSION

In the end, it is important to note that an imperative corollary to helping trafficked victims and combating the challenges globalization offers in this context is that exploitation of women will diminish if other factors come into place. This will require very active civil society–governmental intervention—most important, overall poverty reduction and changes in societal mores. Civil society can target the changes needed in deep-set patriarchal and societal mores, but help will be required from the government in bringing about changes in terms of overall poverty reduction. Some of the approaches highlighted above have tried to undertake this to an extent by undertaking programs/activities in collaboration with respective and related government departments.

Though the efforts are many and varied and have met with varying degrees of success, there is still hope that with increased coordination and collaboration between civil society stakeholders and governments in South and Southeast Asian countries, buttressed by the respective governments' obligations in relation to the various U.N. Conventions on trafficking, labor, children, women and rights issues and complemented by international awareness on the issue, some progress will be made in addressing trafficking issues, especially at the inter-country levels. Finally, it is a recognized fact that migration and globalization will witness continued growth, but as long as women and children are not victims of this phenomenon and as long as coordinated efforts are put in place to address those who *are* victims, there is still hope for such unfortunate sections of our society.

NOTES

1. Peter Stalker, *Workers Without Frontiers* (Geneva: International Labor Organization, 2001).
2. Stalker, *Workers Without Frontiers*, 2001.
3. Ruchira Gupta, "Trafficking of Children for Prostitution and the UNICEF Response," www.asiasource.org/asip/gupta.cfm (13 May 2005).
4. Information on both TRIPS and TRIMS can be found on the World Trade Organization (WTO) website, http://www.wto.org (15 March 2003).
5. Tasneem Siddiqui, *Transcending Boundaries: Labor Migration of Women from Bangladesh* (Dhaka: University Press Limited, 2001).
6. The SAARC Summit was held in Kathmandu in 2002 and all seven of the member countries attended—India, Pakistan, Bangladesh, Sri Lanka, Nepal, Bhutan, and Maldives.
7. The Andhra Pradesh State *Devadasi* Act was passed by the State Government of the southern Indian state of Andhra Pradesh to ban all practices wherein young girls were "sacrificed" at the altar of God in village temples as per the local custom and then auctioned to the highest bidder. The girl is then taken to nearby cities and towns and forced to become a sex worker.
8. As part of my observations while undertaking a consultancy assignment with Christian Aid, evaluating the effectiveness of EMPOWER's programs targeting women and child sex workers, in July–August 2002 in Thailand.

SELECTED BIBLIOGRAPHY

Siddiqui, Tasneem. *Transcending Boundaries: Labor Migration of Women from Bangladesh.* Dhaka: University Press Limited (2001).

Stalker, Peter. *Workers Without Frontiers.* Geneva: International Labor Organization (2001).

• 12 •

Fighting against Trafficking in Women in the North of Israel

Rita Chaikin

$\mathcal{A}$ $2 billion-a-year sex trade, one of the biggest of its kind in the world, has sprung up in Israel during the past decade. Every year since the lifting of the Iron Curtain, thousands of women from Eastern Europe and the former Soviet Union are trafficked into Israel. Israel was first exposed to this phenomenon in the early 1990s following the breakup of the Soviet Union and the collapse of the Socialist regimes in Eastern Europe. The trafficking is linked to organized crime taking root in Israel as a by-product of mass immigration from the former Soviet Union. According to latest research in 2003, 72 percent of the women are trafficked in across Israel's border with Egypt, which runs along 320 kilometers of desert that is difficult to guard against trafficking.[1]

The women are recruited for work in the Israeli sex industry by diverse methods. Some are promised decent jobs (including waitresses, models, and nurses) that offer higher pay than they could ever hope to earn at home. Few had ever worked as prostitutes before. Even those who knew they would be employed in the sex industry had no idea what it was like or in what conditions they would be forced to work (based on in-depth interviews). In rare cases, some of the women were abducted against their will.

In response to pressure from Israeli and international women's groups, there were additions to the Israeli criminal laws in 2000–2001 that mandated minimal punishments for those found guilty of trafficking in persons. Also, a law introduced in the Israeli Parliament is to be passed against such human trafficking. In spite of this, there is still no meaningful, effective deterrent within the laws, and punishments imposed on convicted traffickers continue to be extremely light. Victims of such crimes often find themselves in Israeli police custody, held in prisons or detention centers, only to be deported to their countries of origin to face the danger of being met by the original traffickers.

In the last three years, the campaign against "trafficking in women" has gained increasing momentum worldwide, in particular among feminists in Europe and the United States. This current campaign is not the first time the international community has become concerned with the fate of young women abroad. Feminist organizations played key roles in both past and present campaigns.

Isha L'Isha—Haifa Feminist Center initiated the Fight Against the Trafficking of Women in Northern Israel Project in 2001 to deal with two primary areas: first, by providing support to the women victims, and, second, to raise public awareness of the phenomena. This preliminary report will provide the reader with a deeper understanding of the phenomena and the ways in which Isha L'Isha has set out to fight against trafficking. Statistical information provided in this report has been taken from a comprehensive research survey, which was conducted in a joint effort with The Hotline for Migrant Workers and the Adva Center for Social Research.

HISTORY AND BACKGROUND OF PHENOMENA

Trafficking in women in Israel has existed since the beginning of the 1990s. It was encouraged in a large part by the collapse of the FSU (Former Soviet Union). The huge wave of over one million immigrants to Israel from the FSU allowed panderers, pimps, and agents of trafficking to easily slip through as new immigrants. In the early years, the pimps were small-scale operators, most of whom were native Israelis. However, survey results conducted in 2001 by The Hotline for Migrant Workers found 90 percent of them were from the FSU.[2]

Although the wave of Russian immigration brought with it a wealth of culture, academia, and sports, it unfortunately also contributed to the growth of trafficking of women and their transfer from countries suddenly poverty-stricken with severe economic troubles to the Israeli market. In the beginning of the 1990s, Israeli government, law enforcement, and the general public showed ignorance and disinterest in the existence of this phenomenon.

The Israeli Women's Network (IWN) published a detailed report in 1997 on the situation, which did not even cause a ripple of reaction concerning the information included therein. On the other hand, reports about Israel's involvement in the sex trade were circulating and causing more than a stir within the international community. The United Nations Commission on Human Rights studied the actions taken to put into practice its 1998 Declaration of Rights of Citizens and Politics and criticized Israel for its attitude toward victims of trafficking. Amnesty International published a report, "Woman: For

Sale" (May 2000), detailing violations of law regarding the trafficking of women from the FSU into Israel for the sex industry. In 2001, the United States Ministry for Foreign Affairs published the reports, "Victims of Trafficking and Violence Act 2000," and "Trafficking in Persons 2001," which categorized Israel along with the other countries who have not stood up to the minimal criteria of the United States legislation against trafficking in women. Only after the latest report was made public and warnings from the American government that no support payments would be paid unless Israel take concrete steps to address the problem, did Israel begin to take parliamentary and governmental action.

ISRAELI LEGISLATION AND TRAFFICKING IN WOMEN

The trade in women includes a whole host of related crimes that are forbidden by the Israeli Criminal Code—including pandering, forced prostitution, kidnapping, holding people against their will, rape, assault and battery, forging of documents, and illegally confiscating documents. However, up until the year 2000, the law in Israel did not pay any attention to the specific problem of trafficking in women. The Israeli Basic Law on Human Dignity and Freedom (1982) states in Clause One: "Basic human rights in Israel are based on the worth of the person, the sacredness of life and the right to live in freedom." Clause 4 states: "Every person is entitled to protection of life, freedom, and dignity." In light of this, the State of Israel is obligated to protect the lives of the victims of trafficking and to act on their behalf to preserve their freedom and physical safety. Unfortunately, this has not been the case and further amendments to the law have had to be established in order for the judicial system to begin enforcing these basic rights. In 2002, revisions were made to the law concerning equal rights of women; the law was amended to state, "Each woman has the right to protection from violence, sexual harassment, sexual exploitation, and the sale of her body." However, as this has not been added to the Criminal Code, no sanctions have been encoded in the law to convict felons.

Finally, on July 21, 2000, the Knesset (Israeli Parliament) passed criminal sanctions in which Clause 203a states: "The seller or buyer of people for the purposes of prostitution or an agent of such transaction shall be sentenced to 16 years imprisonment." For our purposes, this covers anyone who is a "seller or buyer, in return for money, services, or any other benefit" (Amendment 56 to the Criminal Code, 1977). In June 2001, the Knesset passed on first reading (obligatory second and third readings have not yet been passed) a proposal by Knesset Member Yael Dayan, which demanded a minimal punishment of a quarter of the maximum punishment for such crimes. This in actuality puts the crime of trafficking under the minimum sentencing system of the Criminal Code. However, the sad reality has shown that there is still a large gap between what the law states as convictions and the actual punishments given to offenders.

WHAT IS BEING DONE TODAY:
ISHA L'ISHA (WOMAN TO WOMAN)

The non-profit organization Isha L'Isha—the Haifa Feminist Center was founded in 1983. The goal is to advance women's status and to aid women in any way, as part of the struggle for women's equality and advancement in Israel. Since 1997, Isha L'Isha has worked with various other organizations against trafficking in women in Israel. After it became clear that not enough was being done in the north of the country, Isha L'Isha activated projects in 2001 directed towards this struggle.

The Project

Isha L'Isha initiated a project to deal with two primary areas in the North: (1) to provide support to the women victims, and (2) to raise public awareness of the phenomena of trafficking of women. Providing support to the women victims includes emotional, practical, and legal support. We visit the women in detention centers, listen to them and find out what they need and are available by phone whenever needed. Every month we receive an average of 50 calls. Some of the victims talk to Isha L'Isha staff by phone on a daily basis. We encourage women to be screened for STDs and AIDS and if needed, provide proper medical treatment to the victims.

We also provide the women with activities to fill their hours of detention time and organize social events at the detention center. Practical support includes clothing, hygienic items, phone cards, bags, etc. Isha L'Isha also explains their legal rights, helps the victims' families locate them, work to shorten the time the women spend in detention centers and facilitate the women's return home by expediting the process of submission of deportation documents through our extensive contacts with consulates and foreign ministries of the FSU source countries. In addition, we use our connections with NGOs abroad to arrange safe returns and to find shelters or professional training programs that the women can join upon their return home. We provide women with information on sources of support in their homelands by distributing pamphlets in three languages—English, Romanian, and Russian—about hotlines of organizations abroad that operate shelters.

To ensure that the authorities treat the women properly, we provide women with legal aid and information regarding their rights, and if needed, file complaints against the authorities in Israel. The legal aid we provide includes notifying the women that they have the option of testifying as prosecution witnesses against their traffickers and pimps. We inform the women that in the event that they testify, they are entitled to be transferred to the newly opened (early 2004) government shelter for prosecution witnesses and to stay in Israel legally during their testimony and for a certain period afterwards. We assist women who want to testify, walking them through the legal process and translating when necessary. We have succeeded in preventing the police from sending women to prison after they testified; instead, they were returned to the hotel where they stayed while testifying.

To raise public awareness in the community, our staff gives lectures about trafficking of women and the work of our organization to police, wardens, judges, lawyers, laymen, and schools. We collaborated on the joint publishing of a report on trafficking in Israel with The Hotline for Migrant Workers and the Adva Center for Social Research and formed a network with other NGOs in the former Soviet Union and the surrounding Arab nations in an effort to work together to stop and limit the smuggling of trafficked women into Israel.

Isha L'Isha representatives have participated in a number of international conferences in the FSU and the U.S., sharing knowledge and experience with other NGOs involved in anti-trafficking work. As a result, we have formed working relationships with many NGOs and coalitions around the world. These contacts allow us to help facilitate safe returns for trafficking victims and influence governments in source countries to take steps against trafficking. In addition, we work with the Israeli Foreign Ministry, educating them about trafficking and urging them to become involved in preventing trafficking. As part of our prevention efforts, Isha L'Isha wrote a Russian language flyer, together with The Hotline for Migrant Workers and the Association of Rape Crisis Centers, designed to educate potential victims by debunking the myths about working in Israel. The flyer presented the facts about what is in store for women smuggled into the country, as well as information about their legal rights in Israel and the NGOs' contact information for those who decide to come anyway. The flyer was widely distributed to NGOs in the former Soviet Union, many of whom the Foreign Ministry learned about from Isha L'Isha.

Program Results

In 2002, we visited, aided, and supported a total of 83 women victims. Legal council was provided to 47 of the 83 women, 13 of whom we guided in testifying in a court of law. In 2003, we assisted 340 women. We assisted 332 victims in 2004, received over 300 calls on our hotline, helped 6 victims receive the court-ordered compensation payments from their traffickers, transferred funds to three victims who returned home before payment was made, helped 157 victims return to their native countries by coordinating with local NGOs to meet the women upon arrival, arrange transport to their home towns, provide temporary housing in a shelter, and/or receive rehabilitation treatment, and gave a total of 29 lectures to 2,489 people. Partially as a result of Isha L'Isha's advocacy efforts, the government opened a shelter in February 2004 for victims who are willing to testify against their traffickers. In addition, the government has shown new interest in fighting trafficking. In 2004, the police closed down numerous brothels and "massage parlors." There was a large increase in the number of women who testified in anti-trafficking cases. We educated police officers about the harsh realities of trafficking and urged them to treat victims with greater compassion. We established a network of organizations that work together in the establishment of stricter legislation to fight the trafficking phenomena.

On the negative side, the closing of brothels has led to an increase in trafficking victims being kept in "discreet apartments," which are harder for the police to find and close. The crackdown on trafficking has also led to an increase in domestic prostitution.

FIELD REPORT

Who Are the Victims?

According to interviews conducted with victims, a large majority of victims of trafficking come from countries in the FSU—countries where, after the Soviet Union's disintegration, both the regional economy and the social support service networks collapsed completely. Many citizens of these countries found themselves employed at jobs with dismal salaries or without jobs altogether. Minimum standards of living could not be met. In these situations, women are among the first to lose their jobs and are the first victims of economic and social breakdown. Women, therefore, are often severely pressed to find employment outside their home countries and often accept enticing jobs without investigating too deeply about their exact nature.

There are a number of countries that lead the list in supplying victims of the sex trade in Israel: Russia, Ukraine, Moldavia, Uzbekistan, Belarus, and increasingly, Kazakhstan. The women are usually in their early to mid twenties. For many young women, the economic and social distress, their need to support their families, and the hope for a better future urge them to search for work abroad. Agents in the sex trade often contact women through advertisements and classified job ads in local newspapers, promising employment abroad with high salaries. Interviews conducted in 2003 by volunteers from Isha L'Isha and The Hotline for Migrant Workers show that 33 percent of the women stated that they did not know they were being recruited for prostitution; rather, they were promised employment as waitresses and maids. Approximately 66 percent of the women interviewed knew they were being offered jobs as prostitutes but reported that they were promised good working conditions, such as a low number of customers daily, freedom to leave their employer after their debt for being smuggled into Israel has been paid, and the promise of earning up to $1,000 a month.[3] In late 2004 and early 2005, we started seeing a new trend: trafficked women who were expelled from Israel and returned a second time, or women who arrived in Israel after working in the sex trade in other countries.

Education and Skills of the Women

In 2002, interviews with the women show that most have 11 years of schooling, or have the equivalent of a high school education. Fifteen percent were students at a university when they came to Israel, 10 percent were in the process of getting graduate degrees, and 15 percent studied a trade or profession. They reported earning salaries ranging between $8 and $175 a month at various jobs in their home countries, such as retail, sales, secretarial, teaching, tailoring, etc. Only 9 percent were working in the sex trade before their arrival in Israel. It is clearly understandable why the promise of $1,000 per month would be so appealing to these women.

Women and Their Families

Statistics from our joint survey show that a large majority of trafficked women are single (72 percent) or divorced (15 percent) and only 6 percent are married.[4] Seventy percent of the women have no children, 20 percent have one child, and 4 percent have two children.[5] Partial results show that many of the women were raised in a single-family home which the father left when they were young.

Reasons Women Come to Israel

The main reason women give for coming to Israel is economics. The poverty and hopelessness in the women's home countries, balanced against the promised opportunities for earning a very large amount of money in a short time, provide the perfect bait for desperate women. Other factors contributing to the decision to come to Israel include internal family problems (i.e., conflicts with parents, the need to prove independence, rebellion of young adulthood), history of domestic violence and sexual abuse, a feeling of being caught in a dead end, the wish to separate themselves from the grinding day-to-day reality, a lack of education, and lack of sexual education, some or all of which provide the additional incentive to leave their homes in search for a "better life."

Recruitment in Home Country

The many interviews conducted show that recruitment of women for the sex trade occurs in various ways: newspaper advertisements, friends, neighbors, and women who have themselves returned from having worked as prostitutes to their home countries.[6] The recruitment is done both "actively" by agents who approach women appearing to fit the physical profile for prostitutes and "passively" through advertisements and notices. Trafficking victim U.E. from Uzbekistan describes her recruitment as follows:

I am my husband's second wife. We had a baby this year and he is now 7 months old. I didn't work; I just took care of the baby. My husband, who lived with his first wife, would come once a week and bring us food. At some point, he stopped coming and I had nothing to eat and no money. My milk had dried up and my baby was hungry. At that point, I was desperate. My sister told me that there are people that arrange cleaning work in Moscow and that I would earn a thousand dollars a month. I thought that with such money, within six months, I would be set for a few years. If I had known that my future would be to be sold as a prostitute in Israel, I would have preferred to starve along with my son in our village.[7]

Here is another testimony:

When I was 9 years old, my parents divorced. My mother married again when I was 16 to a man who would beat me regularly and brutally. One day, after a particularly severe beating, I left the house and went to sit on a park bench and cried. A young woman approached, sat down and asked me what was wrong. I told her and she said that she had an excellent proposal for me that would allow me to earn a lot of money and I wouldn't have to see my family for a long time.[8]

THE JOURNEY TO ISRAEL

In the 1990s, women were brought into the country in a variety of ways,[9] such as fictitious marriages, forged documents of Jewish immigrants, and day-trip sea excursions into Israel's ports.[10] Today, we learn from interviews that victims of trafficking in women are brought to Israel across borders through one or more intermediate countries (71 percent) or via the airport (17 percent). These trafficking paths are also used to transfer agents of trafficking, drugs, weapons, and illegal foreign workers for various industries.[11] Most women destined for the sex trade are smuggled by way of journeys that can last several days, depending on the type of agents and the level of vigilance of the Border Patrol and the Israeli Army at the border points to be crossed. A trafficking victim described the process of her entry into Israel to parliamentary investigators:

They put us in a single-file line, one after the other . . . they counted us like we were sheep. Only afterwards I knew why they counted us like that. It was because for each girl who crossed the border they received $1,000. We walked like that for half an hour—once we sat, once we ran, once we were told to lie flat—until we reached barbed wire. It was in March and the sand was very cold. Then they told us to climb over the wire. On the other side of the barbed wire, a jeep passed and they told us to get in. But the jeep didn't stop. He kept driving fast, 40–50 km an hour, and we had to leap onto the moving jeep. They covered us with canvas. There was no air and so much dust because they drove on an unpaved road. Some of the girls lost consciousness.[12]

During the journey to Israel, Bedouin, some of whom view prostitutes as women with whom anything is acceptable and whose permission for anything is unnecessary, rape many of the women. Y. B. has testified the following:

In spite of the fact that I was promised work in Israel as a dancer, by the time I had been taken to Egypt I had figured out that I was to be sold as a prostitute in a brothel in Eilat. I tried to run away but the Bedouin caught me and beat me. That evening a group of Bedouin (four men) took me and each of them raped me in turn. I lay there and after the second, I couldn't feel anything. The same group came again and again. I lost consciousness and I woke up only the next morning in a tent with other women.[13]

The Selling Methods

Women are sold currently by one of three ways.[14] In the home country—these women arrive in Israel already aware that they are "attached" to a particular pimp or agent. This is especially common in the cases of women who are returning for a second time to Israel. Private sale—upon their arrival, most of the women are transferred to a private apartment, whereupon they begin receiving "customers." Public sale—when a number of women are available for sale, "customers" can choose and negotiate a price for them. H. A.'s testimony describes the latter method:

When we entered Israel, I was still convinced that I was to get work as a maid. I didn't understand where they were taking us in the middle of the night. But, when I saw that in the same apartment there were many half-naked women, I started to understand . . . They put three of us into a separate room and asked me to lift my shirt so they could look at my stomach and my breasts. At this point, I was in such shock; I urinated in my pants from fear. The two girls who were with me were sold immediately and I stayed to sleep alone in the room. I didn't stop crying all night.[15]

Once the women arrive in Israel, they are often again sold. A woman in Israel is bought for between $5,000 and $10,000. The price is determined according to age, appearance, and the forged papers she holds.[16] If a pimp or agent does not have enough money for a "whole" woman, there are instances when a woman can be sold as "common ownership," and sometimes rented from one brothel to another or to an individual for the fee of 500 NIS per day. Another practice is a "switch trade" in which one woman is traded for another.[17]

DAILY LIFE IN A BROTHEL

Work Conditions

From testimonies taken from women in brothels, life is dark and difficult. Work hours can stretch 15–17 hours a day on average (the "morning shift" is from 10:00 a.m. to 3:00 a.m. the next morning). The women get very few rest days, if at all, and are forced to work during menstruation. Their wages average less than $5 per customer, after they have repaid their owners their purchase price. A series of fines are levied against them and are deducted from their wages. As a matter of course, the women are subjected to a wide range of violations of their human rights: rape, being held against their will, kidnapping, assault, starvation, and more. Any chance of escape is blocked; a woman's pimp knows where her family lives in her home country and she is threatened with violence and death to her family should any attempt be made to escape or testify against her owners.

The Pimps

Statistics collected from questionnaires show that 60 percent of the agents and pimps came to Israel from the FSU as legal immigrants. Most of the pimps are immigrant men; in a number of cases, the position of pimp/agent is a woman.[18] There are pimps and agents who run a "family business" in trafficking, in which the partners are husband and wife,[19] or father and son.[20] These people are not necessarily criminals with previous criminal records; nor are they necessarily involved concurrently in other criminal activities. Many of them use their trafficking business as a "second income" in which they engage after regular business hours and on and off during the day out of a standard office at their regular jobs. Sometimes they became involved in such trade after they had lost "normal" jobs and could not find other employment.

The Rule of Terror

Most of the women are locked inside the brothels. They are not allowed to leave without being escorted by bodyguards, nor are their basic needs such as sufficient food, medical care, and rest provided. In addition, according to testimony and various national newspaper articles, the lives of the women in brothels are controlled by a system of threats, violence, and verbal and physical abuse from the pimps, those working with them, and clients.

Clients

It is estimated that there are approximately one million visits a month to brothels in Israel.[21] According to interviews with women who came to Israel knowing that they were to work as prostitutes, they were promised an average of up to 7 customers a day. No one prepared them for the reality that they must service up to 30 customers a day, every day of the month. Although there are women who have 3–4 customers a day, most have many more, up to 47 customers a day.[22] The exact number of customers depends on the level of popularity of the brothel and of the woman herself. The attitude of the customers toward the women range from kindheartedness (assisting them, even rescuing them at times, creating way for them to contact the "outside," etc.) to brutal rape against the women's clear wishes.[23]

Wages

The pimps earn between $30 and $140 per hour per customer. The type of service purchased by the customer determines the price. Most interviews reveal that the women themselves earn approximately $4–$5 per customer, and there are reports of women who were given $11 per day. Often the women are given no wages at all and sometimes owing their pimps money for the price of their purchase and smuggling.[24] Such is the testimony of Y.M.:

My pimp demanded that we have all kinds of sex and she paid us only 10 NIS (just over $2) per customer. She said she wouldn't waste even a penny on us and she's just losing money on us. She forced me to take part in orgies together with other girls when the customers wanted it and told us that she would go bankrupt if she paid us over NIS 10 on that kind of sexual service; that's why she wouldn't pay.

Physical and Emotional Health of Victims

A study conducted on the health of women[25] working in the sex trade showed that one-third of the women suffer from symptoms of depression, with 19 percent requiring clinical care. Twenty-six percent of the women had post-traumatic stress disorder symptoms. A number of these cases directly stemmed from working conditions experienced by prostitutes, while other cases were related to previous sexual attack, childhood abuse, or rape. Approximately 40 percent of the women were prevented from getting medical care and most of those who did receive it were forced to pay for any doctors out of their own pockets, some using falsified identity papers to receive health care. Women who got impregnated were generally dependant on the mercy of their pimps who would ultimately decide whether to allow them to have an abortion, to continue to work, or to be sent home.

CONCLUSION

Since Isha L'Isha's project began in 2002, it has had a tremendous impact throughout Israel. Public awareness has increased significantly, a legislative parliamentary committee has been established, traffickers are now brought to trial, and punishments have become more severe. Law enforcement agencies have begun inviting Isha L'Isha to provide lectures, demonstrating an increase in willingness to learn about the problem and the means of dealing with it. Isha L'Isha has become the primary address for information on trafficking for the police, the judicial system, attorneys, law students, and municipalities. We have also become the main source of support for the victims of trafficking. Conditions in detention centers have improved due to our constant involvement and requests. Among the positive changes seen in 2003–2004 are the following:

- Anti-trafficking legislation and bills were passed and precedents were established for fighting trafficking.
- Increased numbers of trafficking cases were brought to court and 20 percent (2003) to 30 percent (2004) of victims were willing to testify.
- Victims are granted compensation and work permits are granted to those willing to testify.
- Conditions within detention centers have improved.
- Two anonymous health clinics have opened, government shelter opens for victims testifying and four detention centers operate in Israel.
- NGO report was published raising public awareness.
- Conditions in brothels have improved.

Isha L'Isha will continue to work to assist victims of trafficking and to fight to end trafficking of women. Issues of concern that will be the focus of our work for the coming years include:

- Lack of a dedicated police task force and Russian-speaking women investigators.
- Traffickers' plea bargains that result in no compensation for women victims.
- Absence of a witness protection plan.
- No repatriation and rehabilitation programs in Israel.
- Proposed legalization of prostitution.
- Second and third waves of trafficked women—why do they return to prostitution?
- Need for improved cooperation between Israeli police and foreign consulates.
- Need to allow more time before deportation.
- Need for increased preventative work in the FSU.
- Need to send Israeli police investigators to the FSU to take testimony.

NOTES

Without the generous contributions of our devoted volunteers, members, charitable donors, and foundations, we would not have succeeded this far. Special thanks to the Ministry of Internal Security, U.S. Embassy, Kvinna till Kvinna–Sweden, American Friends Service Committee, U.S. Israel Women to Women, Global Fund for Women, Women's World Day of Prayer–German Committee, Boston Jewish Women's Community Fund, Mama Cash, and the Friedrich Ebert Foundation. This article is based primarily on research undertaken by Nomi Levenkron and Yossi Dahan for their report "Women as Commodities: Trafficking in Women in Israel."

1. Nomi Levenkron and Yossi Dahan, "Women as Commodities: Trafficking in Women in Israel," Hotline for Migrant Workers, Isha L'Isha—Haifa Feminist Center, the Adva Center, 2003: 22.

2. Nomi Levenkron, "Trafficking in Women in Israel—An Updated Report," 2001.

3. Levenkron, "Women as Commodities," 2003.

4. For an additional 6 percent there are no statistics.

5. For an additional 6 percent there are no statistics. According to specific evidence given by the women interviewed, agents and pimps prefer women with children. They are thought to be more obedient than single women.

6. A phenomenon that exists in Israel, as well as in many other countries, is the "second generation" of trafficking (i.e., women who have bought their freedom from their owners by agreeing to recruit other women).

7. H.A.'s comments were collected by a volunteer from The Hotline for Migrant Workers on January 1, 2003, in a hostel for State's witnesses in Tel Aviv. In line with the policy of the Israeli Immigration Department, she was held in jail for two and a half months before she was deported as the agents who employed her had taken her passport and she was unable to pay the Uzbekistani Consulate the required sum of $25 (equivalent to NIS 118). The Immigration Department refused to pay the sum in her name and preferred to incur the costs of her incarceration for 74 days, totaling NIS 22,000.

8. From interviews conducted by a volunteer from The Hotline for Migrant Workers on December 30, 2002, which took place in a hidden location.

9. Annual Report of The Hotline for Migrant Workers, 2001.

10. In certain circumstances, women were not actually brought into Israel for purposes of prostitution, but were kidnapped after they were already here. Such is the case in the *State of Israel vs. Asher BenBaruck* (case pending) 97 (1) 336: "The defendant and the accused met two Russian citizens who were looking for an apartment in which to live, locked them within the apartment, and forced them by threats and beatings to work as prostitutes, and to hand over any monies earned."

11. Illegal foreign workers using these routes pay non-returnable fees of thousands of dollars to be smuggled into Israel. According to The Hotline for Migrant Workers statistics, workers from Moldavia and Romania pay on average the sum of between $4,000 and $5,000 to enter the country.

12. Statement #20 from Parliamentary Investigation Session on the Subject of Trafficking in Women, December 26, 2001, testimony from victims of trafficking.

13. Y. B. was interviewed by volunteers from Isha L'Isha in Kishon Prison, Haifa, April 15, 2002. It must be stated that according to another testimony received by Isha L'Isha on February 5, 2003, the Bedouin involved in trafficking told a Muslim woman from Uzbekistan that she would not be raped because of her religion.

14. In addition to the methods of sale described here, in at least two instances women were "inherited" by another pimp after the one who owned them died. Information based on interviews conducted by volunteers from The Hotline for Migrant Workers in Neve Tirza Prison, May 23, 2002; and, on March 19, 2003, from within a hostel for State's witnesses in Tel Aviv.

15. Testimony of H.A. as it was given to volunteers from The Hotline for Migrant Workers on January 14, 2003, in a hostel for State's witnesses in Tel Aviv.

16. Report from the Inter-Office Commission, page 9.

17. Haifa Court Case 4299/01, the *State of Israel vs. Alexander Shreiper*, Case #4117, 4111 (3) 2001.

18. *The State of Israel vs. Hannah Dvir*, Case #1119/01, Tel Aviv-Yaffo Court, 43917(3).

19. *State of Israel vs. Ben David Yaish*, case #70(3) 2002; *State of Israel vs. Sergei and Irina Shechtman* (unpublished); based on the facts described, the couple traded in women for purposes of prostitution.

20. *The State of Israel vs. Rami Biton*, case #1578/99, 476(4) 2001.

21. Statistics are from estimates of approximately 3,000 women currently working in prostitution in Israel, working 30 days a month, who have about 10 customers per day. See also the report of Keren Ilan, Bella Chudakov, R. H. Belmaker, and Julie Cwikel, "The Motivation and Mental Health of Sex Workers," Beersheba: Ben-Gurion University, 2002.

22. From the testimony of A., a citizen of Uzbekistan, to a volunteer from Isha L'Isha in March 2003 in a hidden location in Haifa. Professor Julie Cwikel reported to the Knesset Committee that her research showed similar results: "Most of the girls that we saw said that they were told they would get 4–5 customers per day. They get here to a situation where they must service 12, 15, 20, 25, and 30 customers per day, without any attention paid to their welfare and health or their ability to bear such conditions."

23. This subject can be seen as dealing with the myth that a prostitute cannot be raped.

24. According to the intermediary report by the Parliamentary Investigation, describing fees of between NIS 120–150 per customer. From this fee the brothel owner takes from NIS 100–130. According to the intermediary report, the customer pays on the average NIS 180 from which 40 percent is divided among the brothel, 45 percent to the pimp and only 15 percent to the woman.

25. Karen Ilan, Bella Chudakov, R. H. Belmaker, and Julie Cwikel, "The Motivation and Mental Health of Sex Workers," *Journal of Sex and Marital Therapy* 28, no. 4, 2002, 305–15.

BIBLIOGRAPHY

Altman, Dennis. *Global Sex*. Chicago: University of Chicago Press, 2001.

Anderson, Scott A. "Prostitution and Sexual Autonomy: Making Sense of the Prohibition of Prostitution." *Ethics* 112 (2002): 748–780.

Bales, Kevin. *New Slavery: A Reference Handbook*. Santa Barbara, CA: ABC-CLIO, 2000.

Berkovitch, Nitza. *From Motherhood to Citizenship, Women's Rights and International Organizations*. Baltimore: Johns Hopkins University Press, 1999.

Bishop, Ryan, and Lillian Robinson. *Night Market—Sexual Cultures and the Thai Economic Miracle*. New York: Routledge, 1991.

Caldwell, Gillian, Steve Galster, Jyothi Kanics, and Nadia Steinzor. "Capitalizing on Transition Economics: The Role of Russian Mafia in Trafficking Women for Forced Prostitution." In *Illegal Immigration and Commercial Sex*, edited by Phil Williams, 42–74. London: Frank Cass & Co., 1999.

Doezema, Jo. "Forced to Choose." In *Global Sex Workers*, edited by Kamala Kempadoo and Jo Doezema, 34–51. New York: Routeledge, 1998.

———. "Loose Women or Lost Women?" *Gender Issues* 18/1 (2000): 23–50.

Hauber, Laurie. "Trafficking of Women for Prostitution: A Growing Problem Within the European Union." *Boston College International and Comparative Law Review* 21 (1998): 183–198.

Ilan, Keren, Bella Chudakov, R.H. Belmaker, and Julie Cwikel. "The Motivation and Mental Health of Sex Workers." *The Journal of Sex and Marital Therapy*. Beersheba, Israel: Ben-Gurion University, 2002.

Johnson, Diane. "Trafficking Women into the European Union." *New England International and Comparative Law Annual* (1999): 1–19.

MacKinnon, Catharine. *Feminism Unmodified: Discourses on Life and Law*. Cambridge, MA: Harvard University Press, 1987.

Murray, Alison. "Debt Bondage and Trafficking." In *Global Sex Workers*, edited by Kamala Kempadoo and Jo Doezema, 51–68. New York: Routeledge, 1998.

Nussbaum, Martha. "Whether from Reason or Prejudice: Taking Money for Bodily Services." *Sex and Social Justice*. New York: Oxford University Press, 1999: 276–298.

Sassen, Saskia. "Women's Burden: Countergeographies of Globalization and the Feminization of Survival." *Journal of International Affairs* 53(2) (2000): 503–524.

Strandberg, Nina. "What Is Trafficking in Women and What Can Be Done." Stockholm: The Foundation of Women's Forum, 1999.

Taylor, Ian, and Ruth Jamieson. "Sex Trafficking and the Mainstream Market Culture." *Crime, Law & Social Change* 32 (1999): 257–278.

Trafficking in Women for the Purpose of Sexual Exploitation, Mapping the Situation and Existing Organizations Working in Belarus, Russia, the Baltic and Nordic States. Stockholm: The Foundation of Women's Forum, Stifelsen Kvinnforum, 1998.

Trafficking in Women: Moldova and Ukraine. Minneapolis: Minnesota Advocates for Human Rights, 2000. http://www.mnadvocates.org/vertical/Sites/TraffickingReport.pdf.

Wijers, Marjan and Marieke van Doorninck. "Only Rights Can Stop Wrongs: A Critical Assessment of Anti Trafficking Strategies." Presented at EU/IMO STOP, European Conference on Preventing and Combating in Human Rights, Sept 18–20 2002. European Parliament, Brussels. See http://www.walnet.org/csis/papers/wijers-rights.html.

Williams, Phil. "Trafficking in Women and Children: A Market Perspective." In *Illegal Immigration and Commercial Sex*, edited by Phil Williams, 145–171. London: Frank Cass & Co., 1999.

Women as Chattel: The Emerging Global Market in Trafficking. USAID: Office of Women in Development, *Gender Matters Quarterly 1999*, 1–7.

· 13 ·

The Provision of Protection and Settlement Services for Migrant Women Trafficked for Sexual Purposes: The Case of Italy

Isabel Crowhurst

$\mathscr{T}$his chapter presents an overview of the measures that have been in place in Italy since 1998 under Article 18 of the Consolidated Act on Immigration to provide protection and settlement services for migrant women who are trafficked in the Italian sex industry. More specifically, the aim is to assess methods and practices employed in the implementation stage of this regulation, with a specific focus on the role of non-governmental organizations (NGOs) as crucial actors in the delivery of care and assistance to this target group.

BACKGROUND

Since the 1970s, Italy has become the country of destination for a growing number of people migrating mainly from economically developing countries: between 1991 and 2001 the number of migrants to Italy tripled from 350,000 to one million, and in 2004, only three years later, their presence was reported to be around 2.6 million (that is, 4.5 percent of the population).[1] One of the distinctive features of new migration patterns to Italy is the unprecedented number of migrant women operating in the sex industry who have started to become socially visible since the beginning of the 1990s.[2] The largest groups are reportedly from Nigeria, Albania, Romania, Moldavia, and Ukraine; there are also significant numbers of women from Bulgaria, Poland, and to a lesser extent Colombia and Peru.[3]

There is still no clear estimation of the numerical presence of migrant women in the Italian sex industry; in fact, estimates "rest more on 'conventional wisdom' than on hard statistics."[4] The lack of comprehensive factual data has resulted in schizophrenia of numbers, as shown in the following statistics.

In 1996, the International Organization for Migration (IOM) in Rome reported 20,000 to 30,000 female migrants enter the sex industry each year in Italy. Until a few years ago, the association Papa Giovanni XXIII—an NGO that provides support to women trafficked for sexual purposes—claimed "80,000 girls were forced into prostitution on the streets of Italy"; more recently it reduced that figure to "50,000 or more."[5] PARSEC, an Italian research association on population and social interventions, determined the number of "foreign female prostitutes" in 1998 in Italy was between 15,000 to 19,000[6] and decreased it to 13,000 in 2002; approximately 10 percent are believed to be sexually trafficked.[7]

The inconsistency of this data, and the whole array of other existing data not quoted here, depends on the different bases from which these estimates were derived. If, as the IOM reports, the number of female migrant prostitutes entering the country each year is between 20,000 to 30,000, and according to PARSEC, in a study produced only two years later, their actual presence on the Italian soil amounts to 15,000–19,000, where have all these women gone? Moreover, how did Papa Giovanni XXIII arrive at the hyperbolic figure of 80,000 sex-trafficked 'girls' in their report? The incongruity of the data is a serious blemish in this field and it hampers the necessary effort to make a clear distinction between myths and reality. As stated in a document produced by the UNESCO:

> Numbers take on a life of their own, gaining acceptance through repetition, often with little inquiry into their derivations. Journalists, bowing to the pressures of editors, demand numbers, any number. Organizations feel compelled to supply them, lending false precisions and spurious authority to many reports.[8]

It is evident that serious efforts need to be made in order to monitor closely this consistently evolving phenomenon on a regular basis; only knowledge of the nearest approximation to its real magnitude would allow for the formation of an appropriate response.

The societal reaction to migrant women in the sex industry has evolved rapidly since the early 1990s, when they became progressively more visible due to their increasing numbers and concentration in street prostitution. The local population responded to their presence on the streets with hostility, and it was perceived as yet another element of public disturbance brought about by the migrant population. However, in 1993, the Committee for the Civil Rights of Prostitutes[9] set up a formal structure of support for migrant prostitutes. By 1995, a number of local groups and associations active in the field of social exclusion started to show interest in understanding who these women were, where they came from, and whether they needed any help. Groups of local people established contact with the women and subsequently organized themselves into registered associations of support. By the second half of the 1990s, many of these more or less institutionalized NGOs had instituted various forms of intervention in this field as part of their activities, carried out prevalently in circumscribed local communities and with little support from the state.

New recommendations were soon put forth by the European Union (EU) to promote better cooperation with non-governmental organizations. A series of initiatives to combat the trafficking of human beings, requesting the involvement of non-state actors, contributed to a positive development in the organizational functioning and social and political recognition of voluntary organizations operating in this sector.[10] Moreover, the establishment of a more dialogic interaction between the left-wing government coalition, NGOs, and regional authorities on the issue of trafficking for sexual purposes resulted in 1998 in formal consultation—within a specific steering group—of a large number of third-sector organizations, including many of those that had been working with migrant women, over the formulation of a new legislation addressing the needs of trafficked people. This process resulted in Article 18, which became an integral part of the so-called 1998 Consolidated Act on Immigration.[11]

THE LEGAL CONTEXT OF ARTICLE 18

Article 18 regulates protection services for adult people (for minors other legal provisions are in place) who have been trafficked for labour or sexual exploitations. So far, it has been enforced, nearly exclusively, in the case of migrant women trafficked for sexual purposes. Given the focus of this chapter, in the following section I refer to it exclusively in its application to this target group.

> Article 18 provides for a temporary stay permit of "social protection" when in the course of police operation, investigation or court proceedings . . . , or whenever the social service of a local administration, in the performance of their assistance work, identify situations of abuse or severe exploitation of a foreign citizen. [In this case, the police authority may] grant a special residence permit enabling the foreign citizen to escape from the situation of abuse . . . perpetuated by the criminal organisations and to participate in a social assistance and integration program. [The conditions for issuing a stay permit are based] on the severity and imminence of the danger to the foreign citizen and the importance of the contribution offered by that foreign citizen to combating the criminal organization or identifying and capture of the perpetuators of the criminal offence.[12]

In sum, the basic prerequisites to obtain protection, social assistance, and the stay permit are for the trafficked woman to be in severe and imminent danger and to provide a substantial contribution toward the persecution of her traffickers. In order to benefit from these provisions, there are two options: the so-called social and legal itineraries. The social itinerary is applied when a woman contacts a social service[13] and asks for protection and help. In this case, the organization, after verifying the conditions of "serious violence and exploitation," may request a stay permit. The legal itinerary comes into force when, during the course of a criminal proceeding, it is ascertained that the woman is in imminent danger due to severe exploitation, based on the statements she makes to police or legal authorities. If she agrees to start a legal procedure against the exploiter, she is entitled to request a temporary permit. In both cases the actual granting of a residence permit is subject to the applicant's participation in a program of "assistance and social protection" offered by a recognized social service. The permit, whether obtained through the legal or social itinerary, lasts six months and can be renewed for one year. It gives the holder access to social and assistance services and public education and, in addition, provides registration with the national employment agency. It can also be renewed if, once expired, the woman has found employment.[14]

The "progressive" nature of this relatively new procedure emanates from the fact that it allows the woman not only to benefit from protection and assistance, but also to obtain a stay permit, which in theory[15] is issued based on the abusive and exploitative conditions suffered, her declared intention to start a project of social protection, and not exclusively on her collaboration with law enforcement and immigration officials in investigations and prosecutions.[16]

Article 18 also regulates the allocation of public financial resources to support programs of social assistance and integration, managed by social services. There are currently more than 60 organizations enrolled within a special registry maintained by the Department of Social Affairs that provide such services for trafficked women.[17]

THE MODEL OF IMPLEMENTATION: ACCOUNT AND ASSESSMENT

The program of assistance and social integration is aimed primarily at providing a safe environment for the woman where she can reformulate her project of migration, regain autonomy, and, as the text of Article 18 states, begin a process of integration within larger Italian society. Not all social services structure the project in the same way; however, the following are common practices.

The itinerary starts when the woman establishes a first contact with one of the organizations, either autonomously or through the police authorities. In this preliminary phase, the operators[18] have an informal interview with the woman to inform her about the structure of the project, its time framework, the rules it entails, the required procedure with the legal authorities, etc. All operators interviewed stressed the importance of this first approach and the need to be extremely clear about the difficulties of the itinerary, a necessary prerequisite to be realistically prepared for the phases that come next. The aim is not to be discouraging, rather to give all the information to make an informed choice for the future. As already mentioned, however, for many women, participating in an integration project does not represent a real choice. Either they must cooperate with the justice agency and the social service, or they are forced to go back to their native country. According to the operators, the women who begin the project as an alternative to being repatriated usually lack real commitment and are unable to face the implied obligations, thus many return to prostitution as a preferred solution.

This initial selection procedure also has the function of ascertaining if the woman is in "real" danger so as to avoid any instrumental abuse of Article 18 as a means to obtain a stay permit in the country. If the interview is successful, the woman agrees to start a personalized project of rehabilitation and is accommodated in what is generally referred to as an emergency shelter where the first phase begins. During this time, the woman receives medical care and is assisted with her primary needs. She is asked to evaluate her choice with the aid of a linguistic–cultural mediator. After a number of other interviews, the service prepares a personalized intervention to regularize her legal status in Italy, register for a job placement, build an initial support network, and find a stable living solution.[19] Subsequently, she moves to a private accommodation with other women and social workers. At this stage the procedure to regularize her status in Italy is activated and the woman, with the aid of the NGO operators, will then interact with law enforcement agencies and the judiciary. In addition, she receives language and literacy trainings, participates in cultural and sports activities, and is supposed to begin work. This generally takes place in one of the local factories or social cooperatives that have a special agreement with the NGO in charge. The salary is usually provided through a scheme of "working bursaries" funded by the government. Her introduction into the labor market is an important step, especially when it is the first working experience outside the sex industry. The woman has to learn new skills and adjust to the basic requirements involved in a job, such as respect for the time schedules involved, collaboration with other colleagues, and managing of her own finances. When she demonstrates the achievement of full autonomy, she can move into her own accommodation with NGO operators providing support when needed.

All these phases are extremely delicate in that they imply the passage from one source of income to another, from an illegal to a legal immigration status, the construction of new social and work relationships, and the taking up of new responsibilities.[20]

In addition to the difficulties faced by each woman in embarking upon a new way of life, the program is often hampered by numerous structural problems intrinsic in the implementation of Article 18. First, to reassure the woman and give her the best possible and most favorable conditions to carry out the program, there should be an immediate issuance of the stay permit. However, in practice, the release of the permit by judiciary authorities may take many months, a long wait that is a source of great frustration for the women. Some of the operators interviewed reported on the psychological dependency of the women on obtaining the permit, which becomes the symbol of the beginning of a new life and the necessary requirement to start building trust in the authorities and in the operators themselves.

Indeed, the temporary permit is released in a shorter period upon cooperation with legal bodies. For this reason, even women who started a social itinerary are often encouraged to open a criminal procedure and report their traffickers. Not all of them, however, agree to take this step. Frustrated by the lack of a permit, unable to start a job, and burdened by the new environment and bureaucratic rules required by the program, some drop out and re-enter prostitution networks, in some cases under stricter control by their pimps and without hope in the structures provided for under Article 18.

Another relevant structural drawback to the implementation of this provision is the very limited funds that are made available by the state, hampering the quality of the services provided. For example, the housing that some organizations can afford is often substandard and does not allow for the regular implementation of the program. In one of the cases encountered during my fieldwork, an organization, due to lack of adequate accommodation, placed all women in a "first phase" safe shelter. The basic requirement of a safe shelter is to be in a secret location where, for their own safety, unaccompanied women are not allowed to leave. Those who were already in the second phase of the project and living in a private accommodation had to comply by this rule and felt like being in a state of forced and unjust confinement, not able to benefit from any of the training or work experience which they were entitled to as part of the program. Another organization that lacked funds for a shelter house accommodated women in a house for mentally handicapped children or in a rehabilitation center for drug addicts; in both cases, they had already been staying in these "temporary" shelters for a few months.

Economic constraints also limit organizations from hiring sufficiently trained and professional staff. In many cases, only one employed person manages the project and the rest of the personnel consist of voluntary staff. Cultural mediators are often employed on a consultancy basis. Due to its cost, this kind of support is used only occasionally, limiting the possibility of deeper understanding of the women's background and identity—defined by different cultural practices, religious behaviors and values, relations, work traditions, attitudes, etc.—essential for the formulation of a personalized ad hoc project that takes into consideration their needs, hopes, and expectations. The lack of a proper use of cultural mediation is a very serious shortcoming, especially when one considers the criminalized, racialized, and highly sexualized representations of women sex migrants in the Italian sociopolitical discourse, reproduced in the comments of some male NGO operators I interviewed: "Nigerians are lazy, no wonder it's difficult for us to find them a job. They don't want to do anything." "Nigerians would go with anyone, you just have to show them a banknote and they start undressing." "I mean after all these women were whores and no matter how hard we try, they will always be whores."[21]

The analysis of the initiatives formulated to support victims of trafficking in Italy needs to take into account, in addition to the discrepancies between the law and its administrative implementation and the structural difficulties encountered in daily practice, the ideological diversity within organizations and the extent to which different approaches on prostitution result in different practices. For example, one theory considers prostitution as abjection of the body and a form of sexual degradation that violates the intimate relationship between personality and physical embodiment.[22] "Within this approach, trafficking in women is considered to be just part and parcel of the overall evils of prostitution, without regard for conditions of consent or coercion. So viewed, prostitution and trafficking become practically identical."[23] For those who support this theory, the project is seen as a "salvific itinerary" away from the deviant environment of prostitution, during which the woman is offered the opportunity to change her life and shape it according to a more "proper," "moral" behavior.

Another theory considers prostitution as an expenditure of physical labor that is identical to any other form of labor. Within this frame, trafficking is considered in the perspective of the violence, abuse, and exploitation that it involves, and is viewed as one of the effects of the widespread poor social and legal position of women, that relegates them the informal, unregulated, and unprotected labor market.[24] Within this perspective, the program is generally conceived as an empowerment itinerary, aimed at reconstructing women's self-determination and autonomy, with autonomy meaning not necessarily abandoning prostitution, but "gaining means of control of one's own destiny, by acquiring the capacity to elaborate one's own life story and personal experience."[25]

For the woman, making contact with a particular organization is usually a matter of coincidence rather than a conscious ideological choice and/or statement. However, the formulation of her program of assistance and possibly the nature of her future integration depend to a large extent on the ideological stand of the organization whose services she is benefiting from. She is the unaware subject of an ideological structure, which projects its own desires and assumptions upon her.

CONCLUSION

The analysis presented in this chapter focuses on protection and settlement services for trafficked women in Italy from the point of view of the deliverer in order to highlight the way services are structured and the main problems that result from their implementation.[26] In this respect, it is important to stress that the deficiencies of the law and its application herewith presented should not shed an exclusively negative light on the strategies employed to support trafficked women and the extremely relevant efforts made by non–governmental organizations in this field.

In fact, some of them have acquired a high level of well–grounded expertise in this field. Since the beginning of their activities, they have been improving their level of professionalism by constantly developing their organizational skills, transparency and accountability, and most importantly, the quality of the services provided. Having said this, it remains to be pointed out the need for a more consistent collaboration between associations. The creation of a synergy of improved cooperation and coordination urgently needs to be developed in order to increase the impact and advocacy power of the third sector and the effectiveness of its services, which should not be hindered by the inability to move beyond contrasting approaches.

It is also important to reiterate the inconsistency of data on the phenomenon of prostitution–related migrations. As previously mentioned, according to both IOM Rome and PARSEC, approximately 10 to 15 percent (1,300 to 2,000) of women migrants operating in the sex industry are trafficked in Italy each year. No specific data is given as to how this percentage is ascertained, but more importantly, no mention is made as to who are the women that constitute the remaining 85–90 percent. They do not fit in the category of "victims of trafficking" and therefore are not entitled to protection or a residence permit. Are they forced prostitutes who are unable to denounce their abusive situation out of fear? Are they women who, though abused, do not want to report their situation to the police because they want to repay their debt, or because they are sentimentally dependent on their pimps? Are they women who voluntarily choose to get involved in the sex business? Further research is needed to find an answer to these questions.

Inconsistent discursive dichotomizations between voluntary and forced prostitution have already been mapped out onto the structure of policies and practices—in the case of Italy, by including provisions of services to "legal victims" and by excluding the rest of women sex migrants. As the former UN High Commissioner on Human Rights, Mary Robinson, pointed out, there is a need to "ensure that well-intentioned anti-trafficking initiatives do not compound discrimination against female migrants or further endanger the precariously held rights of individuals working in prostitution."[27] It is imperative that we continue to improve our knowledge of the heterogeneity and complexity of migrant women's patterns by listening with particular attention to the voices and needs of all those who are involved. In Laura Agustin's words: "Let's go out to those in the margins with nothing in our hands and simply listen to them. For, with all the rhetoric about the need to liberate 'unheard voices,' we miss an essential point: those voices have been talking all along. The question is: Who is listening?" [28]

NOTES

This chapter is based on my ongoing doctoral research that analyzes the processes of exclusion and inclusion of migrant women who operate in the sex industry in Italy vis-à-vis their social construction in the Italian public discourse.

1. Caritas/Migrantes, Dossier Statistico Immigrazione 2004 (Rome: Idos—Centro Studi e Ricerche, 2004); and International Organization for Migration, "Italy, the Image of Migrants through the Media, Civil Society and the Labour Market," http://www.iom.int/en/archive/PBN261102.shtml#item2 (15 May 2005).

2. Francesco Carchedi, *Considerations on Foreign Prostitution in Italy*, (Rome: PARSEC, 2000), 3.

3. To be noted is also the fact that more recently a number of women from longer established communities of migrants such as Filipinas, Somalis, Chinese, and Moroccans have started to enter into prostitution, catering almost exclusively to their male nationals.

Esohe Aghatise, "Trafficking for Prostitution in Italy. Possible Effects of Government Proposals for Legalization of Brothels," *Violence Against Women* 10, no.10 (October 2004): 1126–1155; and CABIRIA, Women and Migration in Europe: Strategies and Empowerment, (Lyon: Le Dragon Lune Editions, 2004).

4. Gabriella Lazaridis, "Trafficking and Prostitution: the Growing Exploitation of Migrant Women in Greece," *European Journal of Women's Studies* 8, no.1: 75.

5. The association Papa Giovanni XXIII considers prostitution invariably as a form of sexual exploitation, thus migrant women operating in the sex industry are viewed always as victims of trafficking for sexual purposes.

Associazione Papa Giovanni 23, <www.apg23.org> (15 May 2005); and "Research based on case studies of victims of trafficking in human beings in 3 EU Member States, i.e., Belgium, Italy, and The Netherlands, 2003" http://www.ontheroadonlus.it/pdf/RapIppocra.pdf (15 May 2005).

6. Carchedi, "Considerations," 6.

7. Francesca Bettio and Giulia Garofalo, "Trafficking and Prostitution: Country Report for Italy," NEWR, http://www.newr.bham.ac.uk/pdfs/Trafficking/italy.pdf (15 May 2005).

8. This statement is taken from the UNESCO Trafficking Statistics Project. As part of its mandate to strengthen research, the UNESCO project is conducting a literature review and meta-analysis of existing statements on trafficking, thus tracing the origin of numbers cited by various sources, so as to ascertain the methodology by which these numbers were calculated, and evaluate their validity.

"Trafficking Statistic Project," UNESCO, http://www2.unescobkk.org/culture/trafficking/ev.asp?ev=83&id=86 (15 May 2005).

9. The Committee for the Civil Rights of Prostitutes (Comitato per i Diritti Civili delle Prostitute) was founded in 1983, and since then it has been actively involved in the fight for the decriminalization of prostitution and against trafficking of human beings for sexual purposes.

10. An example of these types of initiatives is the STOP program launched in November 1996 by the European Commission to encourage and reinforce networks and practical cooperation between the various persons responsible for action against trafficking in human beings and sexual exploitation of children in the EU member states.

11. The Consolidated Act was passed in 1998 and brought some order and "consolidation" into the otherwise very chaotic construction of laws and codes on immigration in Italy.

12. Article 18 of Legislative Decree n.286/98.

13. The term *social service* (servizio sociale) used in the text of Article 18 refers to one of the registered organizations entitled to offer protection to victims of trafficking by the Department of Social Affairs.

14. Assunta Signorelli and Mariangela Treppete, *Servizi in vetrina* (Trieste: Asterios, 2001).

15. The actual implementation of this provision is still very problematic. Despite the addition of new government directives in the year 2000, which aim at strengthening the social itinerary, NGO operators interviewed in 2002, 2003, and 2004 still lamented the fact that too often the fastest way for a woman to obtain a temporary permit is to start a criminal procedure.

16. In this respect it is relevant to mention the European Commission proposal for a Council Directive "on short-term residence permit issued to victims of action to facilitate illegal immigration or trafficking in human beings who cooperate with the competent authorities" of July 2002. As already widely criticized, this provision requires victims of trafficking to cooperate in criminal investigations in order to enjoy a protection that lasts only for the time of the cooperation.

17. In addition to projects of integration in the receiving country, the International Organization for Migration (IOM) in Rome runs a program aimed specifically at assisting the voluntary return of victims of trafficking to their countries of origin.

18. The term operators (operatori) refers to NGO staff and is used here in order to conform to the Italian terminology applied on these matters.

19. Signorelli and Treppete, *Services in the Window* (Trieste: Asterios Editore, 2001), 68.

20. Signorelli and Treppete, *Servizi*, 68.

21. From interviews with three NGO operators Italy, 2002 and 2004.

22. Sunder Rajan, *The Scandal of the State* (Durham, NC: Duke University Press, 2003).

23. Wijers and van Doornick, "Only Rights Can Stop Wrongs: A Critical Assessment of Anti-Trafficking Strategies," http://www.walnet.org/csis/papers/wijers-rights.html (15 May 2005); and IOM, "Italy, the Image of Migrants through the Media, Civil Society and the Labour Market," http://www.iom.int/en/archive/PBN261102.shtml (15 May 2005).

24. Wijers and van Doornick, "Only Rights Can Stop Wrongs."

25. Signorelli and Treppete, *Servizi,* 60.

26. Little has been said on how the "beneficiaries" of the services value these provisions, the impact they have on their lives, and the extent to which their integration is successful from their standpoint. This is due to the fact that the current stage of my research is based on analysis of the in-depth interviews I carried out nearly exclusively with NGO personnel during my fieldworks in 2002, 2003, and 2004.

27. UNHCR, http://www.unhchr.ch/huricane/huricane.nsf/0/030C309EBD505F3B802567A7004851E4?opendocument (15 May 2005).

28. Laura Agustin, "The Plight of Migrant Women: They Speak, But Who's Listening?" in *Women@Internet: Creating New Cultures in Cyberspace,* ed. Wendy Harcourt, (London: Zed, 1999).

BIBLIOGRAPHY

Aghatise, Esohe. "Trafficking for Prostitution in Italy. Possible Effects of Government Proposals for Legalization of Brothels." *Violence Against Women* 10, no.10 (October 2004): 1126–1155.

Agustin, Laura. "The Plight of Migrant Women: They Speak, But Who's Listening?" *Women@Internet: Creating New Cultures in Cyberspace,* edited by Wendy Harcourt. London: Zed, 1999.

Andall, Jane. *Gender, Migration and Domestic Service: The Politics of Black Women in Italy.* Aldershot: Ashgate, 2000.

Bettio, Francesca, and Giulia Garofalo. "Trafficking and Prostitution: Country Report for Italy." NEWR, http://www.newr.bham.ac.uk/pdfs/Trafficking/italy.pdf (15 May 2005).

Bonifazi, Corrado. "Italian Attitudes and Opinions Towards Foreign and Migration Policies." *Studi Emigrazione/Etudes Migrations* 29, no.105 (1992): 21–41.

CABIRIA. *Women and Migration in Europe: Strategies and Empowerment.* Lyon: Le Dragon Lune Editions, 2004.

Campani, G. "Immigration and Racism in Southern Europe: The Italian Case." *Ethnic and Racial Studies* 16, no. 3, (1993): 507–535.

Carchedi, Francesco. *Considerations on Foreign Prostitution in Italy.* Rome: PARSEC, 2000.

Caritas/Migrantes. *Dossier Statistico immigrazione 2004.* Rome: Idos—Centro Studi e Ricerche, 2004.

IOM. "Italy, the Image of Migrants through the Media, Civil Society and the Labour Market." International Organization for Migration (IOM). http://www.iom.int/en/archive/PBN261102.shtml#item2 (15 May 2005).

Lazaridis, Gabriella. "Trafficking and Prostitution: the Growing Exploitation of Migrant Women in Greece." *European Journal of Women's Studies* 8, no. 1: 75.

Rajan, Sunder. *The Scandal of the State.* Durham, NC: Duke University Press, 2003.

Signorelli, Assunta, and Mariangela Treppete. *Services in the Window.* Trieste: Asterios Editore, 2001.

Wijers and van Doornick. "Only Rights Can Stop Wrongs: A Critical Assessment of Anti-Trafficking Strategies." http://www.walnet.org/csis/papers/wijers-rights.html (15 May 2005).

UNESCO. "Trafficking Statistic Project." http://www2.unescobkk.org/culture/trafficking/ev.asp?ev=83&id=86 (15 May 2005).

Index

About the Contributors and Editors

ABOUT THE CONTRIBUTORS

Arun Kumar Acharya is presently pursuing his PhD at the Instituto de Investigaciones Antropologicas at Universidad Nacional Autonoma de México (UNAM). He received a masters in Population Sciences (2001) at the International Institute of Population Sciences, Mumbai, India.

Carolina S. Ruiz-Austria was the cofounder and executive director of the Women's Legal Education, Advocacy & Defense Foundation, Inc. (WOMEN-LEAD Foundation, Inc.). Presently she is lead counsel, Reproductive Health Advocacy Network (RHAN); professorial lecturer, Women & Law, College of Law, University of the Philippines, Diliman, Quezon City; and a member of the Board of Advisors, BUKLOD-Olongapo.

Upala Devi Banerjee is currently the Asia-Pacific regional coordinator for the Lessons Learned Project in the UN Office for the High Commissioner for Human Rights in Bangkok, Thailand. Previously, she was coordinator of the Child Development Fund of the Canadian International Development Agency in India and the consultant director of programs of Educate Girls Globally, a United States–based group working to educate girls in developing nations. She was a fellow with the Institute of Development Studies at the University of Sussex, England (2002), and a Ford Fellow with the International Center for Research on Women (2002).

Vu Ngoc Binh was born and lives in Vietnam. He is presently the Vietnam Project Officer for the United Nations Children's Fund (UNICEF) directing the office's efforts to promote the human rights of women and children. Prior to this he spent four years with Swedish Save the Children (Radda Barnen) in Hanoi. He was also the program officer in the country's Ministry of Education and Training in the 1980s. Mr. Binh has published and lectured extensively on human rights, governance, child protection, human trafficking, and gender issues.

Rita Chaikin is presently the project coordinator of The Fight Against Trafficking in Women at the Isha L'Isha—Haifa Feminist Center, a nongovernmental organization in Israel. After serving in the military, she went on to receive a BA in Education at Tel-Hai School of Education, Kiriyat Shmona, and furthered her education at the Intelligence College where she studied professional development marketing and management and at Haifa University in Certified Group Facilitation.

Isabel Crowhurst is currently a PhD candidate in the Department of Sociology at the London School of Economics in London, England. She is presently the research assistant for the Centre for Civil Society and personal assistant to the Convener in the Department of Government at the London School of Economics. She has interned for the European Commission of the Directorate General Personnel and Administration, Non-Discrimination and Equal Opportunities Unit, in Brussels, Belgium, and the United Nations, Office for the Co-ordination of Humanitarian Affairs (OCHA), New York.

William Ejalu is a lawyer and political scientist. Presently he teaches at Eotvos Lorand University Faculty of Law and Political Sciences and is also the executive director of the International Law Research and Human Rights Monitoring Center in Budapest, Hungary. Mr. Ejalu is also the senior legal consultant to Kadaga & Company Advocates in Kampala, Uganda, and works as legal advisor to various human rights organizations.

Austin Choi-Fitzpatrick completed his graduate work in international human rights and international security at the Graduate School of International Studies at the University of Denver. He is an outreach associate with Free the Slaves in Washington, DC, and the Community Outreach Coordinator of the B-SAFE Program, an anti-trafficking component of San Diego Youth and Community Services, San Diego, California.

Anne Gallagher is Team Leader with Asia Regional Cooperation to Prevent People Trafficking (ARCPPT) in Bangkok, Thailand.

Md. Shahidul Haque, a Bangladeshi, was born in Pakistan and is currently serving as the regional representative of International Organization for Migration (IOM) for South Asia, based in Dhaka, Bangladesh. He graduated first class at the masters and honors levels in Social Welfare from the Dhaka University and later obtained an MA in International Relations from the Fletcher School of Law and Diplomacy, Tufts University. He is a Fellow of the Center for International Understanding, Missouri.

Zarina Othman is presently an assistant professor for Strategic Studies and International Relations at the Universiti Kebangsaan Malaysia. She received her MA (1996) and PhD (2002) in International Studies from the University of Denver in Colorado. Prior to that she received an associate degree in Studies in Islamic Political Thought from the Studies of Islamic Sciences (ABIM), Kajang, Selangor, Malaysia.

Abbey Steele is presently a PhD candidate at Yale University in the Department of Political Science. She was the cofounder and Latin America Regional Coordinator of Free the Slaves in Washington, DC, and Bogotá, Colombia. She has also served as a congressional intern for U.S. Representative Dennis Kucinich and interned for the Center for International Policy in Washington, DC.

Saltanat Sulaimanova is presently a PhD candidate in Public Administration at the American University in Washington, DC. She served as a consultant for The World Bank, Global Development Gateway, Washington, DC; the International Organization for Migration (IOM), Bishkek, Kyrgyzstan; the Protection Project at Johns Hopkins University (SAIS); and the International Research and Exchanges Board (IREX).

ABOUT THE EDITORS

Karen Beeks, coeditor, is founder and executive director of Global Partnerships for Humanity in Highlands Ranch, Colorado. She is a political scientist with a masters degree (1995) from the University of Colorado in Denver.

Delila Amir, PhD, coeditor, is the founder and coordinator of the Women's Studies Forum and is sociologist emeritus at the Department of Sociology and Anthropology, Tel-Aviv University, Israel. She has an MA degree in Sociology and Psychology from Hebrew University and a PhD from Pittsburgh University.